MONEY VALUES

MONEY VALUES

HOW TO BE FINANCIALLY MINDFUL

MAARIT LASSANDER

Prometheus Books

Essex, Connecticut

 Prometheus Books

An imprint of The Globe Pequot Publishing Group, Inc.
64 South Main Street
Essex, CT 06426
www.globepequot.com

Copyright © 2026 by Maarit Lassander

All rights reserved. No part of this book may be reproduced in any form or by any electronic or mechanical means, including information storage and retrieval systems, without written permission from the publisher, except by a reviewer who may quote passages in a review.

British Library Cataloguing in Publication Information available

Library of Congress Cataloging-in-Publication Data available

ISBN 978-1-4930-9838-5 (cloth)
ISBN 978-1-4930-9234-5 (paperback)
ISBN 978-1-4930-9235-2 (ebook)

CONTENTS

Preface vi

Part I: The Beginning
CHAPTER 1: We All Have Our Story About Money 2
CHAPTER 2: The Society 21
CHAPTER 3: The Neuroscience 42
CHAPTER 4: The Emotions 57

Part II: The Values
CHAPTER 5: Guiding Values 72
CHAPTER 6: Money-Related Values 86
CHAPTER 7: The Myth of Happiness 102
CHAPTER 8: Economic Systems and Social Expectations 117

Part III: Roll Up Sleeves
CHAPTER 9: Prepare Yourself 128
CHAPTER 10: Work and Live with Purpose 143
CHAPTER 11: Money Management 153

Part IV: The New Story
CHAPTER 12: Building a Vision 189
CHAPTER 13: Being the Change 208

Final Words 222
Acknowledgments 225
Notes 227
References 234

PREFACE

This book isn't just another collection of financial theories wrapped in academic language—though it does draw on rigorous research to guide your journey. This is a book about the moments that stop you in your tracks, the truths that hit hardest when you're sitting at your own kitchen table. For me, that moment came during a conversation with my eight-year-old, Sam.

We were having breakfast on a Tuesday morning, the kind where I was already mentally rehearsing my packed schedule while pouring cereal. Sam, who had been unusually quiet, suddenly looked up from his bowl. "So how much money do you earn each month?" he asked, as casually as if he'd asked about the weather. I paused, spoon halfway to my mouth. "Hmm, enough I guess. For food and housing and our hobbies. And travel, of course." He tilted his head, considering this. "So, that's what you do with that, nothing else?" "Well, there are other things, of course, but those are the main things. I do save a bit as well." I was starting to feel like I was being interviewed for a job I wasn't sure I was qualified for.

Sam nodded slowly, then continued: "So this is the reason you go to work every day and your shoulders ache and you complain that you are so busy all the time?" "Yes, so?" The defensiveness in my voice surprised even me. He shrugged, but his words carried the weight of uncomfortable truth: "It doesn't seem like you have really thought about it. I mean, why are you doing what you do? What is important to you? How is this world going to be any different when you are done?" I sat there, looking at him and trying to rack my brain for a suitable yet educational and honest enough answer. "You are important," I finally managed. "But I see your point. I will think about it and get back to you, okay?"

So, this is me getting back to you.

Money figures in our everyday choices, but it also deeply influences how we think about ourselves and our ability to get by. Money affects our relationships, our sense of purpose, our happiness, and our ability to make far-reaching, life-building decisions. Yet we talk very little about money, and when we do, it is often about not having enough or how to earn more. What we should know is how financial stress affects the brain and the decisions we make. It is also good to know what kind of financial balance is better for your mental health, what you should pay attention to, why spending money means very different things to different people, and what kind of values guide us. Financial advisers, debt counselors, and money gurus fail to reach people if they ignore what it feels like to experience a lack of money and the shame associated with it.

The first part of this book explores how our relationship with money is shaped by family attitudes, childhood experiences, cultural influences, and gender differences in financial socialization. It examines the neuroscience behind financial habits and stress responses, while addressing the powerful emotions that money triggers and how they affect our decision-making. This part discusses that while our money stories are influenced by our past, we can reshape them through self-awareness and conscious effort.

The second part focuses on identifying and understanding our core values and how they should guide our financial decisions. It explores the intersection between money-related values and materialism, while critically examining the myth that money directly creates happiness. This part emphasizes moving beyond GDP and individual wealth accumulation toward a more holistic view of progress and well-being.

The third, more practical part provides tools for mindful money management, starting with accepting financial reality and making conscious choices rather than reactive decisions. It covers finding meaning in work, distinguishing between wants and needs, and developing practical saving and investing strategies. This part also addresses the psychological aspects of social media's impact on our financial behavior and decision-making.

The fourth and final part focuses on building a personal vision for financial well-being that aligns with your values and redefining what success means beyond traditional metrics. It addresses how to handle financial setbacks with resilience and self-compassion while working toward meaningful change. This part concludes with guidance on using your financial resources and influence to create positive impact in the world, emphasizing that everyone can contribute meaningfully regardless of their economic circumstances.

Writing a book is also a financial choice. Doing things that are meaningful to you can strain the patience of those close to you, not to mention your budget. The most important things in life may well not be free, if you follow them wholeheartedly and with commitment. The ultimate purpose of this book is to convey a simple message:

Your financial actions matter more than you think.

Money-related issues, difficulties, and internal conflicts are common to all people, because we live in a world where a large part of life revolves around money. We also have the responsibility to make the best of it, to understand better how our values can guide us financially.

This book would not exist without the goodwill and generosity that many people have shown me by giving me their time and sharing their ideas and also their most painful experiences. I have met researchers, civic activists, financial advisers, mothers and fathers, enlightened young people, people struggling with addiction, people recovering from mental health issues, entrepreneurs, career coaches, and all kinds of people from different walks of life. I have had the opportunity to follow the work of inspiring and passionate researchers, from whom I have learned a great deal. However, any errors or misunderstandings are my own.

If you want practical financial advice, your questions might be either *Where can I get more money?* or *How can I get by with less?* Expertise on these questions can be found in many reputable sources. Reading this book will not make you rich (unless you think about wealth a bit differently). Nor will you be judged, whatever your relationship with money may be. I hope that you will find something different altogether—how to live a mindful and purposeful life with the resources you have.

When I started writing this book, I really wanted to understand how our shared experiences could create a more conversational and open attitude toward money and financial well-being. How could these experiences and research genuinely support value-led action and sustainable lifestyle—perhaps even bring about social change? I promise not to shy away from topics that are difficult to talk about. At best, you may gain a better understanding of your own story and ways to cope, and instead of

Preface

self-blame, you may find yourself feeling compassion toward yourself, as well as others. Regardless of your financial reality, better choices are at your reach.

Maarit Lassander
Paris, Spring 2025

PART I
THE BEGINNING

CHAPTER 1

WE ALL HAVE OUR STORY ABOUT MONEY

We cannot change anything unless we accept it.
—CARL JUNG[1]

TALKING CURE

A bank in London advertised its services with a prominent TV campaign featuring a variety of families on camera. There was a married couple, a mother and daughter, a father and adult daughter, a grandmother and grandchild, all visibly uncomfortable discussing an unnamed topic. One looked at the ceiling, another looked out the window, a third was intensely focused on tapping the coffee spoon. Viewers might assume they're discussing sex, given the palpable awkwardness. The situations are staged, yet the campaign resonates because the discomfort feels universal. The reveal comes when a friendly bank official announces, "At last, we're talking about money"—but only after viewers call a bank adviser, since these families clearly aren't ready to broach the subject themselves.

With a few exceptions, it seems that most cultures around the world avoid talking about money. Many of us can surely imagine the conflicting, awkward feelings that arise when money is brought up. You may even be feeling them now as you read this. You might feel like dropping the whole subject, putting it off until later, or just glancing through the chapter titles quickly. But I would encourage you to stay with it, and I will try to explain why it matters.

Any topic shrouded in silence harbors hidden structures of power, shame, and guilt that resist examination. Taking control requires the ability to say: "This is my reality, shaped by my past and still shaping my future." When facing difficulties, most often the smartest response is to talk about it. This principle applies equally to well-being and money—and especially to the complex relationship between them.

Some time ago, a friend of mine was in trouble and needed emotional support. Irina is a young adult woman with an interesting financial background. In Irina's family, working hard was highly valued, and doing well at school and in hobbies was rewarded. Irina's mother, despite her good salary, was in constant need of money. She often went out with the children to the town, where she would buy clothes and other things for the whole family on a whim. Irina was happy to go shopping with her mother, enjoying the time together that otherwise seemed to be scarce. Spontaneous shopping trips caused conflict between the parents, however, and the atmosphere at home was sometimes very tense. From an early age, Irina got used to smuggling shopping home in old cloth bags, because then her father would not notice that they had been out shopping. New items were hidden away until they were gradually and carefully brought out, with perhaps half-heedless mention of a trip to the flea market.

Irina's parents divorced around the same time the children moved away from home. Now, as a young adult, Irina finds earning and spending money distressing. She often makes expensive impulse purchases, and the guilt they cause makes her avoid anything to do with money, including opening bills. Irina's sister Lara, three years younger, avoids buying even useful things until they become utterly necessary. Lara oriented herself at an early age toward studying ecological, alternative technologies; she saves a significant part of her salary and considers all purchases carefully. Sometimes she finds it hard to enjoy life, because even buying necessities feels like a distressing experience.

In every family, money has its place at the table. Sometimes it is not talked about, sometimes it is talked about in a roundabout way, and sometimes it is called success. Money is never irrelevant, not even when its importance is not acknowledged. The significance of money is often related to how we think about work, housework, livelihood, personal responsibility, or balanced life in general. And all this, in turn, starts with the people who matter most to us, how they dealt with their own story about money when we were children. This is not to say that all children in the same family are born with a similar way of acting or relating to money. A child's experiences are linked to when they were born into the family, the temperament and personality they develop, and how they interact with the adults in their family.

No predetermined paths or experiences guarantee specific life outcomes. We are all individuals who, through our unique perspectives and tendencies, construct our own understanding of the world and how it operates. Yet it remains true that the more we encounter cultures of shame and silence in our everyday lives, the more likely we are to experience anxiety, guilt, and persistent avoidance when confronting these very issues throughout our lives. Regardless of our financial circumstances, our relationship with money can be—and often is—surprisingly complex.

Another friend of mine, Robert, comes from a poor family. While studying, he worked in a fast-food restaurant, as a mystery shopper, and as a telephone salesman to finance his education. Robert's mother is a single parent who has had to balance a meager income, two jobs, and three children for most of her life. Robert has not asked his mother for money since he was a teenager and often uses his own money to buy gasoline for his mother's car or groceries. He regularly experiences stress and anxiety because he feels he has no control over things and money is always tight no matter what he does. He worries about money, makes budgets, tries to anticipate bills, and checks his bank account balance daily. Sometimes he also wakes up in the morning with money worries. Even though Robert is studying business at university, he fears that life will never get easier.

The idea that our financial situation is entirely our own responsibility can easily lead to strong feelings of guilt. To think that being poor or destitute is our own fault is likely to mean that we have made the wrong choices, but also that we are not as smart as others and unable to look after ourselves. We can be blamed, discouraged, or judged for any of the above in any situation. The burden of poverty is not only a lack of money but also a lack of self-esteem and control over one's life.

If we want to make lasting, positive changes in our lives, this mindset is not a good starting point. Long-term, chronic stress—in this case, caused by financial difficulties—is associated with a learned helplessness, where discouragement is followed by a failure to try to influence one's situation. This is also a clear risk factor for depression and anxiety disorders.² Change requires both strength and faith in the future. To succeed, we need self-acceptance and the understanding that things are not permanent—we have the power to change them.

Poverty makes anyone miserable, I think we can all agree on that. The experience of poverty is strongly linked to the income level of the people around you. In a wealthy neighborhood, the external signs of wealth escalate and encourage people to keep up the same pace of consumption as their neighbors, making them feel poor even on average incomes.³ Poverty is an objective issue only in World Bank statistics, where internationally poverty is defined as an income of less than $1.90 a day. In some countries, the poverty line is set on a relatively high level. In the United States today, for example, it means a monthly individual income of less than $1,000. In India, people are considered poor if their monthly income is less than $15.

Poverty is largely determined by what income is sufficient to live on in each country, but psychological poverty—the experience of what other members of the community have in terms of income—is also a key factor. In developed countries, comparing oneself with others is often a source of competition, and satisfaction is especially felt when one's income is higher than the income of others. In developing countries, the effect can also be the opposite: higher incomes of neighbors and friends can encourage and motivate by example. It is very human to think that "if they can do it, so can I."

Although studies show that people are not happier because of money, they continue to chase it because they *believe* they will be happier. However, we often struggle to identify what truly drives our well-being. One reason for this is the way society talks about wealth. It is assumed that everyone is trying to increase their wealth over a lifetime and at the same time to secure their future—for example, to save for their retirement. Consumption and the products we own are also more than just goods, they are *symbols of* what we want to be or show ourselves to be. For me, it might be important to buy my child branded shoes for winter sports. They are not essentially better than any other shoes, if we are honest, but this consumer choice shows that I care, I am a capable mother, and I attach great importance to my child's comfort and dry feet. On a deeper level, the shoes reflect a warm family life, order, lack of haste, appreciation of nature, and peace of mind. And it really is just shoes. What a feeling of satisfaction, the small triumphs of parenthood! No wonder, then, that among all these different emotions, it's hard to describe one's own relationship with money.

+ + +

Each generation develops its own financial script based on the economic realities of their formative years, creating gaps in understanding that go far beyond simple differences in spending habits. In the West, younger generations may not have experienced poverty and deprivation in the same way as their parents or have a different idea of work and its relationship to income. Economic justice meant something different to those who fought for labor unions than it does to today's young adults campaigning for universal basic income—each generation's definition is shaped by the injustices they've witnessed firsthand.

I believe that younger generations may be our key to breaking free from the prosperity-happiness myth that has trapped previous generations in endless cycles of earning and yearning. We already suspect that as income levels rise, the experience of happiness decreases and stress and dissatisfaction with life increases. Professionals with high incomes can be surprisingly unhappy: studies have shown that lawyers, bankers, and HR professionals are significantly more unhappy with their lives than gardeners and florists, who are happier in their profession than many other groups.[4] One reason for this may be the opportunity to spend time in a natural environment surrounded by plants, but it is certainly not the only one.

Another interesting finding of economic research is that people's satisfaction with their income significantly influences how they subjectively assess their financial adequacy.[5] In other words, if you feel that you are getting a fair wage for your efforts—whatever your actual income level—you are also likely to perceive your income level as better than the neighbor who complains about being underpaid (and probably also undervalued) in their current job.

WHAT WE SEE, WE LEARN

The young couple's winter had been even tougher than usual. There were layoffs at the factory, and loan interests were at an all-time high. To lower expectations, perhaps their own as well, they tell their daughter well in advance that Santa Claus has had so many children with gift lists at his door this winter that he has run out of presents. Santa's bank account is not bottomless, so he may not have enough money to buy more gifts (everybody knew that he did not really manufacture them). For a five-year-old, this is a disaster, and for the parents, it means worry and anxiety.

Children often have an innate ability to solve problems if they do not cause too much fear or anxiety. So the child wraps up old toys for her mother, father, grandparents, and even herself. She thinks she is the hero of Christmas, because there is already so much and opening presents is the best thing in the world. She solves the first problem in their life related to a lack of money and, at the same time, strives to bring joy to her family.

This is my first memory of money.

The story also has a happier ending: Santa Claus had found gifts for the young family after all. The old toys were quietly returned to the children's room, and the matter was never mentioned again.

So why has that Christmas remained indelibly etched in my memory? The memory is somewhat contradictory. It tells of adapting to things that challenge one's understanding. It's about the common experience relative to poverty and insecurity and how they affect the whole family in a safe Western country. Nearly 14 percent (2024) of US children live below the poverty line, but experiences and memories of financial hardship are always individual.[6] Parents' income does not tell the whole story. However, it is important to note that a lack of money is not just a matter for adults and individuals; it deeply affects the lives of families, single people, pensioners, and children. How we feel about not having enough money or spending money sends important messages about our attitudes and values to our kids—and not always in the way we would choose if we stopped to think about it.

Over time, my first memory related to money and many experiences since then reinforced a fixed mindset that I didn't really question, because I didn't even notice it was there. I believed that whether we had plenty of money or just about enough, we would manage and our problems would be temporary. On the other hand, I also believed that the lack of money should be discussed as little as possible, as it is an exceptional and even shameful situation that should not happen to normal, middle-income family. For years, this cement-like and at the same time very unconscious way of thinking influenced countless decisions and choices. I sat in the bank applying for a mortgage, bought a trendy financial guide, spent money I didn't have, did my taxes, and left my finances in someone else's hands. All of this—my own story about money—started very early on.

Families have their own ways of doing things. Financial habits—saving, attitudes toward debt and spending—are also to some extent learned. Research shows that social wealth is passed down from one generation to the next, with an estimated 40 to 60 percent of income levels being inherited.[7] The heritability is slightly higher for men than for women. If we ignore material inheritances—wealth that is passed on to the next generation—what is inherited? Research shows that inherited traits that influence wealth include personality traits, addictions, and cognitive abilities, which in turn can influence educational choices, career choices, work-related priorities, and risk-taking.[8]

Parental influence is surprisingly long-lasting, according to research, and may be greater for young adults' financial learning, attitudes, and behavior than schooling and work experience combined. While in adulthood we acquire financial skills and education, the family legacy is not lost.[9] For example, research shows that parents' debt is of little importance to children's financial literacy, but if parents avoid talking about financial matters, it has a negative impact on the young person's later credit card use.[10] If you are a parent, you have more influence than you think.

Parenthood is one of the most life-changing roles you may experience. A few years ago, I attended a very popular lecture given by mindfulness master Jon Kabat-Zinn. Hundreds of people had packed into a small hall to listen to this pioneer and founder of the Mindfulness-Based Stress Reduction (MBSR) program that combines mindfulness meditation and hatha yoga principles and is designed to help people cope with pain, stress, and illness. At the end of the lecture, he talked about how parenthood reveals more about us than we would like. How children, especially teenagers, know us better than anyone else. They know and understand our every gesture and expression, and, above all, how we react in different situations. They know how to pull the strings and push the buttons that trigger a reaction time and time again. The most challenging task we can set ourselves is to surprise these all-knowing people in our lives. Kabat-Zinn suggested that the next time you find yourself in a situation where you are once again on the verge of being that predictable parent, give yourself a chance to stop and consciously choose how you want to act.

This is, of course, easier said than done—if you are a parent, you may find that it is far easier to fall back on your usual behavior. Conflicts often become bigger than life because there are two of us, an unyielding younger person facing a stubborn older person. Neuroscience tells us about the effects of parenting on the brain: it is a real hurricane. At no other time in adult life do such significant changes occur in the brain as when an adult becomes a parent.[11] These changes are intended to prepare the ground for a connection that gives us the ability to care for, protect, and understand these small creatures. Similar changes also occur in the brains of adoptive fathers and mothers, so it is not just a matter of biological parenthood or the hormonal storm caused by childbirth.[12]

Since parenting isn't easy, it's a shame that we tend to make it even harder on ourselves. In traditional communities, parenting is a shared responsibility for the whole village, but in the modern society it's become a lonely battle for one or two people. When there's no one else to share the responsibility, the entire burden of parenting is distributed very unevenly. At the same time, we become uncertain about our ability to be fully present or engage meaningfully with anyone other than our own children. Ultimately, parenting does not even require having children of your own (who are not, of course, ours in any real sense of the word) but rather taking responsibility, showing interest, tolerating uncertainty and discomfort, and recognizing the child's inner world. I always get emotional when I read Nick Hornby's book *About a Boy*, in which the main character, twelve-year-old Marcus, quite realistically observes that one adult in life is no guarantee of security—more adults are needed, and they should also care about each other.

+ + +

In many ways parenthood today may look like a performance. Parenting is a complex set of tasks in which it is unusually easy to make mistakes and everyone encounters difficulties along the way. William MacAskill is a Scottish philosopher who advocates long-term thinking: the importance of our actions in the present is largely determined by their impact in the long term, even thousands or millions of years from now. In my opinion, this is a truly revolutionary idea from the perspective of parenting. Instead of spending all our energy on hawkishly monitoring our offspring's schedules, taking them to several activities a week, and wondering if it's too late to start Chinese lessons, we could see parenting as a bigger role, a partnership and an opportunity to care for young people and children because they deserve it, not because it makes us better people.

Childlessness will also become more common in the future. Whether this is an intentional or unintentional outcome, it doesn't change the fact that we all—parents and non-parents alike—remain responsible for the world we leave to future generations. Perhaps what is more important is the environment we provide for all the children around us. Is there love, joy, and acceptance? Is it possible to thrive, whether you are a child or a parent?

At the pediatrician's office, parents are often asked if they have a support network, people who not only care about what is happening to them but can also help out from time to time when things go wrong. This is not always a simple question. In our Western societies there are more and more people who feel isolated, whose safety nets have been left behind or broken, especially in larger cities. Families and clans have traditionally provided security in unexpected situations, offering both material and spiritual aid. Social and economic capital are strongly interconnected, and social networks, especially those provided by the family and relatives, are a privilege. The accumulation of privileges is linked to social power and the ability to make decisions about one's own life.

Some parents live without the security of a family or relatives, without a co-parent, or otherwise in difficult circumstances. In such cases, I would like to say this above all: seek support, even if you don't think you need it. A support network or extended family or community is a form of life insurance for all of us that cannot be underestimated. If we are lucky, it will come naturally. Sometimes, however, the people around us who should be there to help are unable to fulfill this role and we have to work hard to build a strong community. The absence of a support network or family reflects circumstance, not personal failing—it's both unlucky and unfortunately common. Developing these relationships requires time, patience, and often creativity, but our capacity for connection grows with practice. We learn to trust other people and to be important pillars of support for others. At its best, the role of parenting could be about giving mutual support to each other, to families, kids, and young people who need it.

Low income per se is not automatically passed on from one generation to the next. However, the heritability of well-being and poverty is a reminder that there are many risk factors for economic well-being among low-income earners, and awareness of these will help to break the intergenerational trend. Models from around the world increasingly favor two-generation approaches that support parents and children simultaneously, helping families get the best possible start during the transition to parenthood.[13]

The extent to which children care for their own parents and the impact this has on their well-being has become apparent. Research shows that parents often underestimate the level of concern their children feel and overestimate the level of optimism. They also judge their children's emotional state as a reflection of their own and may find it difficult to understand feelings of worry from their children's perspective.[14] Families who plan for multigenerational well-being—rather than leaving care arrangements to chance—experience less financial stress and stronger relationships across all generations.

We don't have to have money to form perceptions and opinions about it. We all have the freedom to be aware of and interested in the opportunities that money offers, and children learn attitudes and values from their parents. They may not be able to use their learning because of their age, but it forms the basis for future learning and action. It is often thought that only schoolchildren are mature enough to understand the importance of money and to learn how to use it. However, behavioral scientists Sue Bingham and David Whitebread of Cambridge University looked at the available studies and came to a different conclusion.[15] They found that children adopt money habits before the age of seven and that these habits, acquired in childhood, are not easily changed. This means that as soon as children begin to understand the concept of purchasing power, they also begin to form ideas about money. These perceptions are often based on the everyday behavior of their parents. This does not mean that as a parent of a ten-year-old your child is doomed to a lifetime of debt and impulsive shopping (if only I had known!), but it does mean that our behavior as parents matters.

Each child is an individual with his or her own needs and aspirations. If you want to nurture positive financial behaviors and attitudes, here are a few suggestions for action. They are not all-encompassing truths but observations based on discussions at pediatrician's offices, primary health care, and schools. They are also supported by recent research on how children form their financial awareness.

Talk to your children about their relationship with money. Avoid offering your own opinions or beliefs unless asked. Instead, be interested in hearing what they think. You can also ask what they want to spend money on and what is important to them. Does it make a difference whether we are talking about tomorrow or next year? If they are aware of the family's potential financial difficulties, be open about where you stand and how you feel about them. At the same time, emphasize the security of the family and the adults' responsibilities.

Take your children to the grocery store. Let them compare and make decisions, talk about the criteria for choosing products, make a shopping list in advance, and show how planning can help to avoid impulse buying and get the things you really need.

Avoid telling children that you don't have money if it's not true. Many kids have a very concrete way of thinking about events and their consequences. If you don't want to buy something, tell them directly that you don't want to buy it and why. Also try to be consistent with your own rules if you don't want to discuss them on a daily basis. Kids cannot be responsible for the family's finances, but they may want to contribute—for example, by offering to sell unwanted items at a garage sale. They are often very aware of what is going on in the family but may not want to ask if they think the subject is difficult for you.

Think about your message. Your message will be conveyed not so much through speech as through consumer choices—what you choose and how. Combining financial awareness and practicality is not always easy, but verbalizing choices and the thought processes behind them will also help your kids to make better choices in the future.

Help your children to learn the value of money. Help them to buy things for themselves and to be responsible for a small amount of money when they are ready. Earning a small amount of money through chores helps to understand the relationship between time and money. Saving is a habit that, if learned early in childhood, will have a big impact on how easy it is to do as an adult. You can help your kids to set savings goals and postpone buying a much-anticipated toy, for example, by teaching them strategies that work. If they want a skateboard for their birthday, they can prepare in advance by visiting nearby skate parks or design a board for themselves.

Avoid telling educational stories about money if you haven't experienced them yourself. You can share your own experiences when your children seem interested. In particular, talk about what you have learned through trial and error. Talk about money as you would talk about any other everyday subject. Pay particular attention to how you talk to your partner, and remember that these conversations have long-lasting effects on those listening around you.

Notice that the world is different now than it was before. Your children's experience of growing up in this world is different from yours. Things are talked about and approached differently. Listen to what they are saying and try to learn from it. Be interested rather than omniscient.

And finally, if you want to explore how you (or your child) feel about money, play Monopoly.

When I play Monopoly with my son Sam, he keeps an eye on the situation, and when my money starts to run out, he does everything he can to make sure I don't lose right away. If necessary, he slips me a few bills and mutters that it's a loan. It's not that he doesn't want to win, but wants to win after a long and satisfying game in which we both enjoyed the journey. I accept his loan with gratitude and amusement, acknowledging my mistakes. By contrast, his twin, Elliot, is a born banker. He will play until the bitter end, and only to win, being usually also very good at that. But as I said, it's not about the money, it's about the journey.

PERSONALITIES

Imagine that you have made an appointment with a bank adviser and arrive a little early. You are directed to sit in a comfortable armchair and given a questionnaire to fill in on a tablet. You flick through the answers and finally receive a summary that maps your personality against five different traits. This summary also provides you with information on how you can practice skills that will support your financial well-being in the future. You can choose whether you want to keep the conclusions you receive or use them in a meeting with your bank adviser.

Answering the questionnaire may remind you that because conscientiousness is not your strongest trait, you tend to sign papers without reading them thoroughly. You may also find that because you find it difficult to trust the economy to develop in a good direction, you avoid taking out a loan, even though it might enable you to realize a long-term dream. By recognizing your own patterns of behavior, you will be able to assess what they bring to your life.

Personality is a set of unique psychological characteristics, such as how we think, express emotions, and act in different situations. Personality begins to take shape in early childhood and adolescence, and is shaped by genetic factors and early environmental experiences, social relationships, and neurobiology. Personality evolves throughout life, although certain basic traits remain relatively stable. The five major personality traits (neuroticism, extroversion, openness, conscientiousness, agreeableness) have long been the most common way of defining personality, but in recent years broader definitions have been proposed.

In addition to emotional experiences, personality also influences whether we live with enough money and feel financially secure.[16] Of the individual personality traits, conscientiousness and neuroticism may be particularly relevant to financial management, so I focus on them here. Conscientiousness can be described as orderliness, planning, reliability, and responsibility, and its opposite is indifference. Neuroticism is the tendency to experience unpleasant emotions such as anxiety, loneliness, worry, guilt, and fear, as opposed to being emotionally balanced. If we are overwhelmed by worry and anxiety, we may not have the courage to seize the opportunity, prepare for the future, or be confident in our own abilities. To be able to act at all, we need to believe that our actions matter. This is all made more difficult by the neurotic nature of our character.

Several previous studies have concluded that personality traits remain relatively stable throughout life. However, more recent studies have shown that personality does change, albeit slowly, and generally in a positive direction. One of the most interesting studies on changes in human personality began in Scotland in the 1950s. Teachers of fourteen-year-old students filled out a questionnaire that assessed the young people's self-confidence, perseverance, emotional control, conscientiousness, and motivation to learn. About sixty years later, the researchers met with 674 of the original study participants, who assessed themselves using the same questionnaires and also asked a friend or relative to do the same.[17] The consistency of the questionnaire responses was very low, almost nonexistent. This is perhaps not so surprising when you consider sixty years of life experience, but according to the researchers, even in a much shorter period of time, fundamental changes can occur.

What if you ask yourself how likely it is that in the next five or ten years you will have changed significantly as a person? If you are like me and many of your fellow human beings, you would not consider this very likely. However, according to research, it is quite likely, even if we do not notice the change ourselves. It also seems that the more time passes, the more comprehensive the change may be.

Personality changes are often related to the social roles and responsibilities that people take on over time.[18] For example, people generally become more conciliatory and conscientious when they take on responsibility in different areas of life. One such responsibility is parenthood, which for many seems to be one of the biggest changes in life, also in terms of self-perception. The good news is that emotional stability seems to increase with age.[19]

One study of young adults suggests that conscientiousness predicts better financial well-being and neuroticism predicts financial distress.[20] Similar results have been found in other studies, and the importance of conscientiousness in particular has been noted many times. This result is perhaps not surprising, but it is important to recognize its implications. On a positive note, studies have also shown that both conscientiousness and neuroticism are mutable traits. Sometimes they are modified by life experiences, sometimes they can be influenced by a determined effort. Because personality traits change and can be changed, they do not directly dictate the direction of life or who has the opportunity for economic prosperity.

+ + +

Research on personality and economic well-being is important because it seems that by promoting the mental health of children and young people, we can invest in their economic future. A sense of security in childhood supports development and capacity to explore the world with confidence in one's own abilities. The less young people experience depression, anxiety, and constant worry, the more opportunities they have to acquire skills and knowledge about how to make positive financial decisions. Positive conscientiousness is based less on external rules or fear of breaking rules and more on internal motivation. A conscientious young person can have the courage to make their own decisions and pursue the goals that feel right to them.

In addition to conscientiousness and neuroticism, other personality traits also have an impact on financial well-being. For example, it has been found that spending according to one's personality traits increases happiness. Outwardly oriented people experience more pleasure when choosing, for example, a restaurant night out with friends, while more introverted people may experience pleasure from a good book and an evening at home.[21] So knowing yourself and making choices that respect your own psychological needs can contribute to a balanced emotional life.

The best thing about life, however, is that when we find ourselves drifting down unfamiliar paths, it is always possible to stop and ask ourselves whether we have lost something particularly valuable. Personality is not permanent, neither in youth, adulthood, nor old age, but conscious change requires conscious choices. If we want to bring something new into our life, we need to have a meaningful goal. This meaning, purpose, or goal gives us a reason to acquire new skills, meet new people, and try new things. Without a meaningful landmark, change is like throwing a boat into the waves without oars or a rudder. It will move, but we cannot influence its direction.

THE STATUS OF WEALTH

Status is often strongly associated with financial success. There's a cruel irony at work: if your mental image of financial success doesn't include people who look, sound, or act like you, your brain will sabotage your efforts before you even begin. Success becomes "something other people do"—people who apparently share none of your characteristics.

WE ALL HAVE OUR STORY ABOUT MONEY

That's all in the past, you might think. Modern civilized countries are different, we are not shackled by such relics of the past. When we think of developments over a few generations, we tend to underestimate how centuries of tradition still guide both popular culture and people's daily lives. I listen half carelessly as my eldest son plays his latest favorite song on Spotify, where a successful young male artist takes his (hot) chick to Mallorca because women like it when you show you've got some guap (money). This, of course, leads to a conversation where the young man wisely states that he understands my point of view and escapes to his room (headphones on) as soon as possible.

How far are we really from economic gender roles when they are presented to us in popular form as acceptable and entertaining? How many of us really question the catchy melody or the infectious rap that is used as an excuse to serve us the world of the past in a new wrapping? In more statistical terms, according to YouGov 2024 profiles (USA), 25 percent of men earn over $100,000 compared to just 12 percent of women.[22]

Status cannot be held by one person alone; it is always comparable to others and requires a community and an understanding of what is valued by the members of that community. Status isn't portable—it's like currency that loses value when you cross borders. Your corner office commands respect at the board meeting, but at the PTA potluck what matters is whether you can coordinate the book fair. This constant status-shifting can be jarring for those accustomed to deference, while low status can create a ripple effect of social insecurity that spills into every interaction.

Status anxieties take root in highly connected social media. According to studies conducted half a century ago, nearly 10 percent of our thoughts during the day concern social comparisons we make between ourselves and others,[23] and it's much higher today. After all, we have countless opportunities to do so.

In general, comparing oneself to others is a natural way of measuring one's own performance and achievements, especially when other benchmarks are not available. Regardless of the focus of the comparison, it is harmful to us if it becomes excessive and compulsive, which social media also makes possible. The pursuit of adequacy is a pandemic in our psychological world, and children and young people who feel they have to prove themselves endlessly are particularly susceptible to it. Young women who always see something better on social media; young men who cannot find friends; mothers and fathers who see their children suffering; people at the peak of their careers, influencers, multitaskers. According to a survey conducted in the United Kingdom (2019), four out of five young adults feel inadequate.[24]

According to research by Robert Sapolsky, the blood vessels of higher-status monkeys calcify more slowly than those of lower-status monkeys, and they live longer.[25] High status also appears to increase lifespan and health in people at work, especially when status is based on respect and prestige. No wonder the pursuit and valuation of status is inherent in humans. When a status is either developed over time or earned through achievement, it can become central to one's self-concept. Many successful artists, athletes, politicians, and leaders find it difficult to give up the status that their accomplishments confer.

Paul Gilbert, on the other hand, has studied the links between status and depression and found that shame, social anxiety, and depression are common among people who are involuntarily relegated to a lower status in their own group.[26] The Whitehall studies, which began in the 1960s and have followed British civil servants to this day, repeat the findings of Sapolsky's monkey studies: higher status at work increases life expectancy and improves health if status is based on natural achievements such as experience and human leadership.[27] Research shows that status based on respect and esteem is associated with better well-being.[28] Such earned prestige is also good for the community, as it motivates leaders to pursue prestige through fairness, clarity, and effective relationships. If status is linked to external factors such as money or inherited status, competition is created, with negative effects on society.

The acquisition of status is inherent to human beings. We tend to judge ourselves by external factors and try to increase our value compared to others. However, if high status is thought to come from financial success alone, we end up with problems. When status is based only on the size of our wallet, it says little about our values, experiences, or success at work. As a thought experiment, we might consider whether, for example, a low-paid paramedic is inherently less committed, experienced, or skilled at his or her job than a highly paid company director. Another questionable idea is that if people are measured by money, different people will inevitably have different values; you can test the problematic nature of this idea by trying to rank your children or loved ones. People are unique individuals, singular and valuable in their own right.

The third problem is that achieving and maintaining status based on money is a source of real anxiety in Western societies. This anxiety leads to constant worry and evaluation of one's own performance. When we doubt our abilities, we feel compelled to constantly prove ourselves and behave in ways that match the status we're pursuing.

High and low income separates people, but status based on materialistic values has an even greater impact. It breeds a lack of trust and distances people from their social and pluralistic community. Security is based on small reference groups, so-called bubbles, where people feel understood through their common background and experiences. As people distance themselves from the community, this is associated with an emphasis on individual values and autonomy. We are then simultaneously alone and yet increasingly subject to criticism from people we do not know. "Why would you put your self-worth in the hands of strangers?" asks actress Helena Bonham-Carter in an interview with a weekly magazine, referring to auditions. This question captures a defining feature of our media-saturated age: every day we put our sense of self and self-worth in the hands of people who don't really know us. It is very easy to get feedback on the way we are and live through social media. Social pressure also increases social anxiety. When relationships are fleeting and short-lived, an idealistic and, in a way, superficial image of what so-called normal life can be is accentuated.

At its best, status is a way of rewarding activities that benefit the whole community. At worst, it is a personal prison. Status built on competition creates an endless cycle of self-promotion and reputation management. Where the PR department is responsible for a company's media image, today we are all responsible for our own brand on social media, building and maintaining status for an imaginary audience. Status can be based on followers, notoriety, life management, or expertise, but often its value proposition is also based on financial success or decision-making power. There are exceptions to this. Sometimes status also comes from the ability to articulate and normalize people's experiences, thoughts, and feelings in a way that touches and creates hope. This form of status is perhaps the most difficult to achieve, as it often requires throwing oneself into the ring and being vulnerable in the public arena.

Income inequality also contributes to money being used to boost status. The more important it is to demonstrate our worth through wealth, the more we feel insecure, experiencing the constant need to compare, the need to earn more because our neighbor seems to earn more, and exhaustion when life is focused on maintaining status, work, and its monetary value. According to some researchers, economic inequality increases people's experience of insecure status, which in turn undermines trust in others.[29] The more our status in society is based on external and materialistic factors—where I live, where I work, what I wear, how I spend my leisure time—the more pressure there is to do better and create a better first impression. The greater the income gap, the more pronounced and visible the differences in status. If economic inequality is a risk factor for everyone, then everyone should be aware of these side effects.

Status hierarchies also affect our thinking and our ability to act. Our own expectations of our financial and social abilities influence how children from low-income families do on exams, how women perform in math, what jobs we tend to take, what responsibilities we dare to take on. When status matters greatly and income inequality is high, economic growth slows—meaning the apparent success of privileged groups ultimately undermines their own prosperity.[30]

CHAPTER 2
THE SOCIETY

Sorry! The lifestyle you ordered is currently out of stock.
—BANKSY, GRAFFITI ON A STREET IN LONDON

THE CULTURE WE ARE

On a Sunday afternoon, Julia enters an apartment building where a dozen women are already waiting. The atmosphere is cheerful and boisterous, the table laden with all kinds of delicacies they have brought with them from different cultures: potato chips, baklava, potato and egg casserole, ham and cheese pie, blueberry cupcakes. . . . Julia throws her scarf on the bench and hurries into the living room, where an office is set up at the table. One of the women collects the envelopes the guests have brought. She counts the contents and writes the numbers in a large black notebook. Today is a party for Julia's friend Nadine, who is going to visit her relatives in the Basque Country. Nadine hasn't traveled since the pandemic and misses her family. But she's also survived long periods of temporary and casual employment. Everything is in short supply, and she has had to give up the extras.

Julia lives in Montpellier, France, and is part of the "tontine" circle. There is no direct equivalent for the word *tontine* in English, but it can be described as a "savings group" or "common savings pot." Julia's group is a community of twelve women who act as a small-scale bank. Its members deposit a small amount of money each month in an account. Each month, they also get together to celebrate one of them receiving these deposits. The celebrations are like little monthly birthday parties.

Members of the ring have used their deposits to buy things that would normally take them longer to save for: a new washing machine, tickets for a summer holiday, a computer. Of course, one might ask if they couldn't just save the money in their own accounts. They could, but the fun of the tontine ring is that sometimes you hit the jackpot even if you haven't had time to save anything, and other times saving together motivates you to set goals.

This kind of joint savings group requires trust and commitment but also the courage to be honest about your own finances. All of the women are involved because it is meaningful for them to save and use their savings for the things that matter to them. They don't have stocks and shares, big buffers, or the ability to make expensive purchases without a lot of planning. They sigh with relief if they don't have to go to the bank and convince others of their financial capabilities, take out quick loans for life's unexpected situations, or look for hire-purchase options with interest rates that bring tears to anyone's eyes. In our communities we could help each other in many ways if we asked for help more and with ease.

The history of money is also the history of social development.[1] Any object or thing that society has defined as a medium of exchange can be so-called fiat money (*fiat* is Latin for "so be it"). Many of the laws of economics are common conventions, can be modeled, and have concrete applications. Did you know that in 1949 economic data were analyzed by a hydraulic computer? The machine pumps water into pipes and tanks to simulate the economy. Fourteen of these MONIAC machines remain, and you can watch them in action in a video online. The MONIAC machine's pipes and tanks represent different parts of the economy, such as banks, consumption, people's personal savings, taxes, foreign investment, and so on. It is still enlightening to see how the parts of the economy are interconnected.

Physical money has taken many forms and has not always been regulated by states. During the Western Han Dynasty (200 BCE) the Chinese used horseshoe-shaped gold ingots as money, and around 600 BCE the Greeks introduced a coin made of an alloy called electrum, or green gold. Peter the Great (1672–1725) introduced the beard coin, which was given to bearded men who had paid the required beard or moustache tax. The cryptocurrencies of the modern world, on the other hand, are created by computers solving complex mathematical problems.

Money carries different cultural meanings—from a tool of independence in some societies to a symbol of family obligation in others. In some cultures, there is a strong belief that an individual must try to earn as much money as possible to survive because society's safety nets are inadequate. In the Nordic welfare states, on the other hand, there may be a greater reliance on social support, and once a certain level of income is reached, money means much less. In Pakistan, the law stipulates that 2.5 percent of income must be given to charity (Zakat), emphasizing individual responsibility for the underprivileged in society. Consumption may be perceived as either increasing (as in Russia) or decreasing (as in India) life satisfaction.

Although countries and cultures differ, one thing emerges from conversations everywhere. While many people understand economic theory, few have received practical guidance on managing their own money. Understanding our own finances is a life skill with far-reaching implications. It affects not only the control and independence of our own life but also the ability to understand the financial problems of others.

Research shows that wealth appears to be a protective factor in social relationships, with wealthier people less likely to be lonely. One explanation for this could be that wealth enables people to maintain social relationships.[2] Financial constraints can isolate us: we cannot afford to participate, to travel, to acquire knowledge and skills, or to spend time away from work. On the other hand, studies have shown that social relationships can protect against the negative effects of financial deprivation. Trust in others is one of the most important pillars of well-being and is worth holding on to.

Prosperity and status as determinants of life can also be crippling. Why are financial setbacks and bumps so stressful? Financial insecurity is inconvenient to say the least, and sometimes even a threat to survival. But it does not explain the shame and silence that often follows bankruptcy. One of the reasons why financial stress is particularly hard on us may be our own culture. Culture and brain develop in interaction with each other. Culture plays a large part in determining what causes us stress, determining whether we see ourselves as independent entrepreneurs or as members of a community.

A comparison of Western and Eastern cultures has shown that practical demands, such as communal rice plantations in Asia, have forced people to develop communal skills and thinking.[3] Elsewhere, where farming is more of a family and individual enterprise, individual-centered culture has taken hold. Individualism and community influences everything we do, even whether we look first at the person in the picture or the context in which they are placed. Our brains learn through a lifetime of practice to prioritize culture, because without it we cannot be a full part of the human community.

Many people believe that money and wealth influence people's personalities and attitudes. We easily believe that wealth protects us and makes us unbreakable, but does it make us indifferent to others? Joseph Henrich has written about the Western man as the strangest creation of mankind.[4] Several statistics, metrics, and time series show how the Western normal differs significantly from other inhabitants of the planet. And yet we may think it is the most natural way for humans to exist. Henrich also challenges the common perception that differences between countries and cultures are specifically related to wealth and that wealth has made us psychologically different. In reality, he argues, wealth has had a relatively small impact on people.

Of course, various strategies, forms of interaction, and goals are different in less affluent environments, where social safety nets ensure survival even in unexpected crisis situations. But it is still too early to assume that money and wealth are the beginning and end of everything. The forces of religion and culture have led us toward a society in which independence, survival, broken family ties, and decreasing trust in society (welfare state) have also made us more vulnerable to the lure of money and wealth. It has become a way of securing one's life and standard of living, as families and communities have done for hundreds of years.

Where families used to be our financial safety net, today more and more people feel responsible for their financial realities alone. When finances are tight, being alone can feel particularly heavy and shameful—how to tell friends and acquaintances that we can't afford the same things they can. Surprisingly, many people seem willing to live on a small budget and compromise on small pleasures but don't want to admit they are poorer than others. The stigma associated with poverty is particularly strong in our own minds, although we know that financial hardship has caught up with those who previously did not seem to have money worries.

The last few years have treated us all very differently, and debt has a long track record. It is therefore important that we are kind and considerate toward each other, that we consider any economic concerns that are not always visible on the surface, and that we limit our consumption in a way that is not only socially sustainable but also humanely necessary. If the cost of participation becomes an obstacle to doing things together, we might ask what is most valuable—enjoying each other's company or not giving up a certain lifestyle. In my childhood, growing up in Northern Finland, people were extremely wary of talking about elite sport or club memberships because it goes against the ideal of an equal society. This has changed, of course, over the years, but my beliefs and attitudes have been shaped by this narrative. Not everyone has the opportunity to join in, and it depends on your own beliefs whether you think they should have.

EXPECTATIONS, HOPES, AND AMBITIONS

On an autumn evening in October, I walked along a cobbled path covered by wet maple leaves. I tried to make out the house numbers that were hidden in the shadows of the dark branches until I arrived in front of a small, decorative house with a red door. It looked inviting, and I took a deep breath, knocked on the door, and waited for footsteps. The door opened, and a flood of scents and warmth poured out.

I have lived a large part of my life outside Finland, and especially during my years in England, I felt like a stranger in a foreign country, where my partner settled more easily as a postgraduate student. I longed for something of my own that would allow me to build a normal life in a small British town. Eventually, I joined a choir, not so much because of my modest singing skills but with the intention of finding a group of people with whom I could share everyday experiences. I attended rehearsals diligently, sang the St. Matthew Passion conscientiously in local churches, and pushed myself to better understand the lives of more-senior women and men with full lives and families.

My commitment was rewarded one weekend with an invitation to dinner. Despite all my good intentions, the dinner felt like an endless series of painful events. Since I had come without my partner, there was a sad empty seat next to me, which the hostess occasionally glanced at with a sigh. I had forgotten to mention that I was a vegetarian, and the roast beef gave me stomach cramps, which I tried my best to hide. The couple seated next to me devotedly discussed golf swings, a topic completely foreign to me. The priest sitting on my other side was for some reason interested in my hometown congregation, about which I knew less than would have been reasonable. The drinks were stronger than me, and I felt a vague desire to pour them under the table, where a gentle-eyed beagle was watching me.

The approval of others is one of the strongest motivators for adopting external values, whether they feel appropriate or not. I wanted so badly to fit into the space I had been offered that I was willing to change myself and my reality to fit it. Even though a few years have passed, I can easily relive all the feelings and thoughts, the inadequacy, the shame, the desire to escape, and at the same time try to be something other than what I was.

The legacy of previous generations, or transgenerationality, can also have a strong influence on how we think about ourselves and our purpose in the world. In Western, individualistic societies, we sometimes find it difficult to understand how history, family ties, and expectations live on in Eastern cultural traditions. My friend Emily, a Chinese woman born in Australia, describes balancing between the two worlds. China, with its dynasties, is an ancient culture, and Emily's family members are children of this culture. In Australia, on the other hand, most people seem to come from somewhere else—everything is new, young, mobile, and modern.

The country you live in, its society and traditions, can also influence who you are in their own way. Emily considers herself to be very efficient, creative, and hardworking but at the same time people-oriented and family-centered. She works for a technology company and is an experienced communications and talent development professional. Emily's grandparents are from Hong Kong and moved to Australia over fifty years ago. In adapting to their new environment, immigrants often face various challenges: culture shock, language barriers, and sometimes discrimination. Emily grew up in a very traditional Chinese family community, where it is important to respect your parents, speak when spoken to, and perform well in life, especially at school. Outside the family, in Western culture, creativity, individuality, and well-being were valued. For Emily, values are shaped by ethnic and cultural background, family history, and the expectations of family members for younger generations.

Identity and values can emerge from the pressure of these background forces in response to the expectations and ambitions of previous generations, or through interaction with loved ones. The people around us influence the formation of our relationship with the economy and finances. Many of us compare ourselves to people who are similar to us, such as our peers, friends, or coworkers. Comparison helps us see how we relate to others and what qualities we value in ourselves. At the same time, other people's reactions and feedback influence how we perceive our financial goals. Positive feedback helps us see our own skills and strengths, while negative feedback may limit our courage to try new things or take risks.

Some people have a stronger need to adapt to situations, while others ignore the pressure. However, humans have a naturally social brain that strives to give us the tools to function as well as possible in different social situations. The culture and society in which we grow up and live strongly influence the formation of our identity. Cultural norms, values, language, beliefs, and traditions create a sense of belonging to a particular culture or group.

Emily's life took a dramatic turn ten years ago when she met her future husband, Raphael, a French wine expert whose family owns a vineyard in Southern France. Emily moved to the vineyard, following her heart, as she says. She worked on her husband's family farm for three years, learning about grape growing, accounting, and wine marketing, and did everything possible that wine producers do to make a decent living. Living on an idyllic vineyard, which might seem like a dream come true to many, often felt very hard for Emily. She had few friends, and in a small town it was difficult to meet new people, even though she spoke the language. Having left her job, she was financially dependent on her husband, and her career-oriented life suddenly became quieter, with time spent with her husband's family and working on the vineyard.

Emily had to reinvent herself; everything was new, and she needed to learn completely new skills. She learned about winemaking and viticulture easily by day-to-day work, but it was much more difficult to adapt and find people she could talk to and share things with. She no longer had the same social pressures, the need to succeed or advance in her career, but Emily felt like a stranger in her new home. Things that she valued were no longer needed. New environments and social networks require us to question our established identity and search more consciously for our place in the world.

Emily eventually returned to Australia to be closer to her family, but she still reflects on how living in different cultures has changed her as a person. She particularly appreciates France's centuries-old culture, the balance between work and leisure, and the more humane pace of life. The experience has helped her let go of one-dimensional social values where hard work defines success in life, especially in relation to her own family. She has learned to listen more to her own motivation and needs, which is important to her. Nowadays, she is learning to recognize wines for fun, practicing traditional Eastern wellness methods such as Reiki, and dreaming of a break from work, with more time for herself and her interests.

A recent study in social psychology shows how social expectations and changing circumstances affect the identity formation of children and young adults. Whereas families used to expect a great deal from them, young people now also expect miracles from themselves.[5] Anxiety among young people is often linked to the misconception that anyone can become anything they want. This illusion does not correspond to reality and puts pressure on young adults. Everyone should become something "significant," and the search for meaning starts from what society considers valuable or admirable. Social media provides a platform where they can compare their own success with anyone else's and where context is forgotten. Young people feel pressure to define and achieve their own goals and dreams, which can lead to identity crises and mental health challenges. In a large international study, researchers found that one in four young adults (24 percent) reported that they want "to find out who they really are" in the coming decade. Many seem to feel isolated or are seeking to discover their place in the world.[6]

DOES GENDER MATTER?

Gender makes economic sense, says Emilie Bellet, a former Lehman Brothers analyst and current gender equality activist. Gender is linked to our deepest beliefs and perceptions about the differences between people. The perception of biological sex is also socially constructed and varies from one community to another, from one person to another, and even within the development of the same individual at different times. Although economic gender equality has taken giant leaps forward in the last hundred years or so, it has still not been achieved.

Financial skills are an area where women have been proving themselves for decades. Financial decision-making and investment skills have been passed down from generation to generation more to men than to women. Women's access to economic and financial education has been limited. The percentage of women majoring in business or economics education is currently 30 to 35 percent in the United States and approximately 22 percent in Europe.[7] Similar gender differences apply in technical and engineering disciplines, often linked to economic and industrial sectors. In many countries there is still a pay gap between men and women, which may affect how women are perceived as economic actors. In the media, women are often portrayed as economically ignorant or impulsive consumers. Yet several studies have shown that women can be as skilled as, if not more skilled than, men in financial decision-making and investment.

Women and men seem to have different ways of investing and spending. Women spend more on family and community development, such as health and education. According to the World Bank, women are also more concerned that their investments have a positive and measurable impact, are aligned with their values, and are not unduly risky.[8] This way of investing also seems to be in line with the strategies of many successful investors. Studies show that women take 80 percent of the responsibility for short-term family decisions—that is, day-to-day running of the family—but only a small proportion of the responsibility for long-term decisions such as investing (23 percent).[9] It may also be that women feel a greater sense of responsibility for the whole, for the community and their immediate family, so that financial risk-taking affects more than just one person. However, it is just as possible for men to adopt a community or risk-averse investment strategy, and women are not automatically better at money or investing. However, if women do not have the opportunity to use their talents, it turns into a loss for everyone.

In her work, financial adviser Alicia O. meets both wealthy and low-income people, men and women. When discussing gender, she stresses that it is difficult to generalize and there are always exceptions. However, as a man or a woman, there is no harm in mirroring your own actions to others. In Alicia's experience, men are more willing to take risks in managing their finances. Women often think of finances in terms of plans and goals, and they reflect on them over time and commit to them. Women often experience more conflicting feelings about whether they spend money on themselves or on others. Age matters too, as older generations find it difficult to talk about money. When silence and secrecy prevail, managing finances realistically and asking for advice is a huge step. It is particularly difficult when one spouse is left alone and must take responsibility for the finances, perhaps for the first time in their life.[10]

Risks are part of life, and it is rarely possible to avoid them. Often it is even necessary to face the challenge, to be able to deal with both the bad days and the good days, our own human imperfections, and the pains of learning that come with being on unfamiliar ground. What happens when women are discouraged to take risks, fail, try again, and learn? Girls are not necessarily forbidden to take risks, unlike boys, who are both encouraged and restricted by rules and prohibitions.

According to one study, risk-taking by girls is ignored in kindergarten.[11] Researchers found that when boys were given tasks beyond their abilities, they often overreached themselves. When girls were given a similar task, they performed worse than in other situations.[12] The challenge becomes a demand that prevents girls from making the most of their abilities. This is by no means because girls are in any way less able than boys in many school subjects, quite the opposite. Their knowledge and skills may be better, but they do not come to the fore when risk factors are placed in the context. Girls and women seem to learn early on that risk-taking is less likely to lead to perfect outcomes.

Risk aversion is often accompanied by a tendency to do things better than well. This tendency can lead to a self-image that does not include average performance and failure. Striving for perfection is a way of managing and securing life, and in times of uncertainty it feels particularly relieving as a way of dealing with difficult emotions. It can also be a very damaging way to act, both for oneself and one's environment. Achieving success often requires the ability to tolerate uncertainty and imperfection, and the ability to balance ambition with self-compassion.

Perfectionism predisposes one to exhaustion, because no one can master everything, but many people burn out trying. It is therefore important to recognize when the pursuit of perfection starts to limit personal and professional development. Setting goals close to perfection can lead to constant stress about whether you are close enough to succeed and to difficulty in dealing with setbacks. Fear of failure can also lead to avoiding and postponing challenges by staying out of areas of discomfort. In creative fields, the desire for perfection can prevent people from trying new and innovative solutions. If perfectionism extends to social relationships, the perfectionist's constant need to be accepted and exceed expectations can become burdensome.

The 2019 study by Thomas Curran and Andrew Hill analyzes the perfectionism of more than forty thousand British, Canadian, and American university students between 1989 and 2016.[13] They found a significant increase in social perfectionism over this period. Social perfectionism differs from self-directed perfectionism, where a person sets high standards and goals for themselves. Social perfectionists feel pressure from outside, from society or from other people, to be perfect or to meet certain standards. They fear not living up to the expectations of others or being criticized if they are not flawless. Expectations may be related to appearance, career, education, and social life, and the perception of one's own worth is largely related to one's ability to meet these expectations.

In some cultures and environments, social perfectionism may be more prevalent, while in others, self-directed perfectionism may be more common. Sometimes it is also difficult to distinguish between the two, with people feeling they are demanding a lot from themselves, even though their environment tries to tell them that less would be enough. However, some people have a lifetime history of being rewarded only for perfect performance—whether in academics, athletics, or behavior. Telling someone with ingrained perfectionism to "just relax and settle for less" is deeply frustrating and ineffective. When the environment constantly reinforces certain behaviors, people adapt and act in ways that seem to work best for them.

Perfectionism is not a gender-specific phenomenon, but there are some studies that suggest that women are more likely to be perfectionists in some domains (such as housework, university education, and physical appearance)[14] and more prone to certain psychological traits associated with perfectionism, such as self-criticism.[15] Women often have high expectations in many areas of their lives: they must look good, have careers to pursue, motherhood to manage well, and housework to do. Women may feel, quite rightly, that their worth and competence are judged more harshly than men's, which can lead to a drive to be perfect performers in both their professional and personal lives. Particularly in male-dominated sectors, women may feel under pressure to perform at a high level both academically and professionally to excel or gain recognition in their work.

+ + +

Breaking traditional roles is rarely easy for anyone, but it can be particularly difficult for women. Many societies have long-standing traditions of strict gender roles, with specific expectations for women and men. Women may face pressure from family, friends, or community to conform to these traditional roles, and sometimes they become internalized expectations, inducing guilt and inner conflict. Violating expectations is often considered abnormal or inappropriate and can lead to social isolation, resentment, or even punishment. A woman who wants to deviate from her expected role may face economic hardship, and in some places, certain deviations may even be illegal.

The impact of gender roles is hardly surprising, as it reflects a long-standing social reality. If you ask yourself which parent took financial responsibility for your childhood family's finances, it is very likely that the answer will reflect the gender roles in society at the time. In single-parent families and rainbow families, the situation may be different, but the adoption of gender roles is not always linked to the family form. I would argue that becoming aware of gender roles and questioning them is one of the most worthwhile steps a single family can take. Money matters can be handled together, shared or delegated to those with the interest and inclination. However, when responsibilities are shared, informed choices reduce financial risk and strain for all involved.[16]

DEEP DIVIDES

If you are reading this book in the mid-2020s, the economic and social situation is contradictory. On the one hand, much is well, perhaps better than ever. On the other hand, many problems, such as homelessness and addiction, seem overwhelmingly difficult to solve. My kids started their school in central London, and our daily trek to this establishment passed by the usual haunts of homeless dwellers. They became instantly socially aware, not yet used to the status quo, which makes those less fortunate than us invisible. They strongly believed that people should not sleep on the streets, they should live in houses. I believe this too, but I am used to living my life, which includes people sleeping on the streets. Our lives are full of similar coping strategies, but if they become a permanent condition, we become blind to the reality and humanity around us.

In Hans Rosling's book *Factfulness*, numbers bring home the reality of our planet: one billion people live below the poverty line, five billion live on a few dollars or a few tens of dollars a month, and only one billion live in a welfare state where daily survival is generally not threatened.[17] You and I belong to this last group for the mere fact of reading this book. We are concerned about similar economic issues: the cost of housing and childcare, healthcare, aging and pensions, and increasingly about our environment and how it is changing—our choices and their economic consequences. The extent to which these issues occupy our thoughts depends on our own financial situation, needs, and values. It also depends on the generation we are born into. Many things are better than we think, but it is good to look beyond and through the small and large imperfections and focus on the things that need attention. It is especially important to see when we can bring change through our own actions.

In *Zero Degrees of Empathy*, Simon Baron-Cohen writes about the importance of empathy as a force for building society.[18] The more we feel separate from others and disconnected from our shared experience of humanity, the easier it is to remain detached from the ills of society. If we focus only on ourselves as the protagonists of life, other people begin to be seen as objects rather than living, feeling, or worthy individuals. This could also be described as spotlights of attention: when our attention has only one spotlight and it is focused on ourselves, we become, so to speak, determinedly self-centered. If we turn on a second spotlight and direct it at another person, we have the possibility to pay attention to ourselves and to the other person simultaneously. The focus of attention naturally varies from situation to situation, and dual perspective is not always needed. However, this ability is crucial to empathy. When we see injustice around us, it changes our thinking over time and there is a real danger that our capacity for empathy will erode. Income inequality begins to look like a natural consequence of differences among people. This happens because the human mind needs to create an understandable narrative about the environment, otherwise we struggle to live in a world that in many ways is irrational.

Because we adapt to injustice, reality becomes like a cardboard box, into which we cut a peephole that suits us. We see only the piece of our environment that suits us and adapt our thinking accordingly. It may be easier to perceive other people through stereotypes: rich people are calculating and poor people impulsive, women are interested in the social environment and men in the economy, old people are grumpy and young people are indifferent. In uncertain times, we gain a greater sense of security when we see financial success as a merit of personal qualities. Indeed, if everything depended on external factors, our position in society would be only one step away from losing it. In the following chapters of this book I will explore the origins of emotions, research showing that the area of the brain that deals specifically with the unexpected and feelings of fear, the amygdala, appears to be larger in people who vote conservative. In uncertain times, many of our behaviors and strategies focus on staying alive. If survival is emphasized, it can increase competition and create distrust between people. It is therefore useful to recognize how our minds behave in these situations.

Changes in the global economy can cause unforeseen upheavals. Without looking far for an example, the effects of COVID-19 were exceptionally felt across the globe and across all social classes. These changes will test the resilience of social safety nets and will also highlight the importance of planning our own finances in traditional welfare states. Everyday financial struggles have an impact on society as a whole, including security and general well-being. If citizens are able to take better care of their finances, this reduces credit risk, increases economic stability at the societal level, and increases labor productivity. Long-term overindebtedness and financial instability are associated with problems that are visible at the societal level: depressive symptoms and disability, poorer performance at work, and increased health problems. In other words, individuals do not manage their finances in isolation from the broader society.

In recent decades, income inequalities have widened in most Western countries as well as in many emerging economies. Income inequality is clearly not the only or the best measure of equality in society, as relatively small differences in wealth may exist in more hierarchical societies (e.g., Japan) or there may be large income-related health inequalities (e.g., in the Nordic countries).[19] However, income inequalities are often measured because they are easier to monitor than other types of social equality. Indeed, many countries track how income inequality evolves over time.

Fifteen years ago, British epidemiologists Richard Wilkinson and Kate Pickett set out to investigate the impact of rising income inequality on a range of other measures of well-being, including mental health, employment, crime, women's status, infant mortality, and so on. In their books, Wilkinson and Pickett presented evidence that greater income inequality is detrimental to all members of society, not just those on low incomes. Inequality increases mistrust and erodes community cohesion. In prosperous Western countries, economic growth cannot increase people's well-being because it fails to meet basic and social human needs.[20] Wilkinson and Pickett's conclusions have been the subject of much debate, and their research has also been criticized for its use and interpretation of statistical data. Critics have now cautiously accepted some of their observations. In a society where income is equally distributed, this seems to increase trust and reduce infant mortality, imprisonment, and teenage pregnancy.

Subsequent studies have confirmed the notion that high income inequalities in society are linked to mental health problems.[21] Carol Graham and Andrew Felton have analyzed research in Latin America over the last few decades and concluded that much depends on how we define equality and the starting points from which we assess it. In Latin America, income inequality isn't just a statistic—it's a psychological reality that shapes daily life. When people experience vast and seemingly permanent differences in wealth with little hope of mobility, it doesn't just affect their bank accounts, it fundamentally undermines their sense of agency and happiness.[22]

Why are mental health problems more likely in countries with high income inequalities? Many factors may play a role. If resources (money, skilled staff) are available and used to promote mental health, it makes a difference. The more you teach mental health skills, increase people's understanding of health and well-being, and strengthen social support networks, the lower the risk factors. Evidence shows that investing in immediate, stigma-free mental health services pays dividends in ways traditional economics can't capture—when help is accessible at the first sign of trouble, both individuals and society save immeasurable costs down the line. However, seemingly equal health services can also mask problems. In the United Kingdom, for example, public health care is free, but access to mental health services is very limited. You can only get help when your situation has become serious. A frustrated doctor in Scotland says that there "simply aren't enough of us [psychiatrists]."[23]

Societies are different and have developed along different paths. This makes them difficult to compare, and the last ten years have seen contradictory results and ideologically colored conclusions.[24] Statistics cannot necessarily tell us about equality in the ways we would like. They cannot resolve ethical conflicts or tell us what human rights are. The studies woven throughout this book reveal a profound irony: our conventional understanding of economic success—what we've been taught creates the best possible life—often contradicts what science shows actually promotes well-being. If we don't ask the right questions, it is difficult to get the right answers.

Wilkinson and Pickett put forward the idea that economic inequality increases people's experience of insecure status, which in turn undermines trust in others. The more one's status in society is based on external and materialistic factors—where I live, where I work, what I wear, how I spend my leisure time—the more pressure there is to do better and create a better first impression. The greater the income gap, the more pronounced and visible the differences in status. If economic inequality is a risk factor for all, then everyone should be aware of its side effects.

Economic circumstances can also shape whether people believe they control their own destiny or see life as governed by luck, fate, or forces beyond their control. Money problems and economic inequality contribute to a sense of having little control over one's life. This in turn increases anxiety, insecurity, and distrust of the society around us.[25] On the other hand, a very strong sense of control over one's life, "I am the master of my own fortune," can be counterproductive when adversity comes along. We cannot control everything, so the sense of personal responsibility can become too heavy a burden.

If the economy and emotions are affected by such powerful forces at the societal level, what would be generally good for us? It is perhaps not surprising that the balance seems to reside in moderation. For most people, well-being is enhanced by having sufficient income and economic security in an egalitarian society with social safety nets.

This can also be achieved by promoting a happier society for all, not just for oneself. Marii Paskov of Oxford University has studied social assistance in European countries.[26] Her findings show that both the poorest and the richest citizens provide less to those in need—neighbors, the elderly, the sick, or the immigrants—in those European countries with the greatest income disparities. So money can alienate us: the more we perceive ourselves as different from the people around us, the more we are excluded from the community. This in turn undermines our well-being. Income inequality is by no means the only factor that separates communities, but it is perhaps the most influential, and it has proved difficult to overcome. Wealth in itself does not make people less helpful, generous, or social, but awareness of the inequalities around us may well do so.

In a society of inequality and high socioeconomic disparities, awareness of these differences is often greater. Poverty, like loneliness, is a source of feelings of shame and insecurity. If poverty isolates a person from the community, the impact is multiplied. From an evolutionary point of view, exclusion and loneliness have meant certain death. No wonder, then, that human biology is strongly socially oriented. We have an overwhelming need to be accepted, valued, and useful in our own pack. Socioeconomic status is not so much influenced by an individual's own talents and intelligence but by chance and luck and by the environment, which allows us to claim and develop our own inclinations and talents. Poverty is not genetic, but transgenerational factors play a major role, as the early environment shapes the whole of a person's life.

THE LONELINESS OF POVERTY

Childhood poverty leaves a wide range of traces and also affects a child's cognitive skills and learning; the longer poverty persists, the greater these effects.[27] However, these effects are largely ignored in curricula and psychological assessments.

A short while ago, a person posting under her own name on social media described how she had been affected by persistent childhood poverty and worries about her family's livelihood. She felt constantly poor, even though she was educated and working. She felt a sense of guilt, shame, and anxiety about poverty that no one who knew her as an adult could understand. Her sense of security was permanently undermined, and she expected any disaster to come around the corner. The stigma of poverty was visible and palpable to her, exacerbated by the fact that she had no acquaintances with similar experiences.

Poverty in today's Western society can be extremely lonely. According to one expert, poverty is "a daily worry about having enough money"; according to another, it feels like "being a pawn in the system, waiting indefinitely in fear and uncertainty."[28] Our brains sense that we have strayed from the herd, experience interpreted as a special kind of emergency. A participatory research project in the United Kingdom, the United States, Tanzania, Bangladesh, Bolivia, and France has summarized the messages that people and communities want to highlight about poverty.[29] For example, poverty is too often seen as defining the whole person, when in reality we are talking about disparate individuals, each with something to contribute to society. The research project also showed that the people who know the most about poverty are the people who live with it. In the fight against poverty, it is vitally important that they are the ones who are involved in making a difference.

Nearly one in three Americans who don't identify with either major political party consistently avoids participating in surveys, leaving them beyond the reach of traditional research methods.[30] These are people who do not respond to opinion polls, do not agree to be interviewed, do not write letters to the editor of their daily newspaper, and do not say who they intend to vote for in elections. Economic vulnerability, poverty, and the constant struggle to make ends meet make participation not only difficult but also less motivating. In sparsely populated areas, people do not necessarily come into contact with researchers, and participation is limited to mail or telephone. Surveys do not always take into account the requirements of multiculturalism, and part of the population is thus excluded from research. Mistrust can also cause fear and uncertainty about whether the information is really secure and the responses anonymous, or whether the responses and the time spent on them are really useful to anyone.

People outside surveys are unknown to us because they do not share their wishes and needs in common forums. Yet they too may have a need to be heard and seen, to feel that they belong somewhere. Many of them may feel that they are outside society, powerless and invisible. The role of invisibility is as real as any other role, but its consequences can be many times more dangerous. That is why it is our task to reach out to, understand, and see the people who remain outside our everyday lives. It is our task to also be interested in what feels unfamiliar, because any one of us could be invisible in a different society.

One way to break out of your everyday bubble is to be interested in different people and interact with them. Another good way is to read widely, including different texts, stories, and books. The world is full of interesting publications that will really surprise you (in a good way). One human lifetime is not enough to gain all the experiences and insights that can be acquired through reading. Instead of reading, you can also meet, talk, ask questions, and listen—not only with those closest to you but also more broadly.

Poverty is not a way of life. It is not a choice, it is a situation that can be entered into for a variety of reasons and it is not easy to get out of it, no matter how hard you try. Sometimes, but not always, poverty is accompanied by addictions, such as substance abuse or gambling, and sometimes by other mental health problems. However, poverty can also be a series of unfortunate events that come into play when financial safety nets are weak. In good times, economic growth sustains many, but in bad times, setbacks—unemployment, illness—are particularly hard on those who lack the wealth to cope.

The stigma attached to the experience of poverty is particularly difficult. In recent decades, the world has become more equal to some extent, but at the same time it seems to have become more difficult for Westerners to understand why people living in poverty do not improve their situation themselves. Until a century ago, poverty was seen as an undesirable but understandable state of affairs, largely due to the heredity of status and wealth. Today, poverty may be seen as a weakness of character or laziness, as an exploitation of social benefits, or as an exclusion from the community. Society extends unlimited sympathy to poor children, recognizing their powerlessness and potential. Yet the wealthier the community becomes, the less empathy it shows to poor adults—as if reaching adulthood magically transforms poverty from a systemic failing into a personal one.

The skills and contributions of low-income earners struggling on the margins of actual poverty are often overlooked by society. As long as we associate traditional economic success with success in life, it is difficult to see how many of the most important functions of society are the responsibility of low-income people. There is a constant stream of volunteer work, low-paid work, and seasonal or part-time work that contributes greatly to the well-being of everyone. If all this work is valued, it is easy to conclude that economic growth in the traditionally high-paying technology, trade, and finance sectors is also partly based on work that is done for very little or no pay.

Low income may also have positive side effects that should not be ignored—for example, enjoying more relationships, caring, and interaction. The higher the income, the more positive emotions are focused on the person themself, such as self-confidence, life satisfaction, and realizing their own potential.[31] These emotions emphasize a person's individuality and autonomy. Researchers have interpreted this distinction to mean that the fewer resources a person has, the more dependent they are on their social network, so it is natural to nurture emotions that are important for community, such as compassion and love.[32]

An individual's ability to cope with setbacks and hardship is no substitute for the structures and practices of society. The truth is that very little of the resilience of a nation's character or its ability to cope with major challenges can be attributed to individuals alone. When the structures of society support trust and confidence in the future, it allows for perseverance, persistence, and ingenuity. Trust in the future cannot survive without communities that support, protect, and encourage.

We can be almost certain that poverty is a health hazard: it shortens life expectancy and undermines physical, mental, and social well-being. The 2019 Nobel Prize in Economics was awarded to the distinguished poverty researchers Esther Duflo, Abhjit Banerjee, and Michael Kremer, whose research unpacks the huge challenge of poverty and explores these smaller issues experimentally. They have shown that people's lives can be affected by practical measures that reduce poverty and its side effects. Their research relates to the broad question of where society is wise to spend money and what will deliver the most positive results. One, but not the only, essential answer is to promote schooling for children in developing countries.

+ + +

Poverty is a human rights issue and a social problem rather than the ability of an individual to earn money. The strategies I discuss in this book serve a dual purpose: improving your own well-being while deepening your understanding of how economics and values shape our world. Though they won't pad your bank account, they can make you more responsive to social problems around you. But let's be honest: attempting to end poverty through individual action alone ignores the structural forces that perpetuate it. Personal resilience-building is worthwhile, but it's no replacement for the broader social changes we desperately need.

CHAPTER 3

THE NEUROSCIENCE

Even fleeting thoughts and feelings can leave lasting marks on your brain, much like a spring shower can leave little trails on a hillside.

—RICK HANSON[1]

THE CHANGING BRAIN

In early spring in Northern Lapland, it's easy to see where most cross-country skiers are heading. The most popular runs are well plowed, sometimes even embarrassingly slippery, after being polished by hundreds, even thousands, of pairs of skis. You can also tell a good ski run because it is well maintained and well lit. There are also several side trails leading off the slopes, with a range of options to suit all levels of fitness and skiing ability. The more the slopes are used, the faster and more convenient they become for the skiers.

Something similar happens in our brains every day. Our minds follow certain, familiar paths. The more the trail is used, the easier it becomes to follow. At its best, it in turn activates whole networks that reinforce the main path and the progression toward it. Finding an alternative track or direction rarely feels meaningful, as it could mean trudging through a cold and dark forest without knowing what's available at the other end of the track.

The brain is conservative in its own way; it tries to save energy and repeats what it has already learned. People often tend to stay in their comfort zone and avoid new, uncertain situations and ways of thinking. The brain may warn us of threats and failure, which in turn discourages risk-taking. This can prevent new ideas from emerging, as the brain tends to protect the existing balance. In particular, the fear of criticism and exclusion from one's community is strong—it is important for people to remain part of the herd and adapt to its climate of opinion. Breaking new ground and developing ideas also requires cognitive effort and resources. But brain resources are limited, and the challenges of everyday life can lead to people not having enough time or energy to experiment, challenge their thinking, or question their social reality.

To understand better how our financial behaviors develop, we need to spend some time here getting familiar with the workings of our brain. Taking on new challenges in life requires people to learn skills and behaviors. The brain rebuilds neuronal networks and the connections between them in response to these new demands. For example, parenting requires learning new skills, such as caring for and interacting with a baby, while adolescence requires a whole new way of coping with separation and conflict. This process can activate neuroplasticity in the brain, and the brain can adapt accordingly.

Similarly, when an individual takes on a new financial role, the brain can adapt to new challenges and responsibilities. It is important to understand that the brain works through experience and learning; it does not cling to a limited sense of identity or ability but always tries to bring us up to speed. By trusting this capacity for change, we are able to take on tasks and challenges in life where fear and uncertainty rear their heads. We may not be ready the moment change happens, but we can allow ourselves to be open to learning.[2]

We humans have only a limited awareness of our own minds and thought processes, of the development of our brains and how they are shaped. This can make it difficult to recognize and understand what is going on in our own minds and to challenge unworkable thought processes. One way of getting to know our minds is to familiarize ourselves with how the brain works in general, something we should all have a basic understanding of. Few disciplines have aroused as much interest, hope, and wonder in recent decades as neuroscience, neurobiology, neuropsychology, neurology, and many other neuro-related disciplines.

Neuroscience studies the structure and function of the nervous system from different disciplines: neurobiology studies the structure of nerve cells, neuropsychology studies the impact of brain function on psychological functioning, and neurology studies the medical treatment of symptoms related to nervous system function. There are many different perspectives, but ultimately it is about the functioning of our nervous system, which we still know too little about and whose research methods are challenging. Much of the research into the functioning of the nervous system is based on animal experiments and brain imaging, which became possible in the 1970s.

Even today, reference is often made to the three-brain theory developed by Paul MacLean in the 1970s, which distinguishes between three different parts of the brain: the lizard brain (instincts), the limbic system (motivation, emotions), and the most developed part of the cortex, the neocortex, which is responsible for logical thinking and decision-making. A simple theory is not always enough to describe how the brain works, but it gives a pretty good idea of how different parts of the brain interact in ways we still don't fully understand.

Although we think of ourselves as rational and autonomous decision-makers, we are strongly influenced by signals and activation in the deep parts of the brain. The fulfillment of basic needs is particularly important. For example, hunger makes us impatient and angry and affects our ability to make rational decisions. Lack of sleep, on the other hand, reduces our willpower and perseverance to see things through. Particularly intense and prolonged brainwork temporarily reduces empathy for others.[3] This explains why many professionals may feel the need to recover after a long day before they can function normally as a parent or partner. It was long believed that the adult brain no longer molds or that changes only occur in the cortex, but both beliefs have been gradually disproved. The brain develops through experience but also loses function with aging, stress, and traumatic experiences.

There are no significant differences in brain function or structure between men and women. Small observable differences become irrelevant when you consider the greater variability within the sexes: men differ from each other as women differ from each other; few people fit into the same mold. On the other hand, many people no longer want to be confined to the boundaries of a generic gender but consciously construct their own concept of themselves as human beings. What is certain, however, is that gender differences are shaped by environment, upbringing, and culture. Gender expectations and social relationships influence how each of us behaves and develops our skills, so gender can also become a self-perpetuating cycle. Generalizing about gender differences, whether in brain function or ability, easily leads to misconceptions about causes and consequence.[4]

Many neuromyths, or misconceptions about how the brain works, also originate from neuroscience and the biased interpretation of research. For example, many people have heard about the differences between the left and right sides of the brain and believe that they mainly use one hemisphere or the other.[5] These differences are also often linked to gender, with men believed to use one hemisphere and focus on a single task, and women believed to be able to use their hemispheres more holistically and do many things at once. This is probably one of the most controversial topics in brain research today and raises questions about the origin of the differences.[6] Or you may have heard of the differences between visual, auditory, and kinesthetic learners. In other words, we compartmentalize ourselves based on brain research, even though it has subsequently been discovered that these compartments do not even exist.[7] Instead, recent international studies have found that inequality has an impact on the structure of women's brains, by increasing signs of chronic stress.[8]

Every day, every experience, thought, and feeling is part of a constant change in the brain. Emotions and memories leave physical traces on our bodies, on our neurons and the connections between them.[9] You could say that our body is the whole of our life and emotions. This change continues throughout the life cycle; it cannot be stopped, and it challenges our belief in permanent identity. Continuous change does not mean that we do not have periods of sensitivity during which we need to learn certain skills. Studies show that children learn to speak English as a second language at a level equivalent to their mother tongue up to the age of ten, from which point onward language learning no longer reaches a similar level of fluency but can still be very effective.[10] Language learning is one of the best proven ways to influence brain structures and protect information processing abilities even at an older age,[11] unlike many brain training programs that have not been shown to have any practical effect on the brain outside of the actual training: the brain muscles grown in training do not help solve real-life problems.

The brain also needs to nurture experience and repetition to organize itself in a way that is useful to us. When we play an instrument, the sensory and motor areas of the brain involved in processing finger movements and auditory sensation are activated and form connections.[12] Although several hours of intensive finger training can produce visible changes in the brain after just a couple of weeks, these changes disappear very quickly if the training stops. The longer the training has been going on, the longer the effect.

The brain is a complex structure, influenced by both genetic and environmental factors. Our genetic makeup influences brain development, such as how neural pathways are formed, how many brain cells we have, and the type and strength of connections between different parts of the brain. They also affect how nerve cells communicate with each other and how neurotransmitters between them work. However, it is important to know that hereditary factors do not determine brain development or individual behavior but interact with many other aspects, including the environment. We have learned, for example, that poverty has a greater impact on intelligence than hereditary factors, because solving economic problems places a huge strain on mental capacity.[13] Environmental factors, upbringing, education, nutrition, stress, and social relationships play an elemental role in brain development.[14]

The malleability of the brain has helped us to live in changing environments and compete with other species. The ability to absorb new knowledge, acquire new skills, and adapt to changing circumstances is vital for survival.[15] This plasticity also allows new memories to form and old memories to be retained, enabling us to learn from past experiences and make better decisions for the future. The brain's ability to adapt to different social situations and environments helps us to recognize emotions, interpret other people's gestures and tone of voice, and form bonds with others. Adapting to an unfamiliar culture requires considerable mental effort, but people typically adjust successfully over time—sometimes so completely that their original culture begins to feel foreign. The brain's ability to mold itself also contributes to cognitive flexibility, the ability to consciously change unworkable patterns of thought and seek new solutions to problems. This is important for coping, especially in situations where old strategies no longer work.[16]

Brain plasticity is not the answer to everything. You may have heard talk about how the human brain is slow to evolve, and in particular how the brain's ability to cope with the demands of the modern world is limited. It is unrealistic to expect the deep structures of the brain to change at the same pace as our environment, but the malleability of the brain can help us when we are looking for solutions to new problems.

In particular, the information overload and concentration problems that many children, young people, and adults face seem to indicate that the brain has not adapted to the demands of the times. Working environments are not designed with the brain's well-being in mind, and overstimulation, chronic stress, and sleep problems are increasingly common signs of brain overload. The limbic system and the old, deep parts of the brain—the primitive lizard brain—guide us to react in ways that are often inappropriate in challenging social and emotional situations. These brain structures are involved in the learning process, including fear and strong emotional reactions. For example, the "flight, freeze, or fight" response is part of human evolution and its important heritage, enabling us to survive encounters with predators. The same reaction in, say, an awkward performance review or salary negotiation could lead to unexpected consequences.

Many other primitive responses, such as self-defense, hunger, thirst, sexuality, and the need to connect with others, are strong messages from human history and part of our biology. At least some parts of the limbic system can change and adapt through experience and learning. Change can be slow and require effort, but it is possible.[17]

The ability to develop new coping strategies can be vital. Better self-awareness and understanding of brain health can help us to identify and respond wisely to stressful situations, assessing what can be changed and what can be influenced through exercise, relaxation, or conscious breathing exercises. Neuroplasticity can help us learn social skills and improve interaction with other people. This is important for coping with the fast pace of society, as strong social relationships provide support and resources.

MONEY STRESS

Let's revisit Irina's story and examine how financial management plays out in her daily life. Irina often feels uncomfortable and anxious when she must access her online bank account and pay her rent or electricity bill. She works as quickly as possible, often using her mobile phone, and only pays attention to her recent transactions. She is often on her way to somewhere at the time, and a sense of urgency helps her to do things efficiently. Then she immediately moves on to other things, messaging a friend or choosing music to listen to on her headphones. Once the unavoidable financial tasks are done, Irina feels a sense of relief and the release of stress is also felt in her body. Her blood pressure drops, her heart rate steadies, her breathing calms down, her muscles relax, and her digestive system returns to normal. Irina is able to concentrate and function again; she goes on with her life without a further thought. The danger is averted.

Irina has learned to fight unpleasant stress reactions by avoiding their source, money management. Many of us will certainly recognize this reaction and may guess the consequences. In Irina's life, avoidance means that she often overdraws her accounts or is unsure of how much money she has available for unexpected expenses. As her income increases, so do her expenses, and she tends to manage her affairs by gut feeling, without much planning for the future. This approach is surprisingly common, but it perpetuates financial stress, which is amplified as it is avoided. The brain learns to recognize the financial threat and becomes increasingly effective in warning of its dangers. Similarly, avoiding the danger gives the brain a dose of pleasure and relief.

The stress we experience in childhood and adolescence affects how our stress regulation works in later life. Early social experiences also regulate which genes in an individual are activated, helping us to adapt rapidly to very different environments during our social development. The genetic potential of newborns is much broader than we often think, as this breadth is designed to ensure the survival of the individual. Many behaviors that also prove problematic are shaped to support the child's ability to cope in challenging circumstances. For example, if a child grows up in an environment where they do not learn to trust adults, have to fight to survive, and dominate others when given the opportunity, the environment is stressful and shapes their development well into the future. Later, difficulties in building trust and a tendency to aggression can be problematic traits, even though in childhood they may have ensured survival.

Constant stress in childhood is detrimental to both physical and mental health, but this does not mean that it is not important for children to face adversity. Psychological resilience is largely the result of facing reasonable challenges in a fundamentally safe world. It should also be noted that today's families are, in their own way, small universes, autonomous systems separate from others. Therefore, survival in the family environment does not tell us much about survival in society. Fortunately, humans are adaptable animals, even as adults, and changes in the social environment shape the structures of the brain and help it adapt to new demands.

Money often evokes intense emotions. It is linked to almost all our basic needs, providing access to housing, food, mobility, work, social life, leisure, and self-fulfillment. It is also often a reminder of our lack of it, and when it comes to everyday stressors, it is usually at the top of the list without exception.

For a great many people, money-related problems in their lives are complex and not easily solved. Whereas prehistoric man faced physical, tangible threats, such as the saber-toothed tiger, the threats in our everyday lives are often complex, uncontrollable, faceless, and difficult to understand. Whether it's a staff meeting, a bank crisis, or the loss of a wallet, physically we experience a very similar reaction to that of our ancestors when confronted with a predator: heart rate increases, sweat glands activate, the body produces hormones such as adrenaline and noradrenaline, breathing becomes more frequent, blood circulation increases, and even the composition of the blood changes. This reaction is called the "fight or flight" response and can also be accompanied by complete paralysis. It limits brain activity, narrows our ability to see the outside world, and focuses on the threat. It is like a funnel, designed to get us to find a solution to a problem that threatens our survival as efficiently and quickly as possible. If running away, hiding in the bushes, and swinging a club were the solution, this would be the best way to deal with it.

The experience of financial stress, like the experience of stress in general, is not directly related to the trigger of the stress. Small difficulties or feelings of uncertainty can trigger a high stress experience, while major financial changes or losses do not necessarily trigger a major stress state. Rather than focusing on the stress trigger, it is more important to focus on how we experience situations and how we interpret their meaning. This is influenced not only by one's own history but also by the overall stress experience: if the stress level is already high to begin with and has, for example, caused insomnia for some time, the individual stress reaction will also be more intense.

Many people live in a constant state of overstimulation, which has become the new normal. The body and mind have adapted to it, but even small setbacks or disappointments can cause an exaggerated reaction for which it is difficult to find the cause. An overstimulated person is constantly operating at the risk limits of stress, close to the point where symptoms of stress begin to show up in everyday functioning. They are left with fewer resources or resilience—the flexible adaptability to act when the balance of life shifts. However, life is inherently unstable, and things happen in ways that we cannot control. It would therefore be proactive and wise to leave ourselves the space and strength to face unexpected and stressful situations. From a financial point of view, it is worth having a small buffer in your bank account in case life takes you by surprise. Even a small safety net can give you greater peace of mind and, in turn, the ability to act wisely.

However, because in our current living environment the issues that threaten us are complex and difficult to resolve—for example, a default on credit reports or the threat of redundancy—rapid emotional reactions can paralyze our natural ability to respond to sensory information. Humans are able to act in the face of uncertainty, but our brain works in different ways to respond to the challenges of the situation. The existence of the two systems is the subject of the well-known and acclaimed book *Thinking, Fast and Slow* by MIT professor Daniel Kahneman.[18]

The first system of thinking is fast, emotional, and intuitive. Many of the decisions and choices we make in emotional situations are quick, and we may find it difficult to describe their rationale in words. They feel right and intuitively wise, and we escape the saber-toothed tiger. Because the fast system can also tap into unconscious sensory experiences and operate effectively under pressure, it is extremely important for human survival. There's no time to deliberate over everything—sometimes intuition offers the clearest path forward.

The second system is slower, more deliberate, and more logical. It requires concentration and time to activate, and benefits from a quiet time and place. The thought processes in this system are more ready to receive external information and use it to make inferences. Daniel Kahneman and Amos Tversky's theory of how people make economic decisions using the laws of psychology was awarded the Nobel Prize in Economics in 2002.

Financial distress or stress is sometimes thought of as the opposite of financial well-being, but they are concepts of different sizes. In financial distress, an individual finds it difficult to meet external financial demands—for example, to have enough money to meet basic expenses.[19] Research shows that chronic financial stress damages physical health and can prevent people from making important life transitions, such as young adults moving out of their parents' home. It also erodes the building blocks of psychological well-being: self-esteem and confidence. You can see this in my friend Robert, whose ongoing financial difficulties have diminished his belief in what he can achieve. It is as if the mind is living its own life, locked into dealing with prolonged stress. Any worrying sign of running out of money poses a strong threat to survival. While his improved circumstances and achieving financial well-being may help over time, Robert remains vulnerable to mental health issues because financial stress has left him unable to envision a brighter future.

While fight-or-flight served our ancestors well, it's largely useless against today's challenges since it impairs our capacity for rational thinking and problem-solving. In Daniel Kahneman's model, this is precisely the "slow" thinking needed to solve complex problems. There may well be many correct answers to such problems. Although our environment has changed over the millennia, our brains are still remarkably similar to those of the earlier humans.

Irina's story illustrates how childhood experiences can make money feel threatening, even when no real danger exists. For Irina, money means spending because it is associated with acceptance, warmth, and positive reinforcement of the mother-daughter relationship. At the same time, spending causes conflict, guilt, concealment, and ultimately anxiety whenever she recalls her childhood family's relationship with money. She wants to avoid anything that reminds her of the tangible existence of money but often consoles herself by buying things she doesn't need. Irina's anxiety makes her paralyzed in situations where she must deal with money from a financial perspective. To avoid an uncomfortable feeling that she cannot fully understand or explain, she tries to have as little to do with money and its management systems as possible.

The opposite of avoidance is worrying. It may seem like conscientious financial management, but worrying is more like spinning your wheels about your financial situation. Worrying is deceptive because it makes us believe that we have done something to resolve the situation when in fact, nothing has happened. Worrying is in some ways easier than taking action, but it is also far more damaging to well-being than trying and failing. If we worry, we think about the situation through negative emotions, which further impairs our ability to process information.[20] Through action, we learn, gain experience, form values, and discover new opportunities. Worrying, on the other hand, keeps us stuck in repetitive thoughts, like a cement block on the road to change.

CARING FOR THE BRAIN

When I started my research into the sources of financial well-being, I met many professionals who are particularly skilled at helping those struggling with financial difficulties. One of my interviewees was Anna, a dedicated social worker. Surprisingly, Anna started our meeting by telling me that she was a shopaholic. She gets a sense of security and enjoyment from shopping. She especially shops online because of the speed of her purchases and the ease of using a credit card. Parcels arrive on her doorstep at such a pace that she sometimes doesn't even have time to open them. It is very difficult for her to distinguish between what she wants and what she needs. Anna compares her own behavior to any addiction but says "getting clean is even harder. You can stop drinking alcohol or gambling completely, but you can't stop buying. It's encouraged everywhere."

But Anna has also turned her own trouble into a win for others. Alongside her day job, she provides financial counseling to clients who are struggling to find help elsewhere. She budgets, goes through bank statements, explains what interest really means, goes along to a car dealership to ask tough questions, and brags lavishly about successes. Anna knows well what it means to have good personal finances. Yet she has the same feelings as any of her clients, and balancing those feelings is how she makes her daily purchasing decisions.

No wonder, then, that strong emotions such as shame, stress, and anxiety take their toll on our ability to process information and limit our capacity to be proactive. Financial stress also feeds on itself, leading to poor decision-making and shortsighted choices, such as taking instant loans or gambling. Thus, financial stress itself is likely to cause more financial stress over a lifetime. In financial crises, the brain does not process information as well as it normally does, as the stress response is linked to problems with self-direction and attention deficits, which in turn makes financial decision-making and planning more difficult. On the other hand, fluctuating monthly incomes reduce both opportunities and motivation to plan your own finances. In other words, a mind plagued by money worries is not the best equipped to solve money problems.[21]

Long-term studies that track people throughout their lives reveal that financial stress is the most persistent stressor people face—and the one that most severely impacts health in older adults.[22] Long-term stress affects the formation of memory traces, and memory problems are more common in older age groups in particular if there have been high levels of stress in their lives. Economic stress therefore has a long and significant impact. A regular, predictable monthly income supports well-being by facilitating independent financial management and reducing the stress of uncertainty. Conversely, poverty and irregular income increase life dissatisfaction and the risk of mental health problems. Financial stress also predicts problems—arguments, misunderstandings, and so on—in social interactions with family, friends, and the workplace.[23]

Stress puts a strain on our thinking, which increases the number of errors in thinking. If you have ever been embarrassed, confused, or unsure of yourself, you may have accidentally told a half-truth. To be honest, you may have told the opposite of the truth. This often happens to people over small things, like when they can't remember the name of the person they're talking to and want to cover it up, or when they don't feel they're on safe ground. A friend of mine told a mother she met in a playground that she was studying psychology, even though she graduated in psychology years ago. Another friend was discussing a donation with a fundraiser for an animal welfare charity and mentioned having a cat (who had passed away a decade ago) but forgot to mention the dog waiting at home. When our attention is divided or overloaded, we experience what researchers call connection or memory lapses, even in routine daily interactions. Under normal circumstances, these are harmless and often amusing mental slips that simply show our cognitive limits. However, severe stress makes these thinking errors more frequent and serious. They can lead to overestimating your budget, forgetting to pay your bills, or investing in something that looks good without checking the facts.

+ + +

Long-term financial stress also lowers the threshold for responding to other stressors in life. For example, divorce or relationship difficulties can be much more stressful with the presence of financial stress and can also have a greater impact on income. The experience of stress is influenced by how people believe they can cope with it, the stress management strategies they have at their disposal, and the support they receive from their environment.

With a secure basic income, the link between prosperity and well-being weakens even more as income levels continue to rise. The connection never disappears completely, but the impact is generally less important than the impact of good social relations or physical and mental health. Interestingly, research has also shown that when financial security increases for one reason or another, stress is reduced, and, at the same time, the experience of one's own health improves.[24] This does not mean that when our economic situation improves, our bodies are immediately better prepared to fight viruses, but we feel better able cope with, say, a common cold or stomach flu. When you feel safer, you dare to rest more, take better care of yourself, and get sick for shorter periods of time. A hopeful and positive attitude toward life can have a tangible impact on behavior and increase physical health.

We all have our own, individual ability to cope with stress. This capacity varies greatly among people, but it also varies somewhat between different stages of life. Life experience and a longer perspective often increase self-awareness and self-compassion, while busy, demanding years can intensify stress cycles. There is a wide variety of ways to manage stress, some of which are clearly counterproductive. Financial stress can lead to avoidance, as in Irina's case, where the strain is managed by ignoring accumulating bills. In Anna's case, the pleasure spike caused by comfort shopping compensates for chronic feelings of financial insecurity.

Stress management tools are not only good or bad; their effectiveness also depends on people and the environment. For example, meditation is generally considered to have positive outcomes, but it is not the best option for everyone and in all situations to promote mental well-being. Scrolling social media, eating ice cream, or binge-watching Netflix might rescue a tough evening, but stretch these habits over a week and their benefits quickly turn into problems. When choosing stress management strategies, it's crucial to consider their long-term consequences. This is also true for managing financial stress.

What if we really wanted to challenge our thinking, to open up new paths and even question the most unworkable ways of calming our minds? What if we wanted to worry less about how inadequate we are in many areas of life and instead wanted to believe that we can do things that we have never been able to do before? While there can be challenges to generating new ideas, there are also many ways that can help foster creativity and new ways of thinking. Drawing on the Socratic tradition of relentless inquiry, we can turn the spotlight inward with probing questions—"Why do I think this way?" "Why do I act this way?"—pursuing each answer with another "why" until clarity emerges. We can turn to varied experiences, exposing ourselves to the new and the strange, working with other people who are set to explore.

One of the most valuable—though often uncomfortable—forms of personal growth is stepping outside your comfort zone to engage with people whose experiences and perspectives differ from your own. Here are a few more research-based suggestions from renowned brain scientist Michael Merzenich:[25]

- Challenge your brain with active learning and new knowledge—this literally rewires your neural pathways and keeps your mind adaptable.
- Practice deliberately and repeat new skills regularly—this builds stronger neural pathways and accelerates your learning.
- Actively seek out diverse experiences, new environments, and different cultures—this energizes your brain's capacity for growth.
- Fuel your brain's potential with regular exercise and nutritious food—your body and mind are deeply connected.
- Cultivate belief in your ability to grow and change—your brain remains adaptable at any age, so start wherever you are.
- Build and maintain meaningful social connections—engaging with others is one of the most powerful ways to keep your brain healthy and sharp.

These wellness principles sound familiar because they are—yet what's remarkable is that each time we nurture our physical and mental health, we're literally reshaping our brain's architecture, expanding our capacity to navigate whatever life throws our way. We hold the illusion that we move through an unchanging world, when in truth the world moves through us, rewriting our cellular composition with each passing moment. The nervous system transforms every experience into biological memory.

CHAPTER 4

THE EMOTIONS

We are not thinking machines that feel; rather, we are feeling machines that think.
—ANTONIO DAMASIO[1]

EMOTIONAL EXPERIENCE

Fifteen years ago, the TV series *Lie to Me* (2009–2011) featured applied psychology consultants who specialized in interpreting microexpressions and using them to identify emotions in other people. The series was based on real research, as people tend to express basic emotions with the same facial expressions: macro-expressions are used to express visible emotions, and microexpressions are used to express hidden or unconscious emotions. The universality of emotions, their humanity, and our ability to recognize them in other people's faces has led to emotions often being seen as experiences shared by all.

However, recent neuroscientific research has challenged this earlier truth.[2] The debate is now about whether emotions are in fact the same for everyone, a kind of preset configuration in our brains and bodies, or whether they are unique experiences shaped by our own life history and environment.[3] If we understand how our emotions arise, we will also have much more insight into the causes of our actions. And, as noted earlier, the money that permeates our entire lives is guaranteed to evoke emotions.

In the foreword to her book *My People, My Beloved*, Nobel laureate Toni Morrison describes an emotional experience that occurred when she quit her job as a publisher to become a full-time writer. She had mentally examined the issues involved and faced her fears of survival. But after making this life-changing decision, she found herself strangely overstimulated, her heart pounding and anxiety taking over. The feeling did not go away, even though she tried to calm herself down and resume normal daily routines. She wondered if some fear had lingered in the back of her mind but then realized that the feeling was confusing but not unpleasant. She was happy, even elated.

Psychology pioneer William James and Danish psychologist Carl Lange developed one of the most well-known emotion theories in the 1800s, which was followed by many other attempts to explain what emotions really are and how they arise.[4] According to the James-Lange theory, physiological sensations in the body give rise to an emotional experience that is interpreted by the brain. In other words, you decide what you feel. In reality, this does not apply to all emotional experiences, as many of the processes of the autonomic nervous system that regulate emotions are very slow, while the thinking brain is fast. Mind and body can also process emotional experiences simultaneously, and sometimes the body reacts but the mind is distracted and blocks the experience.

Emotional regulation involves recognizing your own emotions, how you feel and get the sense of your own body, and what changes and sensations you are able to perceive. Emotions often trigger physiological responses. Each emotional state (anger, fear, happiness, sadness) produces its own unique "physiological signature" measurable through heart rate, skin conductance, and skin temperature. Even voluntary facial expressions can trigger these specific autonomic responses—you don't need to actually feel the emotion to get the physiological reaction.[5] The body as an interpreter of emotions cannot be ignored; ultimately, it is smarter than humans and seeks to prevent, for example, burnout. Listening to the body's signals is in many ways a source of wisdom, as emotions come and go without us being able to choose them. They are not right or wrong, but they are real physical experiences.

Robert, the student we met earlier who was overwhelmed by financial stress, was fortunate that his university offered counseling services when he finally grew tired of living trapped in his anxious thoughts. He found that saving and constantly thinking about his finances did not reduce his worries—quite the opposite. The more he focused on securing his livelihood, the more he also identified risks. Nothing seemed to be enough. Robert's logical mind could see that running out of money wasn't a real immediate threat, but his nervous system did not agree. Freedom came not from convincing his brain but from learning to be present with the fear itself—feeling it, accepting it, until it naturally began to dissolve.

Professor Lisa Feldman Barrett has spent her long career studying the origins of emotions and has discovered that we often find it difficult to tell what we are feeling. It's easier to distinguish between opposing emotions, such as sadness and joy. For many people, however, it is surprisingly difficult to distinguish between challenging emotions such as anxiety, depression, or anger. They all cause us discomfort that we naturally want to avoid, but it is difficult to name them precisely. In fact, very few people are familiar enough with their own emotional reactions to be able to reliably identify and name their nuances. We can interpret broad lines, however: we can distinguish quite accurately between emotional states of arousal—whether we are calm or restless, or whether an emotional experience is pleasant or unpleasant.[6]

Emotions are not things that happen to us that we can always reliably identify or precisely delineate. They are experiences within ourselves that can be described (through bodily sensations felt internally and externally) and interpreted (through experience and environment). We are active participants in our emotions. All human beings share experiences of discomfort and comfort; all the languages of the world have words to tell us whether we feel good or bad. Tiny cues communicate these sensations in the body with unimaginable speed, so that we know whether to approach or flee. Seeing a toy snake in the park triggers a quick avoidance response before we realize we are afraid. A child's smile relaxes and amuses, and it's hard not to respond.

In our own lives, we often act like scientists at work: we predict early and often unconscious bodily sensations and form hypotheses or assumptions about them. This is absolutely essential for survival, because simply reacting to events would be too slow to help. Sensory information from the environment helps us to correct and refine these sneaky predictions: the snake was plastic, so we can calm down; the child smiles back, confirming that this was the right way to respond. The interaction of predictions, memories, and sensory experiences is constant; it happens whenever we are awake. It's what makes our world meaningful. Without it, we would be at the mercy of a constant bombardment of sensory information, adrift as it were, with no sensations to guide our actions.

We all have a need to explain to ourselves why we feel unwell, and the explanation is often related to the outside world. If a child can specify that they are angry, for example, it is not so much a question of correctly naming an emotion that comes from within themself. It is more likely that they have learned to recognize their own interpretation of an innate feeling of unpleasantness associated with certain external events. They may have learned to associate the feeling of anger also with a sense of having been treated unfairly and learned to give the feeling a related word. Using a word for the experience of the emotion is crucial. Using the word helps them to see different—and hopefully peaceful—options for action.

Lisa Feldman Barrett's research team has also found that delineating and categorizing emotions into basic feelings based on facial expressions does not necessarily reflect experience across the world. People tend to interpret emotions not only from facial expressions but also from other cues in the environment, such as posture and background information. The emotion of grief may or may not be visible in many ways in our external appearance. Grief is also felt in many different ways in our own internal experience, although it has been observed that people often tend to feel grief in the chest and upper body.[7] On the other hand, one can also sense that culture influences interpretation, for when a song tells us that "the heart is heavy with grief," it can both describe a shared experience and guide our understanding of where grief is located in us. In any case, the feeling of grief also guides our actions and supports coping: being with grief requires conserving energy and often seeking comforting human contact.[8]

When we look at the emergence of emotions through the brain, there is a similar diversity. No emotion belongs to just one brain area, although some brain areas are activated more often than others in connection with certain emotional experiences. The amygdala has long been considered a fear-activating brain area, but it is also possible to feel fear when the amygdala is damaged. The amygdala also reacts to anything new and unexpected, whether it arouses fear or not. According to a study at the University of London, the almond-shaped form is higher in young adults with a politically conservative worldview.[9] Conservative values have been interpreted as gaining ground when uncertainty increases in society. Studies like this are interesting but should be treated with caution precisely because the link between brain activity and emotion arises from the activation of multiple brain regions. Different parts of the brain are also capable of adapting to different tasks.

If emotions are not universal experiences, evoked by a specific brain area, which always lead to the same expressions corresponding to the emotion, then what are they? Nowadays researchers see emotions are predominantly contradictory experiences, for which they have tried to give a common description, such as "happy," "sad," "angry," or "surprised." These emotional states are not the same or uniform experiences for everyone but rather refer to a human experience that we try to share in order to be understood.[10] Our perception of reality is constructed by everything we sense—what we hear, see, smell, feel, taste—as well as our memories of the various situations in which we have sensed these things. Our perception of reality is not objective or universal but is the individual's unique interpretation of sensory experiences and expectations.

Seeing reality in this way helps us to understand our internal sensory experiences. Stepping on dog poo in the street causes a feeling of disgust, being jostled by a busy passerby causes irritation, and after a long winter, the rays of sunshine on the face cause joy and hope for the arrival of spring. However, the same events may evoke different emotional experiences in another person. In a job interview you feel a cramp in your stomach and it is up to your individual interpretation whether you suspect you ate something inappropriate for breakfast, feel tense and anxious, or are excited and ready to prove your ability. Your interpretation is very much guided by how you think you react in situations like this, and how your experiences have shaped your brain cells and brain structures.

For example, this is how the situations that Irina and Robert ended up in were structured: the emotional experience of money was real to them and built up over a long period of time. The thought patterns that are often activated can be almost automatic, as they run seamlessly and smoothly through the brain, like driving on a well-lit motorway. The more you use this particular highway, the easier it is to drive on and more roads seem to connect to it. It's quite another matter, then, whether this particular road is the one that leads in the direction you want to go. That's why it's important to see where the emotional roadways that guide your own economic decisions lead.

For simplicity's sake, it's often easier to categorize emotions into positive and negative—a bit like stress management tools. This is the approach taken in some parts of this book, even if the classification is misleading and artificial. Emotions are just emotions and cannot be divided into good and bad or helpful and harmful. The effects of an emotional experience always depend on the situation and the individual. Positive emotional experiences do not always have a positive impact on our actions. Feelings of joy increase confidence in one's performance but also reduce accuracy and perseverance in tasks.[11] Similarly, feelings of anger can lead to aggressive behavior but also to concern for safety and resistance to injustice.[12] The pursuit of so-called positive emotions is prevalent in today's world, and their regular occurrence is often associated with happiness.

EMOTIONS AND DECISIONS

A large proportion of people consider sound financial decision-making to be separate from emotion and are often advised to use their rational reasoning rather than their heart when it comes to financial security. However, reason and emotion are not mutually exclusive.

If a professional investor relies solely on "gut feeling," it can lead to a bad decision. Similar problems have been observed in the administration of justice, and a good example of this is Shai Danziger's study.[13] It showed that judges' decision-making was significantly affected by whether they made a decision just before or after lunch. Before lunch, the internal feelings of hunger significantly reduced the number of positive decisions (almost no positive decisions), but after lunch the situation was reversed (65 percent positive decisions). So it is more or less proven that humans are not rational and do not act only on the basis of objective external information. In the movie *Juror #2* (2025), we see an excellent example of a witness who experiences strong positive emotions of being able to help justice and that will end up affecting his perception of the situation. People seek to act in ways that make life and the environment meaningful and understandable. Sometimes this looks rational from the outside, but if we believe that our internal emotional experiences do not shape our thinking, we are prone to make mistakes.

Research suggests that the role of emotions in decision making—including financial decisions—is much more complex and, on the other hand, more useful than previously believed.[14] According to Antonio Damasio's somatic marker theory, emotions are linked to physiological sensations, which can be conscious or unconscious, and the link helps us make faster and better decisions in some situations. In other words, we make more consistent decisions about things that evoke strong emotions in us. The absence of emotional experiences would make it almost impossible to make choices, because things would not matter, they would not be distinguishable.

In some cases, the intuition we experience may be a combination of knowledge and experience that is difficult to put into words. Experience is based on feelings and the most subtle sensations of the body. Especially in threatening situations—whether real or imagined—emotions provide information that is essential for survival faster than our conscious capacity can process. This is the kind of rapid thinking described by Daniel Kahneman, discussed earlier. The human ability to respond quickly and strongly to messages from the delicate system of the emotional center has been vital throughout the evolutionary history of the human species.

When I need to make a decision and I find myself struggling, I usually follow these steps. They might help you as well.

1. Ask myself what the impact of this decision is on my life/the lives of others on a scale of 1 to 10 (10 as the most important decisions, like having kids, getting married, leaving your job). If I feel it has very little impact on anything, I consider mulling over it at length as a waste of time and tend to make a decision according the best of my current knowledge. If later I am proved wrong, it still did not make any lasting harm.

2. Ask myself, How does this decision align with my values? Can I fit it in the sentence "I decided to X because I value X." Obviously this is for the big impactful decisions. Values are supposed to be our North Star, our guide toward meaning. Still, we don't seem to consult them often enough.

Sometimes I find myself muddled, unsure, restless, or anxious—not connected to my values or even to myself. If that happens, I try to find my bearings first, touching the ground, any way that I find deeply soothing. For example, the following exercise might help.

EXERCISE

Myself as an Experience

We know that our bodies, faces, and minds have changed in countless ways during our lives. But what has remained the same? What makes me, who experiences everything that has happened to me during my life?

I suggest that you read and record this exercise, for example as an audio file on your phone. Proceed at a calm pace. Afterwards, you can listen to it and follow the instructions.

In this exercise, we will try a way of understanding the self and its essence. Sit down and get into a comfortable position where you can breathe freely. You can close your eyes if it feels comfortable. Take a few deep breaths and let the tension out of your body as you exhale. Be aware of the sounds, smells, and sensations in your environment and be open and curious.

After a moment, you can turn your attention to what is happening within yourself. Now, curiously observe your own awareness. Awareness is like an open sky in which come and go all your experiences, sights, sounds, and feelings. Everything moves at its own pace, like clouds. Some experiences are regular and continuous, while others are random and brief. The only thing that remains the same is consciousness itself, the open sky. Try to rest for a moment in this experience.

If thoughts come to your mind, just let them pass through the open sky while you rest here. You don't need to react to them or let them carry you away. What is your most intimate, authentic experience of your self? What is it in this moment that is listening and following the exercise? Is it the same self that experienced and observed things in your childhood? What if your body, your thoughts, and your personality are like clothes that have changed many times since you were a child? What if they have little to do with the clear, strong sense of self that you are experiencing right now? Imagine for a moment that this is true and notice how it feels.

We can continue this thought experiment for a moment and consider what might follow. It could mean that your sense of self, your open awareness, is not bound to time in the same way as everything else in your life. You could say that it reaches beyond time or travels freely through time. You can rest for a moment in this thought and in what it means. If you are unchanging consciousness, an open sky, it also means that you are calm and stable in your essence. All experiences, feelings, and thoughts are temporary.

What remains is awareness in the here and now. How does this calmness and permanence feel to you? What if this experience of self is already enough in itself, complete and lacking nothing essential? How does this completeness feel? You can rest in this feeling for as long as you want, don't rush.

This exercise is adapted from Jeff Warren's meditation practice.[15]

MONEY SHAME

Money and financial management always involves emotional experiences. They are both physical and expressible as thoughts. Often they share a contradictory and layered nature and can be a combination of many different emotions. For example, these money-related situations are indicative of a multilayered nature:

> **Satisfied and proud of success:** I got a bonus at work, I deserve this, now I can relax for a while. This has taken a lot of work, luckily I managed. A little worried about what will happen in the future: will I always be as good?
>
> **Relieved and happy:** I finally got my student loans paid and my contract was made permanent, it looks like I'm going to make it after all. Now I have to be careful with my budget, I don't want to get into a debt trap.
>
> **Anxious and stressed:** I can't believe it, my cat's vet bills are derailing my monthly budget and I have no savings. My pet's health is not measured in money, so I wonder if I could borrow some.

Embarrassed: I'm not sure if I have any money in my account, and I'd still like to provide this lunch. What if my card doesn't work? Really embarrassing. On the other hand, it's embarrassing if I don't offer when it's definitely my turn.

Remorse: I shouldn't have bought this apartment, I can't afford anything, and my mortgage payments are always late. How did it come to this? Since the divorce, it has been really difficult to get my own affairs under control.

As interpreters of emotions, we are not infallible. Sometimes we ignore the external reality, focus on our inner feelings, and refuse to change the prediction our brain quickly makes. When this happens, our actions can also be inappropriate and sometimes even dangerous. Emotions play a huge role in what goes through our minds and the decisions we make.

Let us return for a moment to the situation of Anna, the social worker and shopaholic. She had learned to derive feelings of security and pleasure from shopping. These feelings were activated in online shops, department stores, and smaller boutiques. When she felt low, all she had to do was take a walk to a women's clothing or bag shop, where scents, music, soft fabrics, and eye-pleasing shapes made her feel calm. In such an environment, nothing untoward could happen. Walking there, she felt like any woman weighing up her shopping decisions, her biggest dilemma being which color coat to choose this spring.

In many ways, this environment was different from Anna's home and workplace, which were busy and chaotic. The high-end shopping district promised her that peace of mind could be purchased alongside luxury. But this feeling was fleeting and disappeared almost immediately after shopping. The last vestiges of the comforting emotional experience had well disappeared by the time the credit card bill arrived, replaced by shame and regret. The challenge for Anna in managing her finances was how to feel a sense of peace and contentment without new purchases. At the same time, it was a question of how she could see a little further ahead in her own life, and what emotional states she could anticipate if she continued to spend a significant amount of her time shopping.

There is plenty of talk about the movements of money in society and its impact on our environment: the news reports on corporate profits, what social services cost, and what can be achieved with different amounts of money. But little is said about the impact of money on our own lives. Society may have various policies and programs to distribute income evenly or to solve economic problems, but they do not take into account the fact that many people wish that their own personal finances would never be seen by outsiders. In previous chapters I have written about the fact that we all have our own stories about money, and money often evokes strong emotions. Many people keep their finances secret, even from their family and loved ones.

Some time ago in Johannesburg, South Africa, experiments were carried out with different ways of transferring the child benefit to very low-income families. In many countries, the child benefit is particularly well received because it increases equality and improves the well-being of children. In Johannesburg, recipients of the child benefit had to collect a payment order from the school office on a specific day. Both school staff and other parents taking their children to school could see in concrete terms once a month which parents were below the income threshold and had to rely on social benefits. It is probably not surprising that only a small proportion of families eligible for benefits went to apply for a payment order.

Despite their good intentions, policymakers often ignore the overriding emotion that arises when we have to rely on others to survive. Money-related shame is a largely silenced, underplayed, and misunderstood issue. This shame is not necessarily confined to poverty or unemployment but is particularly difficult to deal with when there is not enough money when there should, by all rights, be enough. An acquaintance of mine told me that he rarely lets his children visit friends because they come from much wealthier families and his own children would be used to a different way of spending. This parent was also reluctant to invite his children's friends over because they would see the shortcomings of life in a low-income family. Limiting life because of shame is surprisingly common, although the story behind shame can take many forms.

Ann-Marie is a journalist who has written three books and writes regularly for well-known magazines. She is a single parent with two children, a dog, a mortgage, and an old car. Ann-Marie has a reasonable monthly income, but her expenses are considerable because she has been unable to sell the detached house in the countryside where she moved as a young mother with her husband. Her husband died of a heart attack when the children were young. She has a large bank loan on the house, but because of her job she lives in the city and rents an expensive apartment in an area with excellent music-oriented schools for her children. Both of her daughters are studying music, which takes up part of her monthly budget.

Ann-Marie lives without a financial buffer, so any unexpected expense will derail her finances. She knows what it means to stretch her last tenner to cover a week's groceries; she has to write faster and quickly bill her clients. She can't afford to save or retire. She skips most social events because they often involve spending money. Ann-Marie never discusses her problems with her daughters and is determined to cover up any signs of money problems. This makes it difficult for her to explain, for example, why she doesn't take many family holidays and why her laptop faithfully follows her around even on weekends.

Ann-Marie is not alone in her situation. In the APA's Stress in America 2023 survey, all age groups reported money and the economy as significant stressors and the experience of these stressors had increased since 2019. The eighteen- to thirty-four-year-olds were particularly affected and reported money as a significant stressor (82 percent), compared to sixty-five-plus-year-olds (47 percent).[16]

Money anxiety is the painful feeling or experience that not having money or possessions makes us flawed, worthless, or different from others. In particular, it masks middle-class poverty, which is not so much about low income as about an imbalance between income and expenditure. Often it is caused by similar issues to Ann-Marie's: unforeseen life circumstances, failed housing transactions, losses, evasion of the truth, stretching assets to the limit, and lack of safety nets. Doing meaningful and quality work does not always mean adequate pay. The optimistic notion that "if you follow your passion, the money will follow" can lead straight to financial disaster. Balance demands more than good intentions—it requires actual financial skills, unwavering dedication, and a clear-eyed view of reality. Financial literacy isn't something we're born with—it's a skill set we must deliberately cultivate.

Shame is a necessary emotion because it binds us into a community and guides us to act in ways that strengthen cohesion. It becomes a problem when it affects who we are as people and the things we cannot control. Shame is linked to depression,[17] aggression,[18] eating disorders,[19] and addiction.[20] The experience of shame can be internal or external. Internal shame is caused by the feeling that I am unworthy or unable to live up to my own expectations. Internal money shame is fueled by the belief that I am "bad with money." It is often accompanied by the idea that the lack of skills is a personality flaw and that this flaw is rare. Everyone else around us seems to get along fine, and if they have problems, it is a temporary glitch caused by circumstances.

When consumed by financial anxiety, people rarely have the mental bandwidth or resources to develop money management skills. Most middle-aged adults I encounter—particularly women—tell me no one ever discussed money openly with them as children, forcing them to learn financial lessons through costly mistakes and hard experiences. Money shame also seems to be easily inherited: the more you encounter it in childhood, the more easily it rears its head in adulthood.

External money shame is related to the reaction of the environment to the lack of money. In the 1700s, the Scottish economist and philosopher Adam Smith noted that the basic necessities of life have a psychological and social dimension, and therefore people feel shame at being seen in public without them. External money shame is often linked to being ignored or to the experience of being scorned or discredited—not being able to live up to the expectations placed on us. External money shame is the experience of having our economic situation or status determine our value in society. Researchers have suggested that external experiences of shame can trigger both mental health problems and physical illness. Thus, lack of money or low social status alone is not a health risk, but the shame that comes from this situation would be the powerful emotional experience that triggers our bodies and minds to react.[21]

Many entrepreneurs talk about their own financial ruin in magazine articles—but only after they have "learned their lesson" and succeeded in their next venture. We are much more likely to talk about relationship problems, parenting challenges, and even our own mental health than to admit that the credit card is canceled. The smaller the amount, the harder it is to ask for financial help. Many people cope year after year with financial stress, but when asked, they don't feel they are among the group that needs—or deserves—professional help. More than half of people feel that talking about money is stressful, drains their energy, and lowers their mood. This is also why they avoid talking about money. Brené Brown, a professor of social work who has studied shame, has put forward ways of dealing with shame.[22] Her message is that it is always possible to move on.

If you find that the money shame you experience defines who you are, consider this:

- Shame is a holistic emotion that is psychologically and physically hard to bear. It takes energy, hopefulness, and belief in yourself to change your life. Making positive change is especially difficult when shame has taken over your life.
- Instead of vowing to take control, resolving to cut out all your bad habits, and denying the existence of shame, try to understand yourself. How have you come to this point in your life? Your story is profoundly human and important as such.
- The antidote to shame is empathy. So have compassion on yourself and ask for help; talk about your situation with people you trust.

In interpreting emotions such as shame, it is important to take into account not only our own feelings but the situation we are in. The more we are able to both notice and correct the prediction of emotional reactions produced by the brain, the more present we are in the moment. Emotions are individually constructed through the interaction of experience and environment, through anticipation and interpretation. This influences behavior and in particular economic behavior. Emotions are not just things that happen to us, but the result of our active actions. It follows that we also have the ability to influence what we feel and how we relate to emotions. When we are present in what is happening to us in the moment and open to (but not controlled by) our feelings, we have the opportunity to make choices and act in a way that is consistent with our values. This ability to make informed choices is central to financial wisdom and economic well-being.

PART II
THE VALUES

CHAPTER 5

GUIDING VALUES

Try not to become a man of success but rather try to become a man of value.

—ALBERT EINSTEIN[1]

GETTING TO KNOW VALUES

Decades of cross-cultural research have identified core human values that transcend individual differences. The pioneer of values research, Schalom Schwartz, and his team found ten basic values: self-direction, hedonism, variety, accomplishment, power, security, traditionalism, conformity, benevolence, and universalism.[2] These values seem to manifest themselves in different cultures in broadly similar ways, although generation by generation they change and adapt to the current society.

Our own fundamental values may not be easily recognized in everyday life, but they can be noticed, especially in conversations, where they conflict with the values of the person we are talking to. This leads to the possibility of disagreement and, at the very least, to discomfort, when we find ourselves not sharing the values we believe in. Values can be approached and identified in a roundabout way by asking questions about how we act in different situations and what choices we make between different options. Core values are often relatively stable, due to the dynamics of reinforcement. We reinforce our values by acting on them and interacting mostly with people who share our values. Core values can change mainly in exceptional circumstances and through experiences that shake up our thinking.

Psychologists generally view values as our foundational beliefs and principles—the underlying convictions that define what we consider important and meaningful in life. Personal values can be identified and written down. Values are not just concrete goals that can be achieved, or material things that can be acquired. They are more permanent guidelines for human behavior and choices. Values can be related to relationships, family, health, self-development, independence, creativity, or justice. Your values determine how you prioritize and act—for instance, whether you put your own well-being or that of your loved ones first.

Values are individual, but they also reflect society and how it is changing. They adapt and evolve over time, depending on life circumstances and experiences. It's worth noting that we frequently act against our own values, then craft compelling stories to justify these choices (e.g., even if I consider myself environmentally conscious, I may choose the plane over the train because I tell myself I don't have the time).

What I value is the most important part of me. For years I struggled with values: they were too cumbersome, out of focus, and impractical. How to lead from values to answers to the fundamental questions of life? How to solve even the most mundane problems? If you value your working life, it can be difficult to find time for family. If you value your family, you can't always take the jobs that require overtime and travel. If you value both, you are faced with a conflict. And this conflict is present every day, there is no solution, because values do not smoothly coincide and imperfection is part of human existence. In fact, the change happened for me quite recently, when I realized that values have, after all, something meaningful to say in almost every situation. I started to think of values more as a way of *being* as opposed to a way of *solving problems*.

Often we have limited possibilities to influence how events and situations unfold. Imagine this: You have slept the night ineffably badly because your child is sick, and the next morning you have to give the most important presentation of the year (at least in your mind). Your water bottle opens in your bag, and your phone gets wet and stops working while you wait for an important call from the doctor. A colleague points out an issue that is a sore point for you (has been for years) and which you've been working on in therapy but still hurts. As a result, you are in the eye of an emotional storm and you take the bus in the wrong direction, which makes you late for meeting a friend, even though it is of paramount importance to you.

In these situations, we have no chance of succeeding to the best of our ability. Sometimes we don't even meet the minimum expectations. The only thing we can influence is the way we act. How can I face a situation that makes me feel my own inadequacy in the most pressing way? I don't have to choose the role that is offered to me in my own mind (the failure). I don't have to blame anyone—life happens to all of us, sometimes with heartbreaking twists and turns. But if I can act in a way that is valuable to me, with gentleness, compassion, respect, and honesty, I feel in harmony with myself and my values. Even when I don't reach my goals, I can do it in a way that I am reasonably satisfied with.

Success and failure often transcend our outward appearances. We may perform in ways that impress others and yet contradict our core values and beliefs. When this happens, we're left with the hollow sensation of having cheated ourselves—like a student who copies answers rather than learning the material. Without navigating the necessary challenges or making authentic choices aligned with our true selves, our achievements, however impressive to others, can feel empty and unfulfilling. Nothing has been learned, though nothing has been lost.

EXERCISE

Tune into Your Values

If you want to get in tune with your values, have a go at this imaginary scene.

You are in a situation that is difficult for you. Close your eyes and imagine what it looks like. See yourself in this situation and in this environment, acting in it as you normally do. Follow the events without trying to change them. What comes to your mind?

Now try to see the situation with fresh eyes. See if you can do things differently. How would you act that could fill you with joy or interest? What kind of details would it involve? What kind of gestures, tones of voice, expressions of emotion, words? When you see yourself acting in this situation, how would you describe it to someone else? What does it look like, what does it feel like, what kind of words and expressions come to mind?

Guiding Values

Words carry profound significance, and finding the right ones to express yourself is essential. These might be in your native language, borrowed from another tongue where certain concepts resonate more clearly, or even terms you've created yourself. They might also be visual—a picture or symbol—though naming this image helps crystallize its meaning. The crucial element is understanding what these words represent to you: how your values would appear to others and how they feel internally.

When we act in alignment with our values across various situations, we not only practice these principles but also create opportunities to expand and refine our core beliefs. Personally, I value speaking authentically—saying what I truly mean. This doesn't always manifest as I'd hope; sometimes I find myself mentally absent or avoiding uncomfortable topics by speaking in vague terms that reveal nothing meaningful about myself. When attempting to communicate honestly, I may struggle with fluency as I carefully consider my words. Yet this intentional truthfulness brings greater presence, compassion, and empathy to all interactions—which is why I believe it's worth practicing.

Another way to conceptualize values is to consider what qualities I bring into a room—what energy, nonverbal cues, and attitudes accompany me. What is my unique contribution? Living according to values offers an alternative to rigid role-playing. Rather than adhering strictly to a fixed identity, I can embody whatever qualities help me remain aligned with my core principles. This values-based approach grants tremendous freedom to navigate life's changing circumstances with flexibility, without becoming entangled in external expectations about "right" behavior or "sufficient" performance in any domain.

Parenting provides an illuminating example. I can't always track every school announcement, check each assignment, remember all camping equipment, or arrive punctually at every parent-teacher conference. However, by operating from my values, I manage these responsibilities adequately most of the time, while finding solidarity with other imperfect parents navigating modern challenges. Realizing that parenting would feel natural by the tenth child puts my struggles with my first into perspective—I'm simply at the beginning of a steep learning curve. As a novice, I find contentment in occasional moments of clarity.

Similar realizations apply to any demanding role undertaken with minimal preparation. Sometimes living by our values requires personal development, acquiring skills and experiences that enable us to function effectively in specific contexts. In such cases, values become intertwined with concrete goals. For instance, improving my financial literacy became important to me because it aligns with my value of providing for my family.

In order to move from the present in the direction we want to go, it's important to ask ourselves a few basic questions. Some values are strongly linked to our own cultural and economic background. Values are fluid, not fixed. What you prioritize in your twenties may feel less important in your fifties as life experience reshapes your perspective. Living in accordance with values increases experiences of stability and meaningfulness. Therefore, it is a good idea to regularly check the direction provided by this personal compass.

EXERCISE

Know Your Values

What do you value? What do you care about in life? How do you achieve what is important to you? Below are some of the values that people typically feel are important. Circle a few that speak to you or write down your own.

> Honesty Integrity Authenticity Respect Responsibility Accountability Humility Courage Perseverance Self-discipline Compassion Empathy Kindness Love Loyalty Trust Forgiveness Cooperation Service Generosity Excellence Achievement Success Growth Learning Innovation Creativity Hardwork Determination Leadership Family Health Balance Peace Happiness Freedom Security Stability Adventure Fun Justice Fairness Wisdom Gratitude Mindfulness

Go through your choices and see if you can pick three more that are important. How are these three values reflected in your life? How do they guide your financial decisions?

The "Know Your Values" exercise is important because it shows that it doesn't really matter what we do for a living, what we own, or how others see us. What matters is knowing what we value. Sometimes the line between our authentic self and the image we project becomes so blurred that it's hard to tell where one ends and the other begins. Outsiders' quick judgments are superficial perceptions and interpretations that can also confuse our own perception of ourselves. Moreover, human value is not the same as economic value. It can be refreshing to find value in things that cost nothing. If you find it difficult to distinguish between what you value and what your environment values, try the following exercise.

EXERCISES

Clarify Your Values

(Read Exercise 1 first, then put the book down, follow the instructions, and only then move on to Exercise 2.)

Exercise 1: Close your eyes for a moment, and imagine yourself doing something you really enjoy. It can be a hobby, a chore, a leisure activity, whatever comes to mind. Bring to mind how this activity feels and what sensory experiences are associated with it (what you see, hear, and feel; what smells or tastes are present). Imagine that you are doing this just for yourself, because you want to. How does your body feel when you imagine doing this?

Exercise 2: Close your eyes for a moment, and imagine yourself doing the same thing again. Imagine that you are doing this for someone else because they want or desire it. How does your body feel when you imagine doing this?

Did you notice a difference between Exercises 1 and 2? How did it feel? Could this reflection be helpful in identifying values? What are the feelings associated with the values that you hold?

Some areas of life will always be more important than others, and some things may not feel relevant now but may be in the future. Our whole value landscape changes over the course of our lives; it becomes more nuanced, and experience also helps us to prioritize the values that matter. In many parts of this book, the point has been made that a meaningful and rich life is based on a values landscape that tells us what is worth investing in and what can be ignored. If we put into practice the values that are important to us in our lives, we will not stumble into the conflict of values that often underlies a vague sense of dissatisfaction and emptiness.

For example, if I value time with family and friends above all else but spend my evenings working, I have a values conflict. If I want to play basketball against the best in the world but spend my days fixing airplanes, there is a value conflict. However, many choices are not as easy and black-and-white as I suggest here. Resolving a value conflict can be a complicated, messy, scary, and seemingly impossible but often meaningful phase in life.

COMMUNITY VALUES

Is it possible to break free from your own bubble and start life anew in a place where fresh beginnings are the norm rather than the exception? What better way to challenge old beliefs about yourself and your abilities, or to truly clarify your values?

In the present day, there seems to be few opportunities for such profound renewal. While reflecting on this question, I realized I needed to talk to an extraordinary person I know who has dedicated his life to exploring distant lands and understanding space.

In 2004, Rico was studying space physics in Uppsala, Sweden, and singing. He sang in the choir of the Kalmar student nation, cycled around the city like any other student, went on hiking holidays with friends, and planned a trip to Greenland. Uninhabited and different environments fascinated him, and when one of the choir members visited Norway's islands in the Arctic Ocean, Svalbard, his stories and experience stayed with Rico for a long time. A few months later, Rico was able to visit the place himself, as part of a doctoral student exchange.

The three inhabited islands of the Svalbard became a permanent settlement only a little over a century ago, when the islands' only town, Longyearbyen, was founded. The climate is arctic, and temperatures in

July are at their highest, averaging 39 to 42 degrees Fahrenheit. Since 1975, it has been possible to fly to the islands from Tromso and Oslo. Surprisingly, tourism is one of the main sources of income, together with mining and research. Svalbard has long been a focus of interest for international research groups and a base for polar research. Longyearbyen as a town is open and welcoming, and its inhabitants are mostly young, under fifty years of age.

Twenty years later, Rico is still in Svalbard. He is a space physicist, a teacher, and an enthusiast of sustainable development in space. Dark hair has changed to white, but he still has the same sense of humor and candor as before. The town of Longyearbyen is home to about 2,500 inhabitants, and most of them spend between six and ten months on the islands, sometimes even a couple of years. Newcomers are easy to spot, and the first question to a newcomer often is how long they intend to stay. The more-permanent residents do not always take interest in temporary visitors. It is more important to build a permanent core community, which takes care of its members. The city's pulse is also faster, as people move, and very few stay for longer. Those who do stay have already done all that Svalbard has to offer. It is well known that everyone living in Svalbard has a snowmobile and a gun.

Before relocating to Svalbard, Rico enjoyed outdoor activities and extended hikes, but Svalbard presented an entirely different reality—a winter environment with polar bears and glaciers just beyond his doorstep. Venturing outside the city necessitates carrying a firearm and always informing others of your destination. Yet even extensive experience can prove misleading, and mistakes happen. One can never be too confident about the surroundings; alertness and vigilance are essential. Despite these extremes, daily life follows familiar patterns of work and family. The city houses numerous families, a kindergarten, and a primary school. In the past nine years, only three children completed the entire school cycle, while seventeen transferred to other schools. The town's greatest assets are its compact layout where everyone knows each other and a virtually nonexistent crime rate.

Four months of polar night annually means darkness regulates daily rhythms in ways outsiders struggle to comprehend, yet this doesn't prevent life from being both rich and quite ordinary. Weather challenges become merely questions of appropriate clothing and equipment.

Children participate in hunting expeditions from kindergarten age, ride dog sleds, and develop an intimate understanding of natural laws. Nevertheless, they also sneak off to friends' homes for console games or time on TikTok. Isolated from the wider world, it's sometimes difficult to remember that life elsewhere continues uninterrupted. Without maintaining continental connections, one risks losing those networks upon eventual return—and everyone must eventually return. In Svalbard, there are no senior citizens and no services for aging populations. Eventually, one might long for different experiences.

Rico, having witnessed enough snow and ice in his lifetime, now dreams of sailing warmer waters. Yet Svalbard remains intrinsically part of him—it has made him tougher but also more relaxed. Priorities become clearer when you've hunted for food, melted ice for drinking water, and gathered wood to build fires. Consumer choices are more necessities, and temptations to use money are few.

I confess that sparsely populated places make me somewhat anxious. I find my sense of community in cities, among the bright lights, noise, and constant hum of life. The background chatter especially helps me concentrate and provides a feeling of security. Yet I recognize that interpersonal connections can develop much deeper dimensions when not divided among dozens of people. Rico describes his most profound moments as those spent with his family—particularly with his wife and newborn child. They lived together as a family unit for six months, sharing each day from dawn until dusk. Now, he finds it peculiar to consider spending merely a few hours daily with his child, recognizing how limited that time is compared to what's possible.

This gives me pause for reflection. Many of us spend remarkably little time with those most important to us. Yet paradoxically, the more time we share together, the more meaningful our conversations become. Research supports this idea, showing that quality interactions thrive on reciprocity, sensitivity, and genuine presence.[3] When we focus fully on being with another person—truly listening and working toward shared goals—we strengthen social bonds both within and beyond family circles.

In Svalbard, Rico has absorbed life's most essential lessons: family takes precedence, work remains just work, and sometimes saying "no" is necessary. He's developed a healthy indifference to others' opinions and learned to choose his battles wisely. Rico believes that working in nature

Guiding Values

strengthens his family's resilience and wisdom, though this comes with the recognition that they inhabit a unique world. Visiting the mainland requires a mental adjustment, remembering that different rules apply there.

Rico experiences himself as existing between identities—having homes while simultaneously feeling homeless, belonging nowhere specific. This grants him a certain freedom from societal roles and expectations, as few people understand what decades of Arctic living entails. Though each Svalbard resident's story differs, they share a warm, close-knit community. Meanwhile, Rico stands at a threshold of change, anticipating a return to a different kind of life and society. The future may bring greater ease but also increased complexity—with abundance comes the daily burden of choice.

After my conversation with Rico, I'm left with a lingering restlessness. When different worldviews collide, even gently, they inevitably raise questions. I find myself wondering why Western daily life often feels overwhelming despite its objective ease. Nothing truly threatens my existence, yet many aspects of life seem difficult and burdensome.

The rhythm of everyday life is repetitive—waking up, commuting, working, shopping, helping children with homework, meeting friends, cooking, and preparing for bed. Nothing could be simpler in theory, yet this routine is frequently described as chaotic living—a perpetual cycle of activity with neither beginning nor end, where we work primarily to consume. This paradox of finding simplicity so challenging raises deeper questions about how we've structured our modern existence.

Longyearbyen exists as a place untethered from deep roots or generational history, thriving instead on the strength of its present community. I find myself longing for the experience of a truly supportive community where people help one another, rather than existing in isolated bubbles despite our daily interactions and the diversity among us. Such bubbles can be geographical—small villages and towns distant from the wider world. For many, however, these bubbles are the product of generations defining who we are, where we belong, and what we should become. Yet I wonder: Is it possible to discover a community where closeness and familiarity coexist with openness to a wide spectrum of individuals? Can we create spaces where we know our neighbors intimately while still welcoming diversity in all its forms? Where family, friends, colleagues, and acquaintances would not be separated but part of a shared story? These would be community values that resonate with many.

A COMPASS FOR CHANGE

What happens then, when we have discovered our values and hope to reorient our lives to match them? Sometimes life can feel static despite the passing years. In the tales of *One Thousand and One Nights*, Sindbad the Sailor exemplifies someone who paradoxically resists permanent change while constantly seeking adventure. Six times Sindbad returns from perilous voyages where he repeatedly faces death. Yet upon each return, he slips back into his former lifestyle, seemingly forgetting the transformative experiences of his travels. He resumes a life of comfort and amusement, only to eventually succumb again to the siren call of distant shores, exotic trade opportunities, and new tales to collect. His seventh voyage proves the most consuming—spanning twenty-seven years—leaving his family to assume he would never return. By this point, they had surely learned not to include Sindbad when planning dinner gatherings.

After his seventh voyage, Sindbad claims to have lost his desire for travel, vowing to live contentedly in Baghdad forevermore. Yet his pattern suggests this thirst for distance could never truly be quenched—perhaps because he never genuinely wished it to be extinguished. Following each journey, he would resolve to appreciate his home life and express gratitude for his survival. But inevitably, the troubles, pains, and dangers would fade to distant memories, and before long, his sails would be set again. His life in Baghdad—though prosperous and seemingly happy—remained uneventful between expeditions, offering little true fulfillment.

Sindbad experiences no genuine change or growth until his seventh voyage, when he remains for years in a foreign land. There, he builds a real home for himself and his family, establishing an authentic life. The tourist finally becomes an immigrant. By this time, Sindbad has reached an age where experience has transformed him into someone truly different from the young man who recklessly invested his entire fortune on his first adventure. Through this final transition, he evolves from an eternal wanderer to a man who has found his place in the world.

Change can arise from deliberate choice, but it equally emerges from the necessity to adapt to new life circumstances. Historically, human adaptability was viewed as merely a superficial shift—a role we gradually adopt over time. Yet what begins on the surface eventually penetrates deeper into the human mind. Personality has traditionally been regarded as one of our most enduring attributes. "A leopard cannot change its spots" and countless other proverbs caution against trusting someone who has once betrayed that trust. Much skepticism has surrounded humanity's capacity to truly transform character.

Recent research, however, reveals that human personality is surprisingly malleable under the influence of various life events. Graduating from university increases emotional stability, while starting a first job or beginning a new relationship enhances conscientiousness. In the short term, ending a relationship often diminishes self-esteem while simultaneously fostering greater openness and a desire to please others.

Generally, people tend to become more open-minded and tolerant with age and experience, developing more balanced perspectives. Even challenging life experiences and significant losses do little to alter this overall pattern of development. While many aspects remain within our control, far more rest in the domain of the universe, and we continually strive to reconcile our lives, values, and tendencies with these external forces.

Why is it that the people around us rarely seem to change? One answer lies in our perceptual limitations—we often struggle to recognize change in ourselves, let alone in others. With those closest to us, we may evolve in parallel, growing and changing together at similar rates that mask the transformation process. For distant acquaintances, our memory proves selective and sometimes downright treacherous, preserving outdated impressions rather than updating them with new information. We also tend to interpret what we observe as part of a coherent narrative—when we know someone's life experiences, these become explanatory factors for their personality traits. The mind instinctively searches for reasons behind others' behaviors, creating a consistent character profile.

This creates a significant asymmetry in perception: we often attribute our own actions to circumstance and chance, while viewing others' behaviors as direct expressions of their unchanging nature and personality. This fundamental attribution error blinds us to the genuine evolution occurring in those around us.

What if I long for change, but nothing ever seems to move in the direction I want? If I hope to avoid repeating certain patterns in my life—like Sindbad's endless cycle of departures and returns—something must change outside of myself. Sometimes it's easier to change your environment than to transform yourself. Motivation is valuable, but by itself, it rarely achieves lasting results. Knowledge and skills to facilitate change are also crucial, yet awareness without personal relevance often fails to affect what we actually do. Our environment and the people surrounding us influence us every day, whether we recognize it or not. That's why it's strategic to focus on what we can control—to direct our energy toward the elements of our lives that remain within our power to change.

Sindbad's life remained unchanged between his voyages—he continued celebrating with friends, enjoying the wealth and opportunities his travels provided. Ultimately, his restless soul found peace not merely through changing scenery but by abandoning the role of tourist and embracing an ordinary life in a new country, complete with all its inconveniences.

Reflect on yourself from ten, fifteen, or twenty-five years ago, depending on your age. Most of us barely recognize that person who shared our name, Social Security number, and physical features. Different emotions, thoughts, experiences, values, and goals have widened the gap between then and now. How can I be certain that the person bearing my name twenty-five years from now won't be entirely different? Everything in my body and mind has already renewed itself multiple times over. Plutarch, the ancient Greek philosopher and biographer, illustrated this dilemma with the story of Theseus's ship. The vessel leaves port, and before its return, every component has been replaced. Is it still the same ship? And does the answer even matter?

Whether it's a person or a ship, something persists when everything else changes. Even after years have passed, I can still feel somehow ageless, vividly remembering distant events and feelings as though they happened yesterday. These memories become the great turning points in my life—beacon lights by which I navigate. Simultaneously, they create the illusion that I remain exactly the same person I once was.

In truth, I am like a stranger from the future, different in countless ways, yet I imagine myself unchanged because my memories evoke similar emotions and thoughts. Musician Nick Cave writes in his biography about how, as young people, we construct ourselves with fierce conviction, believing in a permanent self.[4] Over time, this self-image shatters and rebuilds repeatedly. Eventually, with age and experience, we can relinquish this constant search for identity, embracing our freedom to be whatever we wish to become—a real and whole person, interested in more than merely affirming selfhood and identity.

This brings us again to our opening question: What happens when we discover our values and hope to reorient our lives to match them? Perhaps we've been asking the wrong question. Rather than seeking to mold our changing selves to fit static values, we might instead embrace the dynamic relationship between who we are and what we hold dear. Our values, like our personalities, move with life—not betraying our core essence but revealing it more clearly through each iteration. Sindbad's true transformation came not from choosing between adventure and stability but from discovering how to honor both within a single, integrated life.

CHAPTER 6

MONEY-RELATED VALUES

I know who I was when I got up this morning, but I think I must have been changed several times since then.
—LEWIS CARROLL[1]

THE VALUE OF MATERIAL

Writer and lawyer Nathalie Sarraute was one of my inspirations for this book. Her writings made her one of the most interesting existentialist thinkers of the last century. Sarraute was not interested in publicity, preferring to spend her time immersed in books and writing, and kept her family strictly out of the limelight. She presented ideas that sounded new and appealing to many. Especially after the Second World War, many people wanted a new opportunity, and it was important to believe that people can change. Existentialism emphasizes that we are all born into the world without ready-made answers about how we should live—without a goal, purpose, or destiny. We therefore have the freedom and responsibility to make meaningful choices.

Nathalie herself was born at the beginning of the last century in Russia, but she spent her childhood traveling between her divorced parents in Switzerland and France. Even as a child, she always wanted to find out what lay beneath the surface of ordinary experiences. When she tried to write about her childhood, she found that her memories were contradictory and vague, and she found it difficult to grasp what she could actually say about her experiences, what was true and what was a figment of her imagination.

In Nathalie's novel *The Planetarium*,[2] a deceptively simple domestic drama unfolds when a young man named Alain covets his aunt's spacious apartment. When she briefly offers to exchange homes before withdrawing the offer, the resulting tension exposes deeper psychological currents beneath ordinary family relations. Sarraute transcends conventional materialistic commentary by focusing on what she termed "tropisms"—subtle, almost imperceptible psychological reactions that reveal our true relationship to possessions and status. The novel's title metaphorically captures how humans perceive each other as artificial celestial bodies in a constructed firmament, while concealing vast inner universes of desire, resentment, and motivation.

Unlike writers who directly critique capitalism or class structures, Sarraute illuminates how material desires shape our interior lives. Her microscopic examination of the unconscious impulses driving property acquisition, status anxiety, and familial power dynamics offers profound insights into materialism's psychological dimensions rather than its socioeconomic implications.

The word *materialism* has many different meanings, from the earliest philosophers to our current-day cultural understanding. While philosophical materialism refers to the metaphysical position that reality is composed of matter (a radical view in its time), today we use *materialistic* as an adjective to describe people who love and pursue possessions or status symbols (a significantly less radical view).

In everyday language, a materialistic lifestyle has traditionally been defined as the appreciation of concrete products and the desire to acquire them as far as possible. Though distant from philosophical materialism, this thinking still reflects the emphasis on physical objects over spiritual or abstract values. Materialism is not just about whether the things we own spark joy, take up too much storage space, or are long-lasting or short-lived but is also about a broader focus of attention and energy on buying, selling, consuming, and the value of things. Therefore, materialism is strongly linked to needs, wants, and the impact that spending money has on our well-being.

Although the hobby of collecting involves acquiring things, it is not usually seen as materialistic because collecting something tells us who we are and what gives us pleasure. Art and record collections, books, coins, vintage clothes—you can collect anything and feel a deep sense of satisfaction in growing your collection. Collecting can be a pleasurable and well-being-enhancing hobby, or it can be an all-consuming obsession.

Materialism can therefore take many forms, which are neither good nor bad in principle. However, it is worth bearing in mind the impact of materialism when tracing the impact of money and economics on one's life.

+ + +

Time may change the content of materialism, but you can still recognize it by the question "What do others think about this?" Some studies have found that materialistic attitudes are also linked to self-marketing, body obsession, and self-esteem based on appearance.[3] Materialism could also include branding oneself, the ultimate consumeristic commodity. People who prioritize material goods tend to think about their bodies in the same way they think about their possessions—focusing on appearance and external value.[4] When considering the negative effects of materialism, they are not so much directly related to ownership or acquisition but to the fact that they affect human interaction and its quality. In between the human encounter comes the world of objects and brands.

In recent years, the environmental impact of consumption has become increasingly debated, and consumers are being asked to consider and take responsibility for the impact of their own consumption on the environment. By understanding the impact of the choices we make, it is possible to protect limited natural resources. Studies have shown that a large part of consumption is not so much about owning goods but about achieving a certain psychological state of mind.[5] At its most basic level, this is about comfort shopping or about expressing one's values through the acquisition of certain objects. If you want to distinguish between real needs and pleasure purchases, simple questions such as "What do you spend your money on?" and "What do you value in life?" can reveal if there is a conflict between your goals and your spending behavior.

Materialism has been studied for decades, so we know a fair amount about its effects: a materialistic lifestyle reduces well-being. Sometimes it is hard to say which comes first. Is it that materialism provides only short-term pleasure, leaving us needing more and more? Or is it that when people are not well, that increases the risk of resorting to seemingly easy means of getting pleasure, such as "retail therapy"? If someone is unhappy with their work, does that increase the need to consume because at least the salary makes it possible to consume? If you have experienced a lack of money in your life, does that make spending particularly desirable and meaningful? Research seems to confirm the idea that peer rejection and lack of self-esteem increase materialistic attitudes—that is, goods become important.[6] The antidote to materialism may therefore be found in good social relationships, including being accepted as we truly are.

However, materialistic values in life do not automatically lead to problems. A materialistic attitude toward life can also be learned in childhood and adolescence and accepted by the environment, growing into a belief that making purchases increases security and improves quality of life. In this case, materialism is stable and not so much associated with emotional experiences or expectations that happiness can be achieved through shopping. In this kind of materialism, the acquisition of things or products gives pleasure, but the primary purpose is not to make yourself feel better. Even a materialistic lifestyle can then be a value choice that does not necessarily reduce personal well-being.[7]

If materialistic values emerge in an already difficult life situation, problems are much more likely to surface. Often, a materialistic lifestyle is associated with negative emotional states and an attempt to relieve anxiety and strengthen positive self-image. Shopping addiction in particular goes hand in hand with anxiety and depression. It also easily leads to financial difficulties, which in turn perpetuate a cycle of negative emotions. If one's self-image is far from desirable, the contradiction can lead to shopping: new clothes and status-enhancing products are a way of compensating for insecurity and buying a new, better-looking self.

The outside world also tends to reward such behavior, as new clothes, sports equipment, cars, or bikes are easily rewarded with positive feedback. Conversely, something old, worn-out, and cheap can attract amusement or criticism. Nowadays, thanks to social media, feedback can come within seconds of purchase. The more direct and rapid the feedback, the more it triggers reactions in the pleasure areas of our brain and the more likely it is to leave a strong and positive memory. This ensures that we will continue to make similar purchases in the future.

Living according to materialistic values can increase the importance of external motivation, the need for rewards and praise, which studies show do not bring as much long-term satisfaction as the motivation from within.[8] If people are motivated to act and work only by profit or necessity, there is less intrinsic engagement, enthusiasm, and positive-flow experiences in everyday life.

The minimalist lifestyle may seem at first glance to be the opposite of materialism, but on closer inspection it also contains some materialistic aspects. Minimalism focuses on owning (or getting rid of) objects, which may require the purchase of new and better products that support a minimalist lifestyle. Minimalism promises relief not only from the clutter of things but also from a constricted state of mind where unnecessary worry and reflection take the place of clarity and creativity. It thus carries with it a similar emotional connection with physical objects as materialism. There is as yet no research on the effects of minimalism on well-being, and it can be practiced in very different ways from any consumerist lifestyle. Flexibility and the ability to accept the occasional chaos of everyday life are probably good for one's mental health even in a minimalist perspective.

Twenty years ago, two German researchers persuaded a local kindergarten to conduct a three-month experiment in which all the toys in the kindergarten were put into storage. The results of the experiment were positive: children's imaginative play was diversified, concentration and perseverance improved, and noise levels dropped. Even parents noticed positive effects in the children who participated in the experiment. The experiment has not been replicated, so it is not a good basis for drawing far-reaching conclusions, but it offers one perspective on the fact that more is not necessarily better for human development. Many subsequent studies have also argued that reducing consumption and focusing on growing and sharing social capital is an important step not only for sustainable development but also for human well-being.[9]

THE VALUE OF ACTIVE LIFE

The axolotl is a little-known but fascinating animal. I often see them in our local zoo and I would also be happy to see them elsewhere, but being a very rare and endangered species, almost all axolotls today are born in captivity. The axolotl is an amphibian salamander, which is a rare species of amphibian. They often remain in the aquatic larval stage of their development and never become an adult lizard. Axolotls are perpetual teenagers who don't see the need to develop their potential in any direction. These radicals of the animal kingdom refuse to leave their water element behind and remain content to bask in it. What is good is good enough and not worthwhile to go and change.

Few people know, however, that axolotls can also evolve when the environment demands it. Their gills atrophy and they become land animals, different in appearance and especially fond of living in the twilight. So even axolotls can bow to necessity and give up their carefree childhood in the once-clear waters of the Gulf of Mexico.

On a similar note, it is important to give oneself a chance to evolve, as it can open up new opportunities, foster personal growth, and help you achieve your goals and dreams. At the same time, change can be uncomfortable and scary. At certain stages of life, change can be just too much to handle. Often it is a sign that there are too many overlapping uncertainties in life. If that is the case, stick with the familiar and let time pass; wait for that moment when you dare to swim again, don't beat yourself up about it, and trust that the right time is coming.

Life is not a static, permanent entity that we can formulate to look exactly the way it should look in order to be ourselves. The pursuit of a perfect life is often more of an attempt to control and secure the course of life. It has nothing to do with who we really are or will be in the future. When I am too comfortable in my perfect life, I am tempted to say: "I am what I am, I want to do things that feel comfortable and pleasant right now. I don't want to change, challenge myself, or do things that feel difficult." And that too is perfect every now and then, of course, but not always. Happiness researchers have long sought to find out what makes us happy, rather than what we think makes us happy. Warm, close, and meaningful social relationships emerge again and again among the most important things, but also the experience of purpose and challenge can make us feel more alive.

+ + +

A perfect life for me would look like this: I see a big white house with a garden, and cherished pets and people who are close to me. I feel a sense of calm but also excitement. I have a four-day workweek, most of which I spend sitting in front of the window, writing and looking out to the sea. I see the wonderful food that I've for once had time to prepare, and a huge library with all my favorite books. My perfect life as I see it would be privileged in many ways and quite different from my real life, which is full of contradictions, intolerance, compromise, pain, insomnia, unpleasant surprises and wonderful surprises but rarely quite balanced.

Opportunities to direct the course of your life are not only about privilege. If you feel you have freedom of choice and independence to make decisions about your life, you are likely to live in a culture where the individual is important. In communal cultures and traditions, the community, the family, and former generations may be more central. Not everyone has the financial or social resources to live the kind of life they would want. For many people, everyday life is a struggle to survive, and they don't have the luxury of making choices that might lead to the best possible existence. There is also plenty of randomness in life, surprises and events that none of us have been able to foresee. Our control over life is limited, and although we can influence many things, there are also many things that we have no control over.

To return to the life of axolotls, change is not an end in itself, but unlike for salamanders who spend their lives in warm water, it is often a necessity for humans. When everything around us is changing, it places demands on us to adapt and grow, to examine our values and correct our course. In complex environments the direction of action is often not clear; it requires experimentation and learning. There are three things that you might consider, as they have a profound impact in our lives and also in our financial perspectives: volunteering for impact, working for impact, and altruism and activism.

VOLUNTEERING FOR IMPACT

For twenty years, researchers have known that volunteering improves people's well-being and that well people also volunteer more.[10] Volunteering can also contribute to employment or pay, especially in the public sector. One reason for this may be that volunteering is an opportunity to gain work experience and form relationships that can later lead to paid employment. As volunteering is almost always done for different non-profit organizations (e.g., animal welfare or mental health organizations) or social actors (hospitals, museums, or libraries), it provides an opportunity to learn more skills in these areas. In turn, it can improve your overall success in the world of work.[11]

If voluntary, unpaid work has such positive effects, is it worth doing if you want to make your life better? Before rushing to volunteer, it is crucial to consider your own life situation. While volunteering has many positive effects, it should not be a duty among others. When you are in a steady phase in your life, the time may be right and it may be easier to commit.

When looking at volunteering by age, it has been found that it does not increase the well-being of young people; benefits only start after the age of forty and continue beyond. This may be because young people feel that even volunteering is part of compulsory work experience, that it is done instead of paid work, or that motivation comes from outside. Despite this, the well-being of young people who have done voluntary work also increases with age, and the positive effects continue until they are over seventy.[12] It may therefore be that volunteering in youth has positive effects that only become apparent later in life. In that case, volunteering could be compared to saving money. This is also supported by the fact that those who volunteer at an older age are almost always those who have done it before. Volunteering is also an opportunity to engage with people and strengthen community ties. When children are encouraged to volunteer by their family and other close social groups, they are more likely to continue to do so as adults.[13]

If you want to increase well-being through volunteering, it is important that motivation comes from within you, from your own values and needs. While volunteering provides well-being for others, it does not have to be done solely for the sake of others or for social reasons. You can also volunteer because you want more encounters and conversations in your life; those who volunteer are more likely to form friendships. Social relationships are a legitimate reason to spend time with others, as loneliness is one of the fastest-growing health risks in the world. One in three people over forty-five feel lonely, and loneliness tends to increase with age.[14]

On average, people who volunteer live longer than their peers, are more satisfied with their lives, and are physically and mentally healthier. The health benefits can be even greater than those of healthy eating and exercise, although these lifestyle factors are often linked: active older people also take better care of their health.[15] The health benefits of volunteering are thought to be largely due to the fact that volunteers feel they are achieving meaningful things and are satisfied with their contribution. At the same time, it creates links with the society around them and opens up situations where they meet people outside their own reference group. It gives you the opportunity to reflect on your own values and how you can influence your environment. Spending time and energy on work of your own choosing is in itself a social act.

WORKING FOR IMPACT

For many people, work is a meaningful way to define themselves. It is not surprising that we spend a lot of time ensuring stability, control, and security in our working lives. Our plans, hopes, and dreams aim for a state where nothing surprises us too much, where things happen in a suitable and tolerable manner. Despite all this activity, stability is only an illusion. In December 2024, there were 6.9 million people (4.1 percent) unemployed in the United States. In March 2020 alone, during the COVID-19 pandemic, unemployment claims rose to 3.3 million in a single week from 281,000 the previous week—far exceeding the previous record of 695,000 claims in 1982.[16] In 2024, a significant portion of Americans changed jobs. According to a recent survey, the majority—57.65 percent—of American adults reported planning a major job change in 2024, similar to response rates from the previous year.[17]

Many low-profit companies cease operations each year, and in times of economic downturn, these numbers can increase dramatically. People are not necessarily able to continue in the profession they studied for or have worked in for a long time. In economics, this is referred to as "creative destruction," where there is a shift from low-productivity companies to high-productivity companies. Although creative destruction is inevitable for economic development, it can also cause unemployment and economic instability. The concept can also be applied to art, science, and technology, where the new replaces the old. Artificial intelligence is accelerating this process at unprecedented speed, much like the steam engine or computer did in previous eras—except AI's transformation may be even more comprehensive.

Change is constant, but at the same time it is important that people feel that they are important, not just instruments of change or its victims. In theory, social security and welfare state structures provide security for this transition, but in real life, change and the uncertainty it causes also create long-term insecurity.

Of course, many people change jobs or professions or retrain. Everyone has, at least in principle, the opportunity to reorient their working life and try different things at different stages of life. It is estimated that most Americans will have twelve jobs during their lifetime.[18] If we lose flexibility in working life, we also lose our belief in human change and the right to grow and develop over time. Unpredictable life changes can happen to anyone, and the best way to cope is often not to cling to old and familiar ways of doing things but to be open and see other options around us. In these situations there is also an opportunity to pause and reflect on the impact of the unexpected: what is left, what keeps us firmly grounded in life, and what we value.

A career bubble is often a particularly blind spot in life. Many people spend their days with those who do similar tasks, talk about the same pressing issues, complain about the lack of pay raises or the uneven distribution of work, talk about how busy and overworked they are, or celebrate shared achievements. Whether it's financial success, the recovery of a sick person, a breakthrough in research, or a good atmosphere in the classroom, working life is full of big and small victories that feel especially good when shared with your own group. People are more committed to people than to things. For this reason, it is sometimes difficult to see all the opportunities that can be pursued in later stages of life. When you change jobs, your own reference group changes and goals are reformulated, but people carry with them everything they have seen and experienced. Combining different experiences and work environments can lead to unusual areas of expertise and insights that cannot be identified by following the same pattern.

In the United States, working life is still divided into male jobs and female jobs. Women are more likely to work in healthcare and education sectors, while men dominate fields like construction and manufacturing. Women make up over half of all workers in education, healthcare, hospitality, and service sector jobs, while remaining significantly underrepresented in manufacturing, construction, transportation, and utilities.[19] It is also worth noting that human resources and communications/PR are management fields that are predominantly female. Research has shown that the strongest predictor of which gender dominates a college major is students' anticipation of gender-based discrimination. Women tend to avoid academic fields where they believe they'll face bias or unfair treatment, creating a self-reinforcing cycle that maintains gender imbalances across disciplines. This pattern helps explain persistent segregation in fields of study despite broader social progress toward gender equality.[20]

The internalization of gender roles in work probably begins early in childhood. Children are often encouraged to take an interest in different activities and career paths based on their gender. General preconceptions about how women and men perform in different professions can also influence how easily different career paths are chosen. Entrenched attitudes can also influence recruitment and the workplace atmosphere in general.

All of these are very valid reasons, but I would particularly like to highlight an issue that I think is not discussed enough: how we feel we belong to different communities and how we are welcome in a field where we are in the minority. If we take mathematics as an example, many of us think that mathematical talent is innate. However, in addition to talent, there is a sense of belonging to a group, in this case people who are good at mathematics. This feeling can also be measured. In one experiment, researchers divided participants into two groups. In one group, they told young women that mathematical ability is an innate and unchangeable trait that women have less of than men. This understandably weakened the women's sense of belonging in the field of mathematics. The weaker sense of belonging affected their desire to continue studying mathematics in the future and their grades in mathematics. In the other group, participants were told that mathematical abilities are learned and can be learned by anyone. This protected women from negative stereotypes, increased their sense of belonging, and had a positive effect on their intention to continue studying mathematics in the future.[21]

Messages that we don't belong, can't do something, or won't learn are far too common, and by believing them, we give up and abandon things that could be important to us. This phenomenon extends far beyond gender lines—ethnic minorities often hear they "don't belong" in STEM fields, students from working-class backgrounds are told elite careers aren't "for people like them," and racial minorities face subtle and overt messages that certain industries remain closed to them.

Rather than clinging to established paths, those seeking impact should view disruption as an opportunity to "pause and reflect" and potentially redirect their talents where they might create greater value. Creating high-impact organizations requires deliberately cultivating environments where diverse talents feel welcome and capable of developing their skills, rather than reinforcing limiting stereotypes about who "belongs" in particular fields. I will continue this discussion in chapter 10, taking a deeper dive on the meaning of work.

ALTRUISM AND ACTIVISM

No matter whether you are an economist, a psychiatric nurse, or a construction worker, everyone benefits from a society where some of the financial wealth around us comes from social structures, such as taxes, while others come from personal donations or voluntary work. This can also be government supported and endorsed. While altruism plays a valuable role in society, it should complement rather than replace government responsibility for providing basic services—citizens should never have to depend on the charitable impulses of wealthy individuals for access to healthcare, education, housing, or other fundamental needs.

Altruism, or doing good, has always been part of human life. Sharing food with those who cannot afford it, caring for the sick, cooperating and helping with charity work, donating to disasters and foundations dedicated to charity—altruism takes many forms. It is often forgotten that caring for the environment and preserving it for future generations is also an important form of altruism. Small acts of altruism can be performed directly through consumer choices. The almost automatic good is made possible, for example, by campaigns run in partnership with charitable organizations.

Activism can be seen as "reciprocal altruism" on a societal scale—a process where individual efforts feed the health of the larger social organism. Activists often invest personal resources (time, energy, reputation, sometimes money) to create systemic changes that benefit the collective good—for example, basic services becoming government responsibilities rather than relying on private charity. Activism also uniquely challenges power structures rather than simply alleviating symptoms—making it potentially more transformative but also more threatening to existing systems. Research consistently shows a positive relationship between activism and well-being, particularly among adolescents and young adults.[22]

When we talk about economic altruism, we are referring specifically to the use of money and personal resources for purposes that benefit other people, animals, or, more broadly, the environment. The concept of altruism was developed by the French philosopher Auguste Comte (1798–1857) to describe the counterforce of egoism, or self-centeredness.

Altruistic action involves no reward and is motivated solely by helping another person. Since altruism is not reciprocal, paying taxes cannot be thought of as an altruistic activity, even if it does a lot of good for a large number of people.

Although more than a decade has passed since the banking crisis and the deepest years of the recession, the memory of those years remains bitter for many. The managers of the multinational banks were greedy and did not care about the millions of people who were suffering from the economic collapse—this is what the media portrayed as a society lacking altruism and empathy. There are many good reasons for altruism, as moral and ethical responsibility for other people is the glue that holds society together.

A review of research on altruistic behavior suggests that most people are willing to sacrifice their own benefit to help others.[23] In experimental game situations, only about 10 to 30 percent of the subjects acted in a predominantly self-centered way.[24]

The likelihood of altruistic behavior is particularly affected by age. In 2015, Alexandra Freund and Fredda Blanchard-Fields from the University of Zurich conducted a series of studies to determine whether altruism in real-life situations is more common in younger or older people. The results confirm earlier findings that altruistic behavior becomes more common with age.[25] The researchers have explained this finding by the fact that as we age, the acquisition of possessions becomes less important and other values become correspondingly stronger. Young adults have not yet had the opportunity to accumulate wealth, and it is natural from an evolutionary perspective that in adolescence they should seek to earn money for education, a first home, starting a family, or other goals in life.

Altruism is more related to attitudes than to concrete income levels, so altruistic choices by low-income earners also become more common with age, and wealthy young people are no more or less willing to make financial donations than other young people.[26] Altruism is also higher when people feel more connected and less socially distant.

Altruism thus increases with age, suggesting that wisdom is indeed crystallized in life experiences and that we have the capacity to become more empathetic in our actions as well. Economic altruism is related to well-being, at least in the sense that the better we feel, the more altruistic we may become. It may be that doing good for others improves our well-being, but well-being may also enable us to care more about others.

Age can also increase interest in future generations, encouraging good deeds and giving meaning to life.

Economic altruism enhances well-being and life satisfaction, which may also indirectly contribute to increased income.[27] In the link between altruism and well-being, the motivation to act seems to be important. If we act altruistically and do not expect it to benefit us, it improves well-being.[28] A sense of obligation, social pressure, or other external motivation also reduces the rewards of altruistic action.

Generous financial giving represents a form of positive action that produces effects comparable to being helpful, kind, or advocating for justice.[29] When we do positive things, we reinforce positive emotions, thoughts, and behaviors, while meeting our own needs. Doing positive things can also reduce worrying by increasing a sense of control over one's life and turning attention away from oneself. Generous actions and behaviors make people feel part of a community; they also increase interaction with other people and empathy for others. Doing something together with others reduces both feelings of loneliness and the experience of being alone.

It is possible to teach children and young people altruistic ways of acting that promote mental health, such as donating to a charity collection, raising money for a good cause, or protecting nature and animals. These habits are likely to be useful throughout their lives. It is also important to note that it is good for everyone to find a way to be generous that suits them, whether it involves money or not.

All in all, it seems clear that although altruism does not involve seeking benefits for ourselves, it does improve one's own well-being. Another positive effect is the emotional reaction that follows the altruistic act, described as "a feeling of warmth in the chest." The third potential benefit lies in gaining social acceptance and recognition from our community. William Harbaugh's groundbreaking research from twenty years ago revealed what donations actually "buy" for the giver.[30] He found that even when exact amounts are kept private, charities create public donor categories, and donors consistently give just enough to reach these recognition levels—suggesting that altruistic acts are partly motivated by the desire for social validation. This is particularly relevant when considering cross-cultural or international charitable work, where the impulse to "save" or "fix" other communities—without understanding local contexts or consulting those being helped—can transform genuine altruism into a form of cultural imperialism that serves the giver's sense of moral superiority more than the recipient's actual needs.

Looking at altruism from the point of view of the recipient of the donation, one may ask whether it is right to benefit from altruism. I would argue that since the positive consequences of altruism are largely linked to a genuine desire to help, it does not matter if there are spillover effects. Altruism cannot be done just to improve one's own well-being, nor can it be enjoyed if the goals are self-centered. Altruistic acts may increase prestige among others, but this is an acceptable consequence because in society it promotes an ethical and compassionate way of acting. The possible synergies between motivation and altruism could be described as follows:

Motivation to act	Perceived well-being	Positive emotional experiences	Appreciation in the community
I want to help others and be useful.	Improved self-perceived well-being	A warm feeling in my chest	Appreciation for generosity
I want to show I am a good person and benefit from my generosity.	Little or no impact on well-being	Not much emotional impact	Appreciation for generosity

All altruistic actions create value, but they become transformative when driven by intrinsic care for others, living creatures, or the environment rather than external expectations. This doesn't diminish the worth of any charitable act—instead, it suggests we should honor all giving while cultivating the genuine compassion that makes altruism deeply rewarding for both giver and receiver. However, it's important to recognize that altruistic acts can sometimes reflect and reinforce unequal power structures. When charitable giving flows predominantly from wealthy nations or communities to poorer ones, it can inadvertently perpetuate dependency relationships that echo colonial patterns—where the "helper" maintains a position of superiority while determining what help is needed. Truly ethical altruism and activism requires listening to and following the lead of those being helped, supporting local solutions rather than imposing external ones, and questioning whether charitable giving sometimes substitutes for addressing systemic inequalities that create the need for charity in the first place.

CHAPTER 7

THE MYTH OF HAPPINESS

Money, fame and success are pleasant side effects if you know how you really want to spend your time.
—DERREN BROWN[1]

DOES MONEY MAKE YOU HAPPY?

Ten years ago, Paul finished his degree in business. He had been a relatively carefree student, doing odd jobs in the warehouse and spending most of his time on active student life. Paul barely managed to make ends meet each month, as he had no help from his parents, blue-collar workers who had no extra money to spare. Looking back on his student days, Paul feels he never missed out on anything, even though he could not afford to go abroad or indulge in expensive hobbies. He enjoyed his evenings in the student dormitory, where he would reflect on the world with his friends. He cooked with his roommates to keep costs down and watched his movies in a local student theater.

Today, Paul is a marketing professional whose career has been on the up. He has progressed from supporting roles to more demanding ones, and his salary has followed suit. Paul is again looking for a new role, as he feels under pressure to move into a better-paid management position at this stage of his career, even though he might be more interested in working with clients on product development.

Paul's family includes wife Rania and two-year-old Emil. Between work and family life, he has little time for leisure activities, but occasionally he goes out for a meal with colleagues and plays golf in the summer. Paul's social life is linked to his work, and it is difficult for him to separate the two. He earns many times what he did as a student, but he feels that this is not enough in relation to his expenses. He has a large mortgage and debts from the early stages of his career. Paul still feels it is important to maintain the lifestyle he is used to. He feels that he is solely responsible for the family finances, as Rania is returning to her studies.

As Paul reflects on his own happiness, he feels that most of the time he worries about sustaining himself financially. He hopes that in a couple of years things will be better and he will have more time to enjoy his life. At home, financial discussions are tough; Paul knows the topic makes him nervous, and so he has started to avoid talking about finances altogether. He's also coming home later and later, so he doesn't have much time to do that.

A key issue in Paul's life is how happiness seems to be slipping away when everything is better than ever. In fact, happiness is one of the most researched topics of the last decades, and not without reason. Most people hope to live a happy life and believe it is the most important thing for their children's future. As late as the 1900s, the *Oxford English Dictionary* defined happiness as *good fortune*, the external circumstances of life brought about by good luck. Good fortune meant a reasonably regular income, good health, and perhaps a family to support you through life's vicissitudes. It was not until the 1960s that this definition was abandoned, as happiness came to be seen as a *personal achievement* that one could work hard to achieve.

Happiness is a state of being that Westerners in particular actively pursue. Eastern cultures have traditionally sought to accept the experience of suffering and thereby reduce suffering, while the Western world has required feelings of fulfillment, joy, and contentment to live a good life.

+ + +

Ivan is the middle child in the family and has always been the great hope of his parents—smart at school but also creative in social life. He goes off to study law and, after graduating, joins the civil service. In his job, he moves from one task to the next with determination and proves himself worthy of trust. He starts out working in small towns but then gets a judgeship and moves to the capital. He marries and has two children.

Ivan's wife, Pasha, is at home with the children, so Ivan is responsible for the family's livelihood. He throws himself into his work and the evenings get longer. Ivan is deeply interested in his profession and finds it easy to immerse himself in it, sometimes only going home to sleep and eat. Pasha resents this, and they gradually seem to grow apart. Ivan feels that he is not understood, because he does everything he can for his family to secure their financial future.

The whole family's life changes when Ivan gets a promotion and a new job in another town. Everything seems to be going swimmingly. He buys the apartment of his dreams, which is right on the edge of the family's wealth bracket, but Ivan relishes the opportunity to invite friends and colleagues to large dinner parties. Decorating, designing, and shopping for the apartment is a shared hobby for the couple, and for a while they feel closer than ever to each other, at the center of success and social life.

However, once the apartment has been renovated and decorated, their lives begin to feel empty again. Working together has been energizing, and they finally had a common goal to achieve. With everything in place, things gradually return to normal, with Ivan focusing on his work and Pasha on the family. They still live in their dream home, but now it makes them less proud and more worried: how will they cover their expenses? Ivan is also haunted by worries about work, despite his professional success.

Although Paul lives in twenty-first century Providence, Rhode Island, and Ivan, as described by Leo Tolstoy, in late nineteenth-century Russia,[2] their experiences are surprisingly similar. Both feel that they were happier in the past and that financial or professional success has not brought them the satisfaction they had imagined. They both expect things to get better as they take a step forward, and do not stop to evaluate their life choices or values that underpin them. In other words, they expect change by doing things as they always have. The economic hamster wheel will only ever demand better performance, better income, and better status to cover rising costs and a new lifestyle. You could say that their idea of happiness is confusingly similar to luck: they rely on external factors to make them happy. But research shows that the environment has little influence on happiness. Paul and Ivan try to shape their environment in a desirable way, but at the same time they almost completely ignore what their everyday lives are like.

As researchers have pursued the big question of the links between happiness and the economy, the quest has been marked by conflicting results and a lack of consensus among researchers in different fields. Some researchers question the entire study of happiness, pointing out that focusing on the pursuit of happiness does not seem to increase human well-being, but rather the opposite. Buying a happiness book is not associated with feeling better in the future, although buying one book predicts that we are likely to buy another in the future. Self-development can become an end in itself, ostensibly available to all but actually the prerogative of a minority.

Indeed, the pursuit of happiness has grown into a product that sells more than any other form of self-development. Happiness critics often seize on the fact that emphasizing happiness as the main human goal simplifies life and its complexity. Only the individual can choose the pursuit of his or her own happiness as the goal of life. It is also often a difficult goal, as human life is full of emotions, successes and failures, and times when it is difficult to describe life as happy in any way. However, this occasional lack of happiness does not make life itself any less meaningful.

The emphasis on happiness also has an impact on self-image. In the current social climate, people may see themselves as products and brands whose essential qualities are happiness, enthusiasm, and the pursuit of personal growth. Social media profiles glow with passion and expertise. When life is seen as an upward curve, it nudges us to demand more of ourselves, to be better, more successful, and ultimately happier. Extreme examples of the pursuit of happiness urge us to think of ourselves as rich, healthy, and successful in order to achieve these goals. This completely ignores people's different starting points and the social reality that limits and shapes our lives and their potential. Taking such a narrow view of the pursuit of happiness can end up in the opposite direction: feelings of failure and unworthiness.

If sustainable well-being cannot be found by pursuing economic success (if it is not deeply embedded in one's core values) and happiness cannot be found by chasing it alone, where does the secret to a good life lie? The combination of three factors may be particularly important: a sense of meaning in life, a hopeful attitude toward the future, and a commitment to acting in accordance with our values. None of these three elements of a good life confines or defines an individual's life in terms of patterns or expectations. Nor do they require money, a life coach, or effective life management.

A couple of decades ago, researchers found that happiness is largely genetic: it is estimated that up to 50 percent of happiness is hereditary and certain identified genes seem to be linked to perceived psychological well-being.[3] Many have criticized the presentation of such precise figures, given that the environment influences which genes are activated and that people themselves influence the environment. In any case, hereditary factors modify the baseline level of happiness, which is then raised or lowered by environmental factors in both the short and long term. Since environmental factors also influence gene action, the inherited baseline of happiness is not permanent but can be altered by life choices and exposure to different situations and interactions.[4] Environmental influences on happiness are relatively small, estimated at around 10 percent. These findings are therefore a far cry from the happiness of the Renaissance, where the environment was seen as playing a major role. For Paul and Ivan, prioritizing their outward circumstances led to lives that appear fulfilling on the surface but lack genuine satisfaction.

Even if we assume that genes and the environment have a major influence on human happiness, there is still a margin of maneuver. The psychology of happiness is based not only on psychology but also on recent research in neuroscience, sociology, economics, and philosophy. All of these disciplines are trying to answer one question: how to live a happy life right now. Focusing on happiness in the present is easier than thinking about happiness in the future, because people are not very good at predicting their own emotional states in the future. For example, we imagine we will live happily ever after if we can just find the apartment or job of our dreams, but these are only likely to provide happiness for a year or two.

For instance, it's hard for me to predict off the top of my head whether going on a work trip halfway around the world next year will feel challenging or exhilarating. A few months before departure, it might feel like a long-awaited break and an exciting opportunity. A week before, all the arrangements involved are exhausting and irritating. If I want to test this, I imagine in my mind that the flight leaves tomorrow morning at six o'clock so I can get a better idea of how I feel. So it's worth assessing happiness in the present moment rather than in the future, because we're not at our strongest when it comes to thinking about future emotions.

Popular wisdom says that money doesn't make you happy, and often even lottery winners don't seem to live significantly happier lives—many even spend their fortune and revert to their old lives. There is hardly a single explanatory factor in this equation, but one can always speculate: it may be related to the burden of managing possessions, to external expectations, to one's own expectations of the meaning of life, or to work-life balance. In any case, the link between happiness and wealth is related to the entire spectrum of human life, from individual life experiences to social decision-making.

BEYOND GDP

The relationship between happiness and economics is like a complex ecosystem that appears fundamentally different to each scientific discipline studying it. Psychology has contributed the idea of a *set* of default values (*set-point*) to the study of happiness. We tend to judge our happiness as always being at a certain level. Pleasant events increase and unpleasant events decrease our perceived happiness, but after the events we often return to or near the default value. People adapt to life-changing events, such as divorce, the death of a partner, the birth of a first child, or the loss of a job.[5] There are also things that research has shown are more difficult to adjust to, perhaps because they involve strong, ongoing emotions or experiences. Marriage can make us happy or unhappy for decades because we don't adjust to it. If we enjoy the company of friends, we don't adjust, but meeting friends makes us happy again and again. Sex or loud, unexpected noises are examples of events that we don't need to—or should—adapt to.

Adaptation is also influenced by biology and gender roles. For example, studies have shown that men do not fully adapt to unemployment because the negative feelings of exclusion and insecurity associated with it are perpetuated by the constant comparison of their situation with others.[6] So while people have a remarkable capacity to adapt to positive and negative changes in life, the process of adaptation is not always the same. For example, recovery from negative events is disrupted if the events have been traumatic. A traumatic experience is like an intense stressful situation that stays with you and can be difficult to unwind without help.

Positive life events are relatively easy to adjust to—that is, get used to—and happiness soon returns to baseline levels. The "happiness hamster wheel" describes this very process of adaptation and adjustment, where something new and better is always needed to bring pleasure. However, adapting to what is pleasant leads one to wonder whether it is even possible to increase well-being, because we get used to everything in the end. Researchers have shown that it is possible to increase well-being, but the means are not directly related to the amount of money in life.

Indeed, well-being can be increased by consciously paying attention to changes that bring pleasure. A friend of mine was particularly pleased to ride the new electric bus and see how it works, while another participated in the annual cherry blossom event. You can also look for positive events in your life that are different and surprising, as they will hold your attention for longer and leave a stronger memory. I always remember a particularly demanding boss giving me nice feedback because it came in an unexpected situation, was unique, and made me see new qualities in myself. You can also offer these experiences to others; for example, you can surprise your colleagues with pastries on a normal day instead of bringing a bun to the coffee room table every Friday. Positive events can also be retrospectively reinforced by cultivating gratitude. So even in the midst of adjustment, happiness can be practiced through conscious actions such as mindful presence, seeking uniqueness, and reinforcing gratitude.[7]

Sonja Lubomirsky's research on happiness also suggests that the idea of a constant level of happiness limits us unnecessarily.[8] Although heredity and our own personal experience of happiness influence how happy we are, we can think of a range of happiness that we move through in our lives. Our own actions can then influence whether we are in the middle of our range or at the top or bottom of it.

It is important to note that happiness adjustment and happiness enhancement tools apply mainly to people who are already operating at a basic level of happiness and for whom the environment enables them to fulfill their basic rights and needs. If a person lives below his or her own level of happiness—that is, circumstances have a major impact on his or her well-being—then any improvement is a permanent way to increase well-being. People living on the streets need a home, people facing violence in their homes need security, children need a trusted adult to support their growth. There are therefore many situations where well-being can be directly increased by making the environment better and by, for example, increasing the security and financial support provided by society.[9] In these cases, money can and does directly increase happiness.

Once basic needs are met, it would seem that we are quick to adapt to an increase in income. We are particularly quick to adapt if we use the extra money to buy consumer goods. A new mobile phone or a jacket from a luxury brand is barely home when both the novelty and the sense of happiness that the goods bring are already starting to fade. Research shows that if we leave the mobile phone and the jacket in the shop and use the money to promote goals and activities that are important to us, we are able to enjoy the opportunities that money brings for longer—in other words, we are happier. For example, if you shorten your working day to write a play in your spare time, join a fat bike club, spend more time with your family, or start volunteering, you're probably as close as you can get to the happiness that financial well-being brings.[10]

Economics has considered the problems posed by rising expectations. Rarely are we satisfied with what we have, but we move on to the next goal. Indeed, the traditional view in economics has been that more is always the same as better. When we look at happiness or satisfaction from an economics point of view, satisfaction with the economic situation depends largely on the kind of life we are used to and what we compare ourselves to—the economic reality around us. This idea is similar to that of poverty: the experience of poverty depends on the level of wealth in the environment.

This may explain why in countries of rapid economic growth, happiness is easily overlooked. When income inequalities increase and growth is uncontrolled, unexpected consequences arise both inside and outside the workplace. In the midst of rapid economic growth, people may not feel that they are facing life's challenges together with others, but instead a sense of isolation, loneliness, and social bubbles are reinforced. However, humans are social animals, and we need to cooperate and see ourselves in relation to others and with others. So more happiness can be achieved by caring about other people. It also reduces the need to see oneself solely in terms of success or achievement.

HAPPIEST IN THE WORLD

For eight years in a row, the UN's World Happiness Report has ranked Finland as the happiest country in the world. The World Happiness Report studies happiness through a survey in which respondents rate their satisfaction with life on a scale of 1 to 10. The survey has found common features among the world's happiest countries: traditionally higher than average income levels than other countries; better health outcomes; and more social support networks, freedom, trust, and generosity. Interestingly, immigrants' happiness—that is, their assessment of their own quality of life—is quite similar to that of the native population. The happier the country, the happier the immigrants.[11]

In the early 1970s, Professor Richard Easterlin of the University of Southern California wanted to find out how rising income levels affect increased well-being. In his research, he found that if everyone's income rises at the same rate, it does not increase happiness equally for everyone. This finding has been called the Easterlin paradox.[12] His study was the first of its kind and has been criticized by later economists. Some more recent studies suggest that happiness is linked to well-being and not to income, while others argue that the link between well-being and income cannot be proven one way or the other. The results also depend to a large extent on whether you study the development of individuals or nations, whether you look at Western countries or statistics from Asian countries such as China, and whether you look at long-term trends in the lives of the same people or compare low-income and wealthy people. There are many possible interpretations, as the setting of the study has a huge impact on the results that can be obtained.

However, what is true for individuals also gives an indication of what shapes the happiness of entire nations. Average happiness has increased in many countries since the 1970s. At the same time, happiness gaps between people have also narrowed. In particular, policies that keep people employed and increase economic security increase life satisfaction. This finding is similar to the results of research on financial stress: it is easier to experience well-being when you can plan your life—for example, with a regular monthly salary. The exception is China, where economic growth has not increased life satisfaction because of rising unemployment and the breakdown of social safety nets.[13]

In addition to economic growth, there are many other indicators of social development that show that many countries are now living more securely and equitably. While increasing happiness is not easy, it is a natural consequence of social well-being.[14] However, an interesting question is how the surrounding community influences the aforementioned default value of happiness. Is happiness, in fact, a shared story of what it is like to live in this moment and under these circumstances? If the level of happiness of migrants is aligned with the happiness of the rest of the population, this is how it could be explained.

Economic growth does not increase happiness decisively, and the effect is not unequivocal. In Finland, which does well in happiness statistics, GDP is not as high as in the other Nordic countries, so presumably it is not the amount of money but other factors that influence how satisfied we are with our own lives. One factor may be that people adapt and adjust more easily to gains than to losses. The loss of a loved one can permanently reduce happiness, while a pay rise can be a momentary joy but after a year it may feel too small.

Similarly, it is likely that we have become accustomed to many of the benefits that society provides, and that cutting back on them could also significantly reduce our happiness. We do not want to give up the benefits we have gained, but if the situation is good enough, new services may not be missed. For example, it is hard for Finns to imagine paying for primary school or library services, because we have come to regard them as basic rights—which have certainly contributed to putting Finns at the top of the international happiness league tables. In contrast, the United States demonstrates how high GDP alone cannot guarantee happiness: despite its economic dominance, Americans face unique stressors around healthcare costs, student debt, and job insecurity that may partially explain why the world's wealthiest nation often ranks lower in happiness than countries with more modest but more equitably distributed prosperity.

Ruth Veenhoeven is a pioneering researcher on social happiness and interested in the so-called common sense of happiness. According to her, the tendency to happiness is a character trait, like openness or optimism. However, the variation in trait is largely explained by the extent to which we are able to fulfill the needs that are important to us in our environment.[15] Veenhoeven's research therefore suggests that happiness is clearly a social issue, since our environment either enables or hinders the realization of happiness.

Many economists have also abandoned a purely income-based perspective and have come to assess economic well-being through concrete action. They ask whether society enables us to take care of our health by promoting it through healthy exercise, nutrition, and home and social life, and whether we have the opportunity to contribute to the life of the community.[16] Professor Paul Dolan has suggested that we should question traditional ways of measuring happiness. Is it enough to ask how satisfied we are with our lives, or should we also ask how often and regularly we experience positive emotions in our daily lives?[17] After all, happiness is also an emotional experience, not just an assessment of income or personal performance.

WHAT ENOUGH MEANS

A sufficient level of income is necessary for a person to be well. Individual studies show that increasing income increases happiness most for men and people on low income. One reason for this may be the responsibility for providing for the family, which is linked to traditional gender roles and is reflected in the lives of many men. Another reason is probably related to the fact that higher incomes confer a higher status—that is, a higher position in relation to others. Some surveys suggest that in work and friendship relationships, status is more important for men than for women.[18]

In the following chapters I will look further at basic human needs, including the ability to function independently and to use one's own abilities and to interact with others. These basic needs are met by being able to live a life that is consistent with our values, doing things that interest us in different communities—at home, at work, in hobbies, and even at a housing association meeting. We also have the basic need of learning new things and being surrounded by people who are engaging in many ways, from friends to well-wishers. If, on the other hand, you simply want to achieve happiness as a goal, pursuing it is unlikely to lead to an equally good life or to long-lasting, balanced well-being.[19] If you want to explore this insight, I recommend the James Pennebaker–inspired writing exercise at the end of chapter 9. Before you set out to find meaning in life and make changes, turn your gaze for a moment to what exists in the here and now. It is also the starting point for your future.

Setting value-based goals and working toward them creates a sense of purpose in life. Research shows that some people set a goal of a high income from a young age. They are likely to consider salary as a major factor in their career choice and work hard to achieve their goals. High financial goals can provide satisfaction and well-being, but primarily when they are achieved. The crucial factor appears to be the gap between aspirations and actual achievement.[20] Studies also suggest that money boosts happiness because it makes us feel more optimistic about the future. The connection between income and life satisfaction comes partly from these improved expectations rather than the money itself.[21] Money can therefore make an individual satisfied when it is embedded in the goals and values that determine the direction of their life. This does not exclude the possibility that high-income earners also use their wealth for altruistic ends or pursue goals in their lives other than just making money. Prosperity requires a sense of meaning, and meaning can be created in many ways, including through the pursuit of financial success.

Thus, if financial success is in line with our values, it can be rewarding. But what about spending? Consumption and shopping therapy are so common that one might imagine they would increase well-being. However, research has shown that a materialistic worldview that values goods is linked to the fact that people do not perceive their well-being as good compared to others. An interesting series of studies by Monica Bauer and colleagues addresses this question.[22] These studies have considered the extent to which consumption is driven by people's own materialistic values and the impact of the environment that encourages consumption. The researchers gave participants in the experiments tasks and cues related to consumption and found that if the environment encourages consumption, it reduces the sense of community and togetherness experienced by people. An environment that encourages consumption also increases negative emotions in people who do not have a materialistic worldview. Focusing our attention on consumption does not seem to do us any good—regardless of how we feel about it.

HOW RICH DO WE FEEL?

The lack of unequivocal results on the links between well-being and economic growth is also perhaps because the right questions have not yet been asked. For example, is the level of income measured in currency at all related to what is meant by economic prosperity? And if not, should we be aiming for something more than a certain income level?[23]

Tori is about to finish her university studies. She has been working for a nature conservation organization and will continue in the same part-time role but with renewed enthusiasm for putting her studies into practice. Tori has worked occasionally as a cashier in a grocery store during her studies and has managed to make ends meet on student grants. She spends little money except on rent and food, lives in a cheap communal apartment a little farther from the city center, and is into recycling waste food. She also enjoys hiking and volunteering as a dog trainer, which takes up a lot of her time but allows her to be outdoors and practice working seamlessly with her dog. Tori aims to live within her means and uses a bicycle for her daily commute and a bus or train for longer journeys. Her monthly income is low, but when asked how she feels about her financial well-being, she says it is excellent. Tori's circle of friends share similar values and interests, and she rarely feels pressure to increase her spending to be social.

In the past, it was strongly believed that a clear, measurable level of income was the most reliable measure of economic well-being. Many economists still think so, but a large number of researchers have questioned the relevance of money. For example, a longitudinal study has shown that if people experience economic well-being—they feel in control of their lives, their worries are moderate, and they have a vision for the future—this has a positive impact on health, even if their tangible income is low.[24] This has been a turning point: once the link between poverty and health problems became visible, many excellent programs could be created to increase economic equality.

Researchers have cautiously suggested that by measuring how satisfied we are with how we are doing financially, we can get a sense of everyone's experience of their own finances and how to manage them, both at the level of thought processes and emotional experiences. It is then not just a question of what I can afford but *an experience of* what I can afford. For example, Tori feels that she has enough money for whatever she needs. People in a similar financial situation may experience the situation very differently, as their own expectations, environment, social status, and opportunities to change their financial situation influence their experience. Life stage also plays a role: if a young worker at the end of their studies and an experienced professional are offered the same job, they will experience a similar pay differently. For a young worker, the salary may seem sufficient or even a significant improvement compared to living on student support, while an experienced worker may be disappointed if the salary is any lower than in his or her previous job. On the other hand, people also differ in their need to experience economic security or their ability to tolerate uncertainty.[25]

The theoretical model of economic well-being is based on the hierarchy of needs developed by Abraham Maslow in the 1940s, which distinguishes between short-term immediate physiological needs (such as food and housing) and longer-term needs for security (saving for retirement in the case of the economy, investing in the future of the family).[26] This theoretical distinction still has its merits in explaining why, in a challenging economic situation, people need to focus on short-term survival, leaving aside future security. On the other hand, it has also been challenged, as there are situations in which an individual's own values and priorities influence the ordering of needs.

Once physiological needs and security have been taken into account, Maslow places the need for love and belonging to a community as the next priority. Interaction affects all the basic functions of our bodies, and while money allows us to fulfill basic needs—to buy food and shelter, for example—it is not in itself necessary for human survival, unlike contact with other people. In this sense, Tori, for example, lives a good life because she has a place in many social groups.

Financial well-being may vary, but this is not necessarily due to changes in income levels or debt. Even if two people have the same level of income, they may have different values and choices, and thus experience financial well-being very differently. For example, Tori's well-being is affected by the fact that she is a young woman who does not yet have a family of her own but has an active circle of friends. She is educated, a university graduate. She also has a strong sense that material resources are limited and believes she can find ways to live respecting the environment and consuming wisely. All of these factors contribute to Tori's personal well-being and financial balance. She also lives in a reasonably secure and balanced society with a good labor market situation, so she is fortunate in this respect.

Our immediate environment also plays a role in how satisfied we are with our own economic situation relative to others. The lives of those in Tori's social circle are very similar to her own in terms of values and behavior. No one in her circle of friends is homeless or in serious financial difficulty, and no one is truly wealthy. Their relationship to work and its remuneration is very flexible.

Studies have shown that those who are satisfied with their income level also rate their income level higher than those who are dissatisfied with it, and this has nothing to do with the actual objective income level.[27] People's experiences, values, and life goals shape their perception of what kind of life they want and what constitutes a good-enough financial position. This can be influenced by a number of external factors, such as family and friends.[28] Broad societal factors also play a role: if a society values environmental awareness, people are more willing to compromise their quality of life in order to make choices that support sustainable development. The different stages of life also inherently shape what kind of life is expected.

People tend to see the future in a more positive light than the present.[29] This is not surprising, since it has already been noted that hopefulness is one of the building blocks of a happy life. As human beings, we need to see opportunities around the corner, daydream, and look forward to the wonders of the future. Having a positive view of the future, or feeling that we can influence our own future, also motivates us to act in ways that will improve our economic situation.[30] This translation of hopefulness into action is important, because simply thinking positively or reading about happiness has little impact on our daily lives. Happiness also requires action.

CHAPTER 8
ECONOMIC SYSTEMS AND SOCIAL EXPECTATIONS

A restorative economy means thinking big and long into the future.... It also means doing something now.
—PAUL HAWKEN[1]

THE SHOPPING HEAVEN AND IMPULSE ECONOMY

Difficulty in recognizing emotions causes a wide range of issues in life. When we have difficulty identifying emotions, especially uncomfortable ones, it can take the form of pleasure-seeking experiences, such as Anna's comfort shopping. A close proxy of such pleasure-seeking is addiction, which is also driven by avoidance of unpleasant emotions. A university in South Korea found that the stress students experienced from their studies increased both negative emotions and the risk of online addiction.[2] Students thus respond to the unpleasant feelings caused by stress by escaping into online surfing. I feel a deep sympathy for South Korean students, for who would not recognize similar coping mechanisms in themselves? Didn't I just google something funny because I was simply bored with work?

However, online addiction is not a good coping mechanism for avoiding unpleasant feelings, as it takes time, reduces sleep quality, breaks routines, and reduces social life. For Korean students, it meant disrupting their extracurricular life, which in turn reduced their resources, making studying more difficult and increasing both stress and the need to throw themselves into the virtual world. Addiction is a coping mechanism that does not provide relief, even if it feels like it at times. Addiction can arise from anything, including healthy eating, work, or even a hobby that sweeps us away from everything else. Our emotions function as an internal warning system—when we learn to read their signals, we can address underlying issues before they morph into addictive behaviors that mask rather than heal.

If you think about the use of money in the most concrete terms possible, payments are largely based on touches and taps. You use your card at a payment terminal or tap the "pay now" button on your phone or computer. In a fraction of a second, you've completed a transaction that a few decades ago would have required a trip to the bank, counting the money, and thinking about the balance of your account. We live in a so-called impulse economy, where payment decisions are faster and easier than ever. Any need or desire can be fulfilled with a few taps, and a purchase could arrive on your doorstep this afternoon. Any reason that forces you to wait for a pleasure to come true seems too long, because we're used to having our desires fulfilled immediately. As payment has become virtual and abstract, the value of money has become increasingly difficult to comprehend. Every tap and touch takes from your account a certain amount of money you have worked for. But work done is not abstract—it is an activity that you spend your day and perhaps your life doing.

Cryptocurrency offers another example of how the digital economy challenges our psychological wiring—digital money that exists only online and uses computer technology to secure transactions without traditional banks or government oversight. Unlike traditional investments, cryptocurrency combines several psychologically challenging features: extreme price volatility that can see values swing dramatically within hours, markets that never close and demand constant attention, social media environments that amplify both success stories and panic, and an abstract digital format that makes losses feel less tangible. Research shows that these unique characteristics create mental health challenges rarely seen with conventional investments. They can trigger anxiety, sleep disruption, and obsessive monitoring behaviors that impact daily life and relationships.[3]

Comfort shopping or retail therapy is often taken lightly. Returning to Anna's experience, she tells me that you can't stop shopping altogether, you are encouraged to shop, and even most of her friends didn't see shopping as a problem. This makes pleasure shopping, or outright shopping addiction, a particularly persistent behavior, as shopping itself is generally accepted. Few comfort shoppers really think about whether they can afford it. Online shopping is also very easy and has built-in addictive factors, such as lack of social contact (you can leave the checkout at the last minute without explanation), the speed of the shopping transaction, and the fact that new products are always just a few clicks away. Research shows that online shopping addiction is highest among people who also suffer from offline shopping addiction, as well as general online addiction. These behaviors are also strongly associated with low self-esteem and negative emotional states that are avoided.[4] It is therefore a similar cycle to that of the Korean students.

It is human nature to seek to satisfy needs and to look for pleasurable experiences. However, it is often difficult to distinguish between transient desires or wants and underlying needs. Buying certain kinds of products can feel like a relief, providing a momentary answer to the question of what I need to feel safe, valued, part of a community, or just entertained for a while. Sometimes these feelings are part of life. A new computer won't solve the overload and uncertainty of thesis work, but it can bring a moment of pleasure and excitement, which in turn helps relieve stress and creates more sustainable ways of working. A new pair of jeans won't take away the heartache, but it will take the mind off things for a while and might provide an excuse to call a friend who will listen and offer support.

Sometimes, even just spending money can produce pleasurable experiences, as the hormones endorphin, dopamine, and oxytocin ensure a natural high and momentary relief. They also store the details of the experience in the body's memory—and tell us that the next time we feel particularly sad, we can fall back on these resources. If the experience of pleasure is very intense and combined with repeated and strong cravings, an addiction can develop.

The key point here is that a very wide range of money-related behaviors seem to be particularly prone to addiction. Such behaviors include acquiring money (gambling or working compulsively just for money), spending money (shopping), and, perhaps somewhat surprisingly, saving money. If saving becomes an end in itself and is used as a pretext to avoid buying essential goods or adequate food, it can turn into a harmful behavior—extreme frugality. Developing awareness of our feelings and financial habits serves as an important safeguard against the addictive potential of money and spending.

Anxiety and depression are risk factors for addiction, which is sustained by the desire to reduce suffering. The brain soon learns to relieve itself of the addictive trigger, whether it is a drug, medicine, food, or shopping. The rat experiments of Canadian psychologist Bruce Alexander shed light on the link between addiction and the lack of social interaction.[5] According to Alexander, highly anxious animals, like highly anxious humans, seek relief from drugs, and isolation from others increases the risk of addiction. These findings have been greeted with caution but have given rise to a research tradition that sheds light on the influence of environment and living conditions on the development of addiction. Many researchers have presented evidence that social support, contact with other people, can also reduce the risk of renewing an old addiction or creating a new one.[6]

How we talk about economics shapes reality itself. When economic discussions focus solely on individual achievement and responsibility, we miss the deeper truth: money often becomes our default solution to problems that require human connection instead. Our fundamental needs for belonging, contribution, and significance can't be purchased—they're fulfilled through genuine engagement with our communities, not through accumulating things.

What to Do When You Have a Shopping Addiction

Addiction is linked to the search for novelty and stimulation. Around 10 percent of the population is genetically more sensitive to new stimuli and responds strongly to the secretion of the pleasure hormone dopamine. However, the brain will enjoy more than shopping if it is exposed to enough new and interesting stimuli.

- The brain can be fooled by window shopping. You can tell yourself that if something you see is still on your mind in two days' time, you can come back and look at it again. Take pictures!

- Try renting instead of buying. In many larger cities, you can rent clothes for a monthly fee and choose without buying new ones. Some libraries also offer loans of leisure equipment.
- Join a peer support community that encourages and supports you in achieving your goals, whether it's a shopping break or financial independence. Share your experiences.
- Make a difference. Distinguish between long-term life satisfaction and short-term pleasure, and seek experiences that have long-term effects.

HOW SOCIAL NORMS SHAPE FINANCIAL BEHAVIORS

A significant recent study challenges the long-held belief that human well-being increases with income until it reaches around $7,500 per month.[7] After that, income was not believed to have a significant impact on happiness or perceived well-being. However, researchers have now concluded that one-third (over 30 percent) of people experience a significant increase in their happiness and well-being even after this point. Around 15 percent of people, on the other hand, do not experience any significant benefits from additional income. This has been explained by the fact that when there are other stressful factors in life, such as health problems, relationship difficulties, or traumatic events, money cannot solve these problems. If, on the other hand, things are going reasonably well, additional income is indeed beneficial in terms of quality of life. In other words, money is not the answer to everything, but it has a greater significance for our well-being than we have thought.

Financial success is often thought of as something that can be easily measured and defined in terms of salary or possessions, equated with personal worth, while financial difficulties trigger feelings of shame and personal failure. However, financial well-being is a broader concept that is influenced by the financial stress we experience and our ability to manage our daily finances and plan for the future. A bank balance alone does not tell us much about how these things play out in our lives.

Why are financial setbacks and hardships then so stressful? Financial insecurity is, at the very least, difficult and sometimes even a threat to survival. However, this does not explain the shame and silence that often follow bankruptcy, for example. One reason why financial stress weighs so heavily on us may be found in our own culture and its priorities. Culture and the brain develop in interaction with each other. Culture has a major influence on what causes us stress. It also affects whether we see ourselves as independent entrepreneurs or members of a community. Through a lifetime of practice, our brains learn to prioritize culture because without it we cannot be fully part of the human community.

We all know what stress is, whether short-term or long-term, positive and energizing or chronic and debilitating. Stress reactions are sometimes necessary, as they help us focus on things and get done what is important to us. On the other hand, stress reduces our ability to function. Stress increases repeating behavior because we cannot think of anything better. It increases aggression and reduces the ability to assess risks. It also reduces the ability to feel empathy toward people outside our immediate circle. In the depths of a stress tunnel, people lose sight of exits and side paths, convinced they must simply keep moving forward and trust they'll eventually emerge. At its worst, stress is a prison that is easy to fall into but difficult to escape and that affects everything we do and think.

Contrary to popular belief, a high income does not protect against stress, although it does make it easier to tackle the causes of stress. In most cases, it is a question of some kind of imbalance between income and expenditure, but there may also be underlying factors such as previous debts, unfortunate guarantees for debts, bankruptcies, long-term unemployment, or health problems. However, most people experience financial setbacks and surprises over the course of their lives that are largely beyond their control. There are also situations in life where it is difficult to control spending because, for example, you want to support a loved one. Whether it is a parent, spouse, child, or friend, many people feel that their own income and needs are not as important as long as their loved ones do not suffer from deprivation. The role of enabling another person's life and livelihood can also feel rewarding and selfless, even if the consequences do not necessarily lead to the best possible outcomes for anyone.

Sometimes the best way to tackle stress and create opportunities for action is to invest in the future. It is true that no one knows what tomorrow will bring, but being prepared and thinking ahead can also have an impact on the present if you do not have to worry constantly about the future. When your basic needs are taken care of, you are free to focus on what is important: living in the here and now. From a financial perspective, planning for the future can also mean making better decisions not only for our loved ones but also for society and future generations. This can mean donating money, volunteering, and making decisions that are good for a sustainable economy but also making meaningful choices in our own work. Sometimes it is easy to see that our work, whether we are highly paid or not, makes the world a better place for many people. This does not mean that teachers, nurses, rescue workers, and many others should not be paid a decent wage. However, work can be seen as a concrete contribution that affects the lives and economic well-being of many people now and in the future.

My work as a psychotherapist has taught me a great deal about how people act when they know what is important to them. I believe that most people have an inner ability and tendency to achieve the best results for their well-being if they are listened to and encouraged but also challenged in their own thinking. Thinking tools are unfamiliar to most of us or are little used. When we are aware of how our brains react to external reality, rewards, routines, surprises, and discomfort, we are also able to make wise choices. Change is possible at any moment, but conscious change as an adult requires reflection, consideration, and sometimes going against the grain. However, the economic situation and one's role as an economic actor are often seen in very black-and-white terms. Similarly, success and progress in life are linked to economic indicators.

There is a conflict between two opposing schools of thought in our society: On the one hand, there is the discourse of sufficiency, which talks about how we are enough as human beings just as we are—enough as parents, partners, children, employees, and citizens. On the other hand, there is the ideology of growth, a strong trend at both the individual and societal levels, which is very reminiscent of the story of economic growth and success. It sounds like a surprisingly benevolent view of human potential, of the ability to grow and develop. But is development more of a necessity than an option? Who determines its direction—do I choose it myself or do I follow guidelines set by others? Am I only rewarded for a certain type of performance? How many people are rewarded for socially critical thinking and questioning established norms? The ideal of personal growth often clashes with the fact that it is not self-determined. The direction of growth may be dictated by societal priorities.

Let's return to chapter 2 and Montpellier for a moment. The "tontine" circle is an example of how to take care of oneself and others financially. No one is just a recipient of help; everyone also gives help to others. Power is distributed equally, and status is irrelevant. No one demands that members of the circle do anything other than their share or to be more successful financially, to work more or to be independent of others. Studies suggest that they would all be happier with their lives if their income were at least $7,500 per month. On the other hand, this might separate them from the community that has become an important part of their lives. Culture shapes our brains and behavior, but we also shape culture. By building communities and communal models of behavior, we can change and question the roles of successful women and men, hopefully for the better.

INEQUALITIES AND BIASES

On a spring afternoon, just as the first tulips were beginning to appear in front of the flower shops in southern Helsinki, after the long winter, I sat down for coffee with Anniina. Anniina is a specialist in an organization that supports people with mental health issues. She has the voice of an angel, is a trained teacher, and has an ability to analyze life, learning, and well-being in a way that can lead to hours of discussion. Our conversations have made me wonder whether we should do many things differently in schools, academia, and working life.

Anniina has reflected on how enormously Western society has changed over the last hundred years. At the beginning of the last century, children were born into a specific role in society, norms and expectations were strong, and the objects of identification and comparison were within the immediate circle. If a person chose to resist these expectations, they could be rejected and excluded from the community. Today, norms are much looser, community roles do not strictly limit the development of identity and the meaning of life, and parents no longer dictate the future, although they certainly have hopes for their children.

Working life is characterized by uncertainty and flexibility, and it is good to be able to manage oneself. Personal agency is emphasized; people can influence their own lives and well-being and find their own path. This is, of course, liberating and offers opportunities. We strive to see the potential in people, their ability to grow and change at different stages of life. At the same time, many people wonder whether they have made their own decisions or have been at the mercy of external expectations.

Anniina and I discuss at length that the dangers of an individualistic culture are largely the same as its opportunities. Questioning one's own life and values takes energy, and life is full of constant choices, the abundance of which can also cause anxiety and aimlessness. A person's misfortune can also be seen as the fault of the individual, while at the same time the influence of the environment, society, and the political climate is underestimated.

Decisions that determine the future are being made at an increasingly young age. The gap between generations is widening because parents are unable to understand the experiences of young people and the conflicts they face. Acceptance is touted everywhere, but many children and young people cannot find their place or feel accepted. Choice, commercialism, and culture are linked to all life choices—what entertainment and products we consume and how they influence what we think about ourselves and how we build trust in other people and society.

So what could help when considering how to promote positive well-being and values in society as a whole? Digitalization has brought certain benefits, with many people finding peer support and identification through social media, but comparisons are made with complete strangers whose backgrounds and realities we have no connection with. Young people have many more opportunities to make choices that interest them but also the pressure to constantly succeed and be "someone great."

Stephen Vassallo, a researcher in school psychology, talks in his book *Neoliberal Selfhood* about how easily we adopt the self-improvement goals of neoliberal and capitalist society, even though they are just one way of looking at the world.[8] Another way of thinking could be to look at life and its stages from the perspective of development and community. What skills do we need to be able to contribute to the well-being of our neighborhood, for example? What kind of adults are needed to ensure that children and young people have a better life? How can we protect our living environment and make choices that are positive and sustainable?

My discussion with Anniina concludes that instead of endless possibilities, it is essential to offer human connection and structure. Children and young people need a strong community in which to grow and develop. We all need the mirror that familiar faces provide—people who reflect back to us who we are, both our light and our shadows, helping us see ourselves clearly. For every child and young person, we could work together to strengthen the skills that complement their temperament and support their well-being.

In his book *Hidden Potential*, organizational psychologist Adam Grant talks about people who encounter an unusually high number of obstacles, setbacks, and delays in their lives.[9] However, mental and physical endurance can grow even in less than optimal conditions, and this should be valued and supported. In fact, when we compare children and young people who have been nurtured in the best schools, had tutoring and educational activities, their skills and abilities are on average at the same level as those who have found their own way in much more challenging environments. Parents who hunt for good schools, neighborhoods, and communities remove obstacles from their children's path but do not necessarily help them develop their own abilities in a way that will help them throughout their lives. In addition to academic skills, so-called character strengths, prosociality, resilience, and empathy also have an impact. Cultivating these skills enables learning, curiosity, and support from the environment. They also allow hidden potential to eventually shine and emerging potential to arise.

PART III

ROLL UP SLEEVES

CHAPTER 9

PREPARE YOURSELF

There is so much I don't know about the future. I only know that I have to be part of creating it.
—JOSTEIN GAARDNER[1]

MAKING A DATE WITH REALITY

Do you know what happens to me when I think about reviewing a tax proposal for deductible expenses? My brain accelerates into overdrive and develops dozens of important and meaningful tasks in an instant that are absolutely essential to complete right now. Among other things, I've found myself in a bookstore looking for playful math exercise books, or preparing an Indian dinner for the first time that includes dozens of different spices and ingredients from many stores. I've found myself finally cleaning out the drawer at the bottom of which are countless old discount coupons for shops that have long since closed. And if nothing else, I can always reply to emails that I have classified as actionable but not urgent—and which, without the tax proposal, I would forget about until they no longer mattered.

All this is done to avoid focusing my attention on an area of life that causes considerable discomfort. Unfortunately, this is also the area of life that is likely to affect all other areas—even those that are most important to me. My family is better off when I have my finances under control. I am in a better mood and more confident and can make smarter decisions.

So when you're thinking about how to get on track to a life of financial well-being, the first step is to see where you are. Personally, I try to notice when I end up avoiding completing a tax proposal. On a more general level, it's simply a matter of noticing what I earn each month, what I spend, what I spend it on, and how happy I am with my finances. In this book, I don't offer percentages or guidance on what your finances should look like, because I strongly believe that this depends on your values, not on what your bank adviser thinks or what I think. Personally, I have a lot to thank my own excellent bank adviser for, but at the same time I know that I have put a lot of emphasis on things in my money management that make me feel better but don't necessarily fit into the recommended savings and investment charts.

And what to do if simply stopping and taking stock of the situation causes anxiety and discomfort? What if you avoid it until there are no other options? What if you have handed over this part of your life to someone else? What if the mere thought of taking stock makes you irritable because many factors are out of your control? You may have been looking for a job for a long time; sold your car; moved to a smaller apartment; struggle regularly with bills, income support, and the associated paperwork; and the future does not look promising. Why even bother?

In his book *How to Worry Less about Money*, British philosopher John Armstrong makes a simple but radical point: when we talk about money, we are talking about our relationship with it.[2] Like many relationships, money can be a complex bundle of expectations, hopes, disappointments, and strong emotions.

At the end of the chapter there is an exercise to help you focus your attention on your money relationship. Consider it a unique and valuable opportunity to do that. During the exercise, you will discover which impulses, thoughts, and feelings are taking your attention away from what you are doing. Let them come and go, but avoid jumping on them. If you need to clean out your junk drawer, make a small note on your calendar and let the impulse go. If you find uncomfortable and anxious feelings taking over your mind and body, give yourself time to notice what they are. If possible, welcome them, give them the best seat in your living room, and offer them a cup of coffee. That may be enough for today; continue the exercise again tomorrow. The important thing is to regularly focus your attention on your finances and manage the direction of your attention.

Wait a minute, you might say. *How is this different from what I do every day, sometimes even in the middle of the night? I'm racking my brain trying to figure out how to make ends meet or how to pay for a car repair/dentist/child's hobby. I don't do much else, and it hasn't helped me much.* At the point when worry and anxiety take over your thoughts, they also color your ability to think about finances in the best possible way—worrying replaces thinking. Your stress levels may be high, you sleep badly, eat what is easy to grab, and focus on the source of your stress, but in reality your ability to solve problems is already impaired.

Unless your intention is to run hard and escape the downward spiral like a caveman from a saber-toothed tiger, your body's reactions are unlikely to help you make a plan for the long term. Only partial solutions will emerge: when one problem is eventually solved, the relief it brings will overwhelm your mind and you'll build up your strength until the next financial worry and concern comes along. With high stress levels, you can't take advantage of slow, deliberate thinking.

So take control of your attention, and practice focusing it when the moment is right. Only then you have the best conditions and resources to make good decisions even at hard times—and stick to them. Make mindfulness a habit, make it a daily routine, perhaps taking just five minutes of your day. While you're focusing your attention, think about the one small step you can take today that will take you toward the financial balance you seek. Maybe you've written it down as a goal.

Once you become aware of your relationship with money, it is also possible to change that relationship. Psychologists Brad and Ted Klontz have studied the different beliefs and behaviors people have about money.[3] When they looked at attitudes toward money, they found four different types. They can be distinguished both by what people think about money and by how they interact with money:

> **The idealization of money.** Do you believe that money is the key to happiness, that more money would make you happier? If you see money as the answer to your problems, you may have a tendency to live beyond your means and take risks. At the end of the month, you only pay part of your credit card bill.
>
> **Money as a status symbol.** Is money the key to success and status for you? Do you feel more valuable if you have more money? Do you often say that rich people don't deserve their money? If you see money as a status symbol, you may have a tendency to live beyond

your means and lose control of your finances, especially if you want to show outsiders how much money you have.

Guarding your money. Does money make you uncomfortable? Is it something you don't want to talk about? Do you believe that money shouldn't be discussed, even in familiar company? If money makes you uncomfortable, you may try to keep it hidden and perhaps downplay what you have bought or what it has cost. Money is a sensitive subject for you.

Avoiding money. Do you see money as a negative thing? Do you think there shouldn't be too much of it, whether it's about yourself or others? Do you believe that you don't deserve money because many others have less than you? If you avoid money, you are likely to avoid managing your finances. Credit cards and spending will only add to your worries.

As you consider conscious financial wellness, it's worth asking yourself whether you identify with one of these financial types—or perhaps more than one? Or do you have a unique mindset that underpins your finances?

Peter had made a big financial decision a year ago: taking out a big loan and buying a detached house. He had a steady job, and his partner Teresa was pregnant. Everything seemed to be going well. They had never lived in a detached house before, so there was a lot of learning involved in managing it. The savings went toward kitchen renovations, but Peter was careful not to take out another loan and spent his evenings budgeting for his future paternity leave and perhaps a slightly lighter working week in the future.

In the spring, Teresa began to experience vague symptoms of fever and shortness of breath. A damp patch appeared in the downstairs of the house and mold was found under the floor. They were forced to move quickly into a rented house, and it turned out that renovating their house into a habitable one would cost almost half its original purchase price. The condition survey had been superficial, so Peter and Teresa had to consider whether to sell the house at a big loss or commit to a long and expensive renovation. The timing could not have been worse. Peter was punching a sandbag at the gym, wondering what he should have done differently. He went over the events in his mind but couldn't find where he had made a mistake. The whole thing felt like a bad dream.

Like Peter's, your financial situation can be tricky, uncertain, complex, changing, and difficult to grasp. But the first step is always to accept reality as it is. Radical acceptance is a different way of approaching reality. It means accepting that things are the way they are. If you think of them as different, it doesn't change your situation or your account in any direction. If you find it difficult to accept reality, your thoughts are likely to go something like this: *This can't be true, this can't be happening, this can't be right. I can't believe this is happening to me. There has to be another way to look at this situation. It's not fair! Someone must be responsible for this. I absolutely refuse to accept this. Where can I complain?* Thoughts can include sadness, anger, disappointment, and a feeling that you really don't deserve life as it appears to you at this moment.

Accepting the situation does not mean that you are at peace with it. It does not mean that you throw in the towel and do nothing. Nor does it mean that there is nothing to be done. Accepting the situation does mean that you stop struggling with reality. Reality is not your enemy. It is the starting point from which you have to struggle, whatever the next step. Things happen, and many of them are not predictable. Often they are nobody's fault. In Peter's life, accepting the situation means that even though his stomach is knotted at times with anger and worry, he sits down, breathes, and goes over the cost estimate for the renovation. He accepts reality as it is and starts to work through the options. He is free to choose, because there is more than one option. If he gets stuck in the "this shouldn't have happened" mindset, there are few options. When you make a date with reality, it also opens up different options for action.

EXERCISE

Focusing Attention

Set aside about fifteen minutes in a place where you know you won't be interrupted. Choose a chair that suits you, where you can sit in a comfortable position. You can also lie down on the floor with your feet up on the chair or against the wall. Make sure that nothing tightens or puts unnecessary pressure on your body. Close your eyes.

Focus your attention on your breath for a moment, whether you feel it in your stomach, chest, or nostrils. Follow the natural rhythm of your breathing for a few (five to ten) inhalations and exhalations. Notice the sensations you feel in your body (e.g., pain, relaxation, weight, warmth, restlessness, tension). Let the sensations come into your awareness, but do not let them distract you. Nothing else needs to be done.

Ask yourself: What does a balanced and good relationship with the economy look like in my life? Let an image or images arise in your mind, and choose one to focus on. Notice what it contains. Is it detailed or blurred? Does it involve people or activities? Hold the image in your mind for a moment, then let it pass. Notice how your body and breath feel now. Has your experience changed? Take three deep breaths in and out, then open your eyes. Write down what you observed and what thoughts the image you visualized evokes in you.

FROM REACTING TO MAKING WISE CHOICES

The previous chapters have discussed how our individual backgrounds, personalities, values, and emotions influence the relationship we each have with our finances. Instead of trying to act like a machine—which is impossible in any case—it is wiser to become aware of who we are in relation to money.

Much of the anxiety associated with managing the economy comes down to our experience of being somehow incomplete, insecure, and incompetent—unlike everyone else. If you've ever stood in a checkout line and heard a little beep when your card has for one reason or another refused to work, you'll catch this sense of inadequacy. Sure, technology can fail and it's not always the card user's fault, but sometimes I'm amused to wonder what explanations cashiers hear. Perhaps this thought will help you to grasp that feeling of uncertainty and confusion when something unexpected happens and you find yourself out of money, even if only for a moment.

Instead of trying to be a machine, a superhero, a financial guru, or completely flawless, try exploring the human condition. It's human to feel uncertain when trying to operate in a complex and in many ways digital world. It is human, common, and even necessary to feel a range of conflicting emotions when you do your best but still feel inadequate.

Being a human is important because it allows us to understand others. If I approach my own humanity with kindness, curiosity, gentleness, appreciation, acceptance, openness, non-judgment, and non-prejudice, it is possible for me to come closer to who I am. At the same time, it is possible to get closer to who other people around me are. If I don't use my energy to deny my feelings as inappropriate, I can find that some feelings help me move forward while others prevent me from acting.

Emotions are the main driving force in life. They cannot be divided into good or bad, because all emotions have a purpose. However, there are emotional experiences that can take over and prevent us from making the choices that will help us live a meaningful life. Acknowledging and living in harmony with these emotions gives us the freedom to make decisions that are important and purposeful.

Focusing attention is also a good basis for working with emotions. Focus your attention on how you feel when you are managing your finances. Write down your feelings and note that these feelings come up or tend to take over in these situations. If you feel shame, guilt, or hopelessness, note that too. If you are angry with the world around you, that is also allowed. If the feeling requires immediate action, stop for a moment and try to stretch the moment. What if I am here, with this feeling, and I postpone action for ten minutes? Ten minutes later, will I still be in the same state of mind, in the same state of readiness to act? The more aware you are of your feelings, the more you are able to make conscious decisions. The philosopher, psychotherapist, and survivor of World War II concentration camps Viktor Frankl has written that "between stimulus and response there is a space. In that space is our power to choose our response. In our response lies our growth and our freedom."[4]

Thoughts about money can be emotionally strong or neutral. As you interpret your emotions, pay attention to which thoughts easily take over, whether they are daydreams or visions of disaster. What kinds of thoughts become growing, self-feeding creatures, snowballs that gather more mass and strength with each turn? Note that the brain likes to tell us stories that relate to previous stories. They discover causes and consequences, coincidences become larger-than-life predictions, and small details can be interpreted into a variety of outcomes. The power of the brain is awesome, for its job is to connect things and make sense of life. Unfortunately, it also often misleads us when we don't question the story our mind is telling us.

For example, many of us recognize the inner critic tapping our shoulder. The critic is present at every important stage of our lives, often pointing out how things could have gone better, easier, or smoother or just look better. In some situations, the critic can help us to be realistic and make improvements, but sadly often the critic is an afterthought, forgetting the progress that has been made. A critic's voice can sound familiar; it can remind us of an authority or an important person in our lives. It can be a combination of many experiences and expectations accumulated over the years. It can be cruel and relentless. Our inner critical voice does not help us make better choices or build a life that suits us. It is incapable of doing so because it lacks the capacity to accept humanity and understand complexity. And that is what change requires.

EXERCISE

The Most Difficult Experience

Now I ask you to think for a moment about the most difficult money-related experience you have ever had. Close your eyes for a moment and go through the details of the situation or event. What was said, what was experienced, how did things make you feel? You can try to see the whole event as a film in your mind: What would it look like if it had been made into a story?

Take a moment to breathe a little deeper and longer, and pay attention to how your body feels. What feelings or emotions does this memory evoke in you? Have the feelings subsided or do you still feel them as unpleasant reactions in your body? If you can, try breathing for a moment, directing your breath to the part of your body where you would place the feeling or sensation. If you feel tense, redirect your breathing while paying attention to the sensations of weight and heat in your body. Continue until you feel relief or relaxation in your body.

Thoughts and emotions are the daily activities of the mind. It's very easy to come to the conclusion that they represent the ultimate self: I am what I think and feel. But I suggest, for the sake of interest, that you take a step back and question these conclusions. Thoughts and feelings are the workings of the mind, but it is reasonably easy to see how the workings of the mind are different at different times and on different days. The more I identify with my own thoughts and feelings, the more at the mercy of the storms they inevitably lead me into. Criticism makes me feel embarrassed, good feedback lifts my spirits and boosts my confidence. But they are received by the same person, sometimes even in the same day.

Taking a step back from an emotional experience or a turmoil of thoughts, one sees more clearly that the "I" is a continuous experience of the self, changing over time but not from moment to moment. My thoughts and feelings shape my actions and, in the long run, how I experience myself. However, they are not the same as me.

By taking a step back, I am able to distinguish between fear and concern about the economy and economic management at the level of action. Fear need not prevent me from making decisions that will help me live a life in accordance with my values. Fear can still be there, and it may have long roots in my own experiences, perhaps also in the experiences of my parents and grandparents. Yet fear and life as a whole can also be looked at from the sidelines for a moment. Then it is easier to see what tools or aids are available. Then I can see which route would be both feasible and best for me.

How do you give yourself space and take a moment to sit back and watch, instead of rushing through the daily grind? The answer lies in the steps already outlined. Go slow rather than too fast. When you want to separate emotion from action, the following steps will get you started:

- Practice focusing your attention and breathing. Pay attention to your feelings and thoughts, let them be, but don't get carried away.
- Ask for help, talk about what you are doing. Don't avoid talking about money.
- Accept encouragement and support, and stop there for the moment.

Prepare Yourself

Decision-making—including financial decision-making—can be a human superpower, but it can also be the sum of many unexpected factors. Imagine this: You are in the live audience of a cooking show, front row of the studio. A well-known and acclaimed chef is talking about his love of chili and the different types of chili legumes. You're not a fan of spicy food yourself, and you can't understand how anyone could enjoy the taste of chili. With a smile, you shake your head at the person sitting next to you. To add a little excitement to the program, the chef tells the audience that he will select a few test subjects from the front row to try a taste of the fiery flavor. He chops up a few small pieces on a plate and approaches the audience. The question is, How do you feel?

It is possible, even very likely, that your body is tense. It could be that these sensations were already present in some form the moment you saw the chili on the table. It is possible that your mouth is dry. You may feel a strange, uncomfortable feeling in your stomach. You may find yourself reacting to noises more strongly than you imagined; you may laugh or even utter a few strong words. It is also possible that you may freeze, make yourself smaller than normal, and sink into the back of your chair. You may feel time slowing down, voices getting louder or quieter, the spotlight of attention searching for you. Chances are you are not the only one having these reactions in the same row of seats.

No one can know in advance how their body will react in a situation where they are not consciously forming any complete thoughts. There are many possibilities. But it is up to you to decide how you act.

Our body's subtle cues tell us what experiences we want to move toward and what we want to avoid. We are often guided by our feelings without having time to make conscious choices. Our bodies, tuned to sustain life, react quickly. In the modern world, however, many choices and situations are complex and contradictory. If you followed your first impulses in the live cooking show, you'd be out the door. If, on the other hand, you take the time to stop, breathe, and notice what your body is telling you but at the same time realize that it is possible to be with these feelings for a moment, you might sigh and admit to yourself that the situation is not comfortable, but it is possible to either refuse to try the chili in a friendly way or, alternatively, accept the challenge. You may also be a little curious. Refusing or tasting are both wise choices, and above all they are choices of the conscious mind.

It is often painfully obvious how strongly connected the economy of different impulses is to different addictions. The ease of spending money makes life smoother, but it is not without risk. Thoughts and feelings pass quickly, but impulsive spending decisions made as a result can have long-lasting consequences. If you're not sure how your emotional experience is guiding you, a wiser choice than reacting directly is probably to take a timeout and postpone pleasure. Remember, too, that sometimes we must also fail to manage our finances. Failure may say more about our financial self-image or our relationship with money than continued successes.

Minimum Changes

Even small changes in financial habits can be surprisingly effective. Try these ways to manage your impulses:

- Think for ten minutes before spending ten dollars. Think for one hundred minutes before you spend one hundred dollars.
- At the beginning of the week, withdraw some cash from your account and commit to spending only that amount on your current expenses for the week. Be realistic so that the amount is large enough to start with. At the end of the week, you may need to be more specific with your budget.
- Act differently from your emotional impulse, but be compassionate with yourself. Find a substitute activity, like going for a walk.
- Set aside a small amount of money from your bank account to spend each month on impulse purchases that bring you pleasure. When you spend this money, there's no need to feel guilty because you've already budgeted for it. You can actually enjoy it.
- Save money in an account that you don't have direct access to or can't withdraw from without taking several practical steps.

MINDFUL ABOUT YOUR LIFE

In 2012, sitting on the edge of a large auditorium at Bangor University in North Wales, I introduced myself as a Finnish psychologist interested in hearing about teaching presence and mindfulness skills in schools. The brilliant and humorous trainers Richard Burnett and Chris Cullen had created a program that over the next few years would find its way into the classrooms of tens of thousands of children and young people around the world. In the auditorium, teachers, youth workers, and mental health professionals from different cultures enthusiastically threw themselves into experiencing and living the nine lessons—not just for the children but for themselves.

Mindfulness skills are part of the research tradition that has also motivated my own journey as a counselor and psychologist. Mindfulness skills refer to directing attention to a specific object intentionally, in the present moment and without judgment. Noticing things exactly as they are and dealing with them in an open and friendly way. In order to truly pause in all the experiences of our lives, we need just such skills. They allow us to be present in our own lives, throughout that unpredictable arc and until the end. Studies have found evidence that using mindfulness skills also increases satisfaction with one's financial situation over time, regardless of income fluctuations.[5]

It is never too late to learn mindfulness skills.[6] You can experience mindful presence in the morning sunshine, watching the ripples of water on the still surface of the pond and letting the first rays of sunshine warm your face. It can mean meditation exercises on a ratty carpet in your own home. It can be a post-sauna swim in the cold springwater. It can also be the moment before a demanding work meeting when you lock the bathroom door, take a deep breath, and listen to your heart beat gradually steadying. When we are present in situations and face them in a very special way, with kindness and curiosity, we can take the experiences as they are.

My friend and former co-teacher Sari Markkanen teaches meditation and mindful presence for a living. She has found in her work that the practice of conscious presence increases sensitivity, compassion, and benevolence toward oneself but also toward other people and life. At its best, this experience translates into compassionate action rather than just individual stress management. As we experience a deepening connection with nature and people, we become more aware of how our choices and actions affect us locally and globally. We can awaken a desire to help. Mindfulness practice often increases our satisfaction with life, and reduces our experience of lack and need. Instead, we can feel that we have enough and have something to share.

Inspired by our conversations, I want to challenge the idea that mindful economic management is only a matter for individuals, as conscious choices also make it possible to be more present in social interactions, to strengthen community and interpersonal encounters. It is not a question of accepting prevailing social ills but of focusing our attention on what is here and now and starting from there.

By observing the present, we can commit ourselves to improving the situation with a view to achieving our goals. If you have kept reading so far, you are likely to have a better understanding of what financial well-being means to you and the life it enables you, your loved ones, and indeed other people on this planet. We are all affected by economic movements; money is a relevant consideration to us all, and taking responsibility for it is important. Inspiring research in recent years has shown that when you have good social awareness skills, you are also capable of empathy and pro-social behavior, which improves the physical or psychological well-being of those around you.[7] When you practice mindful presence in adulthood, the experience can also be restorative for you if you have experienced insecurity and instability in your past. Positive interaction with other people is a fundamental force of presence and should be nurtured.[8]

Professor Carol Dweck of Stanford University has studied attitudes toward change and growth, and believes that we all have the opportunity to grow and develop if we are open to it. Growth and development are not the same as obligation or the idealization of self-fulfillment. According to Dweck, growth does not mean an over-positive "I can do it all if I believe I can" attitude but rather a realistic "learning and development is possible with few obstacles" attitude. People who are open to the possibility of growth are also more adept at assessing their own strengths and weaknesses. This is probably because they have had to face both when giving themselves the opportunity to learn. Therefore, I encourage you to think that change is possible when it just finds the space it needs.

Researchers preoccupied with change have found that our psychological system is remarkably adept at avoiding pain, but paradoxically, it also makes us worry about things we can't control. This contradiction is captured by writing, which I have mentioned a few times in this book. Writing seems to have a unique advantage: it allows us to look at our own internal events as if they were part of a story. Telling a story about myself is a powerful way of structuring and seeing the big picture and of figuring out what my role is in this life, in this moment, in this place. A story also never fully reflects reality but is an edited version of what our minds tell us. Our psychological system organizes our memories into compartments, makes connections, interprets, and prevents some parts of the story from ever forming. A story is good for us as long as it is sufficiently balanced with the truth. It must not be too far from the truth but not so close that its harshness prevents us from acting positively and hopefully.

Writing our own financial story is the first step to identifying mindful money management. If writing doesn't come naturally to you, you can also do the exercise in your mind or even make it a visual map.

EXERCISES

Financial Life as a Story

Exercise 1: Choose a situation involving a financial dilemma. Close your eyes and imagine that the situation is right in front of you, but you take a few steps back from it. You can let the situation unfold as if you were watching a play or a film. Watch what happens, and what your role is in the situation. Consider how this changes your perception of the events, or whether it brings something new to your own memories of the events. Write down your observations.

A broader writing exercise allows you to reflect on your own economy from many other perspectives:

Exercise 2: Set a safe and quiet time and place, and choose a pen you like. Set your alarm for twenty minutes.

Write about the most memorable financial experience of your life. As you write, let your mind wander freely to explore your deepest feelings and thoughts. You may want to relate your experience to other areas of your life, your childhood or your relationships with other people, such as parents, a partner, or relatives. You might link your writing to the future and who you would like to be, or to who you were before and who you are now. You may reflect on what adequate financial security means to you. There may be a number of difficult financial facts or events in your life; you may also write about them.

Anything you write is for your reading only. You don't have to worry about grammar or punctuation, just let the writing flow freely.

When the alarm sounds, stop writing and read what is on the page before you. Whatever it is, do not judge, evaluate, or defend. This is your story, and whatever follows is rooted in your experiences. You are the only one who can make the changes that follow.

This exercise is adapted from James Pennebaker, PhD, in "Expressive Writing Can Help Your Mental Health," https://www.youtube.com/watch?v=SsTzXB8M8fg.

CHAPTER 10

WORK AND LIVE WITH PURPOSE

The more that you read, the more things you will know. The more that you learn, the more places you'll go.
—DR. SEUSS, *I CAN READ WITH MY EYES SHUT!*

THE MEANING OF WORK

Do you remember your first job? It probably wasn't the one you expected to stay in for the rest of your life. Nowadays, people change jobs more often than before, but at some point, your job will often come close to what you thought you would do "when you grew up." Your job may be a profession, a calling, a choice, or a coincidence, and your employment relationship may be permanent or temporary. Most people want their jobs to have some meaning, and feel themselves useful. Consider the ancient Greek king Sisyphus, condemned to push a boulder up a mountain for eternity, only to watch it roll back down each time he reached the top. This myth has become the perfect metaphor for modern workplace burnout. As Albert Camus famously wrote, "The workman of today works every day in his life at the same tasks, and this fate is no less absurd."[1]

In general, work is good for people. A job provides a secure income that enables us to meet our basic needs and also brings status. The continuity of work, the structures it creates in everyday life, and the sense of purpose it brings to life are also beneficial. A European study compared working-age people living in thirty countries who were in permanent, fixed-term, or temporary employment (gig work). The results showed that fixed-term or gig work is not always automatically harmful, but that much depends on the individual's life situation.[2] Many students, for example, do temporary jobs and take advantage of the flexibility. Similar patterns emerge in the United States, where research from the National Institute for Occupational Safety and Health (NIOSH) shows that work arrangements can have varying impacts on well-being, with factors like schedule predictability and job control playing crucial roles.[3] Studies of American gig workers reveal mixed mental health outcomes—some experience stress from income unpredictability and isolation, while others value the flexibility and autonomy that gig work provides.

However, if working life is constantly very uncertain, it is a stressful situation in many ways. Uncertainty prevents us from seeing ourselves in the future: what we will do, how we will get by, what opportunities we will have to pursue meaningful activities. Uncertain employment relationships may also offer fewer opportunities for training, and employers may invest less in their employees' skills, meaning that the work does not meet the need to develop and learn. Work may also lack independence and variety, which are good for people. Uncertainty has the greatest impact on the well-being of permanent employees. This may be due to an unspoken agreement between the employer and the employee: permanent employees are often committed to their work and also expect commitment and care from their employer, not uncertainty.

Studies show that if working conditions are poor, this can be more damaging to well-being than unemployment.[4] Poor working conditions—too much pressure, too much work, poor management, and so on—are the biggest factor contributing to burnout, but when combined with financial worries, the combination is particularly stressful. If other factors that increase resilience are missing from life—close relationships and communities outside work—people are at great risk of burnout. Work must sometimes feel light, and time cannot always be used optimally. The mind also needs rest and moments of ease—even if it is just making a cup of tea. Brain researchers talk about protecting the brain and slowing down. Constant stimulation and the search for meaning can also cause burnout. The brain tries to protect itself from excessive stress and temporarily disengages.

It is also good to know that eight hours of consecutive, concentrated work per day is a myth. The length of the working day was determined in a very different world, where much of the work was routine or physical and considerably slower than today. In practice, our capacity for deep, cognitively demanding work is limited to four to six hours daily—and even that may be optimistic for most people.[5] Overtime is borrowing time from the next day; no one can do it continuously, and it does not lead to good health.

Can we say something about the meaning of work—outside individual experience? One option is to extend the concept of meaning to include a sense of control, appreciation, feedback, decision-making power, financial independence, freedom from fear, freedom of choice, or even the ability to utilize one's own strengths. The broader we view meaning, the easier it is to find it in our own work. Traditionally, meaningful work (organizational work, service professions, human rights advocacy, care work) can lose its meaning if the workplace does not meet the criteria for a good workplace. It is possible to experience feelings of meaninglessness at work, even if the end result is saving human lives or protecting rare wild animals. It is very difficult for an outsider to assess the meaning of work and how it feels from the perspective of the person doing it.

Psychology professor Michael F. Steger has studied the meaning of work and quality of life for a long time and has also created a measure for it. A short questionnaire asks you to consider, among other things, how well you understand the meaning of your life. You can find this questionnaire on his website.[6]

Meaning has become the necessity in working life: work that keeps us alive has been replaced by work that makes life meaningful. Many of us also see this difference as a generational gap, as both our parents' employment relationships and their attitudes toward work were very different from those of young people entering working life in the 2020s. In the past, careers were defined by continuity, security, early choices, and logical progression from one task to another. There were fewer questions and opportunities, but at the same time there was probably less pressure to create a personal brand or develop expertise outside the workplace.

Johann Hari explores the meaning of work as a creator of community in his book *Lost Connections*,[7] and he identifies several psychological needs that are essential for well-being. These psychological needs have been studied for a long time, and they are social in nature, meaning that they are best fulfilled in communities, both at work and in our free time. It is important for us to control how we work or how we spend our time; we also want to be heard and seen for who we are, belong to something, and envision a future that feels both meaningful and hopeful.

If we want our work to feel meaningful, we should do work that we want to do, are good at, and that is needed. Work can also be seen as both a way and a right to participate in the community. If you have at least some financial security, you can also choose not to take on work that you do not want to do, where you feel threatened, or where the principles are unethical. Simply being able to say "no" is a small but significant way of bringing more control into your life. Economic well-being also allows you to make career choices that suit you, to get an education, and to change the direction of your life. If your financial security is weak, you may find yourself stuck in a job that does not necessarily support your well-being. Money can offer you means of increasing your options and making your life better.

People have an internal motivation that drives them to do work that is meaningful and rewarding (what they want to do and are good at) and an external motivation that is influenced by salary and the expectations of others. Habit plays a powerful role here: Researchers have suggested that we become less accustomed to choices and values guided by internal motivation because they provide personal feedback and attract attention.[8] When salary and various incentives are only a means of livelihood, they soon cease to give pleasure, we get used to them, and our level of happiness returns to what it was before. This mechanism is important to understand when facing a decision related to working life. When internal motivation is emphasized, it may lead to longer-lasting satisfaction in life.

Many experts believe that working life is undergoing a major transformation. The economy has changed, and jobs and ways of work are evolving to respond to the new situation. What makes this change difficult is that the latest psychological knowledge about people's ability to process, organize, and handle information at work is rarely taken into account. Workplaces have often responded to the new situation with individual-oriented solutions: instructions on how to cope with work without becoming overloaded and how to recover from work. This is certainly helpful, but there is a risk that it will lead to an increase in self-direction without support, work that is flexible but also more intense, a reduction in resources, and a demand for higher output.

Experts are unusually divided on whether the transformation of work is a fact or a myth, but people's relationship with work and its results have not changed significantly. In the middle of the last century, philosopher Hannah Arendt wrote about active life.[9] She divided it into work that helps us survive (paid work), work that produces lasting and concrete things (such as the work of a carpenter or builder), and other active life, such as political participation. It is interesting to consider how these three parts of active life are realized in our own everyday lives. Is it possible or even necessary to stretch the narrow image of wage labor to encompass human activity? Work itself does not have to be wage labor to be valuable.

This evolving understanding of work's purpose aligns with what historian Rutger Bregman calls "moral ambition"—the idea that we should expand our definition of valuable work beyond traditional economic metrics to include contributions that genuinely improve human well-being. Bregman argues that many of the jobs our economy rewards most highly may actually contribute little to society, while essential work like caregiving, teaching, and community building often goes undervalued or unpaid. His research suggests that when people are freed from the pressure of mere economic survival—as demonstrated in various universal basic income experiments—they don't become lazy but instead gravitate toward work that feels meaningful and socially beneficial. This challenges the assumption that financial incentives are the primary driver of productive work, suggesting instead that given the security to choose, people naturally seek ways to contribute to their communities.

The moral ambition movement proposes that we might restructure our economy to better reward work that creates genuine value for society, rather than simply generates profit. This is certainly true for the work we all need in our lives—sometimes more, sometimes less—but which never loses its essential role in regenerating communities. Care work is performed predominantly by women (75 percent globally) and serves as the foundation upon which all other economic activity rests; without it, nothing else could function. Yet despite this fundamental importance, it remains consistently undervalued in economic theory.[10]

Unemployment does not necessarily make our everyday lives more unhappy, but the loss of status, decline in self-confidence, feeling of insecurity, and loss of human relationships and daily routines do affect happiness.[11] Long periods of unemployment in particular often reduce well-being, but the surrounding community and its attitude toward work also play a role. Perhaps somewhat surprisingly, high unemployment rates improve the life satisfaction of the unemployed, especially men, because many others are in the same situation. The less stigma, marginalization, guilt, and shame unemployment causes, the easier it is for people to cope and be active, for example, in volunteer work or further education.

Education itself has a small but significant impact on happiness, and indirect effects of education, such as better pay, contribute to greater happiness. However, the higher the level of education, the less it affects happiness—and in the case of doctoral studies, the effect is already negative. The comparison group also has a major impact here, as people are on average more satisfied if their neighbors of the same age have a similar level of education.

Work is the most important factor in increasing income and reducing poverty. It also provides an opportunity to belong and participate in the community and society. Work contributes to the fulfillment of psychological and social needs. Through social and economic status, work has a significant impact on both physical and mental health and, ultimately, on how long we live. Because we are social animals, many aspects of work and its status are socially constructed, together with others. Thus, the stigma of unemployment is more harmful to health than unemployment itself. When work is viewed in this way, it is clear that the basic need to participate in community activities can be fulfilled in many ways other than through paid work. The more open we are to these alternatives, the more freedom we have to make choices that suit us.

ECONOMICS OF BELONGING

If you could live anywhere in the world, where would you live? I asked this question to my friends and acquaintances, and I wasn't surprised by the answers. Many would like to live somewhere warmer, beautiful, and close to nature, ideally close to family and friends. The question is intimately connected to "What can you afford?" or even "Can you afford to stay?" Geographic freedom—the ability to choose where we live based on values rather than economic necessity—represents one of the most profound expressions of financial well-being. Often our living in a place determines our economic realities, whether we had any choice about it or not. Yet, even those with the resources and opportunities to relocate often discover that money alone cannot purchase belonging or guarantee happiness in a new place.

Rural areas tend to have a slower pace of life and stronger community bonds. Even though distances are greater, people rely on each other more. In cities, it is easier to blend in with the crowd and find your own tribe. Rural areas and cultures also have their own identity, to which their inhabitants adapt to a greater or lesser extent.

Amy is a lecturer in social anthropology at a university located in Auckland on the North Island of New Zealand. She was born in the United States, studied and lived in England for twenty-three years, and moved to her current home five years ago. When Amy talks about New Zealand, she is both proud and thoughtful. People think this is paradise, Amy says. A sheltered haven where you can finally be close to nature, go hiking, cycle, swim, sit in the shade of lemon trees, and enjoy the important things in life. A place famous for its beauty. A place where the rich build their safe havens. Anything grows here, and you can experience anything. And in a way that's true for those who can afford it.

In reality, New Zealand is not immune to natural or man-made disasters. Earthquakes and volcanic activity are common, and racist attacks, such as the 2019 Christchurch mosque shootings, are possible. Poverty and inequality are significant social and economic problems in New Zealand, and they affect the country's society and economy in many ways. If we look at the situation using the Gini coefficient (a statistical measure used to measure income inequality or wealth differences in society), New Zealand's Gini coefficient in 2023 was 36.2. The Gini coefficient is 0 when everyone has the same income level (perfect equality) and 100 when one person receives all income (perfect inequality). In almost all Western European countries, the Gini coefficient is below 35, while in the United States it is slightly above 40.

In New Zealand, the cost of living is high, so ordinary people, part-time workers, and the unemployed struggle to make ends meet. In 2016, about 15 percent of the population lived below the poverty line. A significant portion of the population experiences material poverty in particular, being unable to afford vegetables and fruit, heating costs, or hygiene products. Although child poverty has declined in recent years, indigenous children face significantly higher poverty rates than other ethnic groups. Paradise has two faces.

In social anthropology, "place of belonging" refers to a place or environment where people feel that they belong or identify with. For indigenous peoples in particular, people and the land are often inseparable. This can refer to a physical place, such as a country or community, but also to a broader social or cultural environment. Sometimes we feel a sense of belonging through a particular culture, language, traditions, or customs. On the other hand, the place where you belong can also be a social group, such as a family, circle of friends, work community, or hobby group, where everyone feels they are part of a whole. Nowadays, a sense of belonging can also arise in virtual communities, such as social media groups or online forums. The place where you belong can be in constant flux and depend on many factors, such as personal growth, life experiences, and social relationships. There can also be multiple spiritual homes to which we feel connected even from afar, across years and miles.

New Zealand has been important to Amy and has changed her life in unexpected ways. Attending academic conferences elsewhere feels strange when you encounter things like dress codes or hierarchy. At Amy's university, you see teachers and students walking around barefoot, everyone trying to be close to each other, no one feeling the need to appear to be anything other than who they are. The culture, language, and heritage of the indigenous Maori people are part of everyday life. The land she lives on is also disputed. The state and the Maori are fighting over its ownership, which Amy feels is deeply unfair. The indigenous people have little chance of turning the situation to their advantage, but the dispute is tearing communities apart and disrupting interaction throughout New Zealand. How can you feel like you belong somewhere that has been taken away by others? When you truly belong somewhere, you have an undeniable right to be there. For people who have moved from elsewhere, gaining acceptance in their new community is crucial—without it, you can't feel secure or truly settle down.

It was only after moving to her current home that Amy understood how important it is to be connected to your community, your ancestors, and your family. In New Zealand, family and *iwi* (tribe) always come first, and it is important to introduce yourself through your family and where your roots are—what is the nearest river, the nearest forest, the nearest valley where your heritage began. This helps you understand life in a different way. As a place where you belong. As soil that has its own meaning. Unlike in the Far North, where people are gradually losing their original homes and identities, in New Zealand they put down roots, becoming part of nature and its continuity, fighting for their right to be where their families and ancestors were born.

Amy knows in her heart where she belongs. She longs to return to Somerset in southwestern England, where her children were born and where she has experienced the most difficult and best moments of her life. It is the place where she belongs and where she believes she will return one day, if luck and the job market allow. Somerset and Glastonbury are magical places with traditions that go back thousands of years. Their magic is also based in the people who maintain traditions and rituals and respect their environment.

The concept of "belonging" reveals how deeply economic forces shape our relationship with place. In New Zealand, as Amy discovered, paradise exists alongside significant inequality—where your economic status determines not just what you can afford but whether you can truly feel at home. This dynamic plays out everywhere: gentrification displaces communities, housing costs determine who can live where, and economic mobility often means leaving behind the places where we feel we belong.

Northern Finland is abundant with traditions, ancient treasures, magic, and wonders of nature that are worth stopping to appreciate. When I was ten years old, I stumbled upon a place where I truly belonged—a small rocky beach in my hometown that felt like our family's secret. My father and brother would take me cycling there, where we'd sit on a large rock, explore the fern forest, and collect stones and shells. This little beach became my spiritual home, perhaps because it felt completely mine, a private sanctuary that taught me how an environment can be immeasurably valuable beyond any price tag.

The stories of Amy and countless others reveal a fundamental tension in modern life: the places where our hearts feel at home are not always the places where we are able to stay. True financial well-being isn't just about accumulating wealth—it's about gaining the freedom to align our physical location with our deepest sense of belonging. Whether it's

Amy's dream of returning to Somerset, constrained by job market realities, or the broader pattern of economic forces displacing communities through gentrification and housing costs, money ultimately determines not just our standard of living but our ability to live authentically. The highest expression of financial security may not be owning luxury goods but rather having the economic freedom to choose our home based on love rather than necessity—to put down roots where our hearts already reside, rather than where circumstance has planted us.

CHAPTER 11

MONEY MANAGEMENT

Forgoing a marshmallow now to eat it in the future felt, in the moment, in a certain part of the brain, literally like just giving the marshmallow to somebody else.
—NATHAN HILL[1]

WANTS AND NEEDS

One of the challenges of human life is that it's not always easy to separate needs from wants. Once the simplest basic needs are met, people can begin to influence the level of happiness they experience. We want many different things in our lives. In order to somehow put these needs in order—and to consider where to spend resources such as time and money—it is crucial to understand the relationships between them.

Basic human economic needs are often thought to include food, clothing, and shelter. Of course, there are many other basic psychological needs, but if we think in pure terms of surviving day to day in the most ascetic conditions, clean water, food, clothing appropriate to the climate, and a place to sleep are enough to keep us alive. In modern living conditions, sanitation, healthcare, education, and access to the internet are also often cited as basic needs.

Basic needs are relatively simple to identify, but a need in itself is not necessarily the same as something we need to survive. Nor does a need always mean the cheapest or simplest possible option.

In looking at needs and wants, we can use philosopher John Armstrong's division of needs, which in turn is based on Maslow's hierarchy of needs:

Higher-level needs	Intermediate needs	Lower-level needs
Intrinsic motivation needs *(they come from your heart)*	Needs for a comparative social life *(you feel that you are not left behind)*	Basic needs for survival *(food, water, warmth)*
Things you need to live a meaningful life and fulfill yourself	Things you need to be valued in your community	A healthy diet, safe housing, a job that allows you to earn a living

Once the needs of the lower level are met, money is the easiest way to meet the needs of the middle level. But these needs have the lowest utility value: the satisfaction they provide is often short-lived, whether it's new clothes, a new car, or a better-paying job—the previous chapter showed that we are quick to adapt to these changes. When the satisfaction disappears, new needs always appear in its place.

So, if the goal is economic and human well-being, it is better not to focus so much on meeting middle-level needs but rather on higher-level needs with much better efficiency. However, higher-level needs such as meaningful life and self-fulfillment are not separate from economic reality, as they may be met indirectly when we make economic choices. For example, having the option to limit working hours may make it easier to maintain friendships, spend time with family, or devote oneself to a vocation that is not work-related. On the other hand, work can also mean friendships and dedication, in which case we need time to focus specifically on it and fulfill ourselves through it.

A purchase can also meet a higher level of need when it is related to who we are and what we want to do with our lives. For me, such a purchase was a new laptop. I had been hanging on for a long time to an old one that had got caught under the foot of a rocking chair. The computer's shattered screen was covered with protective plastic and the text was sometimes unreadable. Since I write a lot for a living, writing equipment is an essential necessity not only for my work but also to bring joy and pleasure to my everyday life. At best, fulfilling higher-level needs creates value in ways that are not related to money—but money can still be a useful tool for achieving them.

HEALTH

Health is one of the most basic needs. The idea that life without illness, injury, and other health challenges is easier than life with health worries can be captured in an everyday way. Studies have confirmed that financial well-being affects a person's health, both physical and mental.[2] When the link between health and money has been studied, four very different connections have been found:

- Money enables access to paid healthcare services. This is not always the case, of course, but in general money increases the range and choice in healthcare.
- Money problems cause stress, and long-term money problems cause chronic stress. Stress-induced biochemical changes in the body increase the risk of illness and slow recovery from illness.
- Exercise, a good diet, a good work-life balance, and other healthy lifestyles are easier to achieve if money is available. If money is scarce, we spend a lot of time struggling with financial problems—and that time is taken away from everything else.
- If physical or mental health problems limit our ability to study and work, they can increase our financial difficulties.

Health is important in the pursuit of life satisfaction: having good health and social relationships makes people more likely to be satisfied than if only their finances are in order. Several researchers have also pointed out that people seem to be healthier in countries with lower income inequality.[3]

The link between economic well-being and nutrition is not necessarily due to income levels alone. For example, many studies have found connections between stress and gut health. The amount of financial stress and one's own experience of managing finances can therefore affect health in more ways than just the amount of money available. However, if the income level is high enough, it allows us to pay attention to diet, to receive nutritional advice, to choose healthy and possibly tastier options, to purchase organic food, and even to have access to semi-prepared food to make everyday life easier.

Financial well-being also affects family relationships, quality of life, happiness, and overall success in life—all factors that are linked to mental health. Health is now widely seen as including mental well-being. Mental health services have become more available and accessible, and therapy has become about taking care of one's own mind. The stigma associated with mental health has decreased, although it has not disappeared completely. Society is spending more and more money on mental health promotion to build on people's resources and strengths to support coping in a wide range of life situations. The most common mental health problems today are depression and anxiety, which most often also manifest themselves in some form of physical symptoms such as fatigue, insomnia, lack of appetite, or pain—another way in which mind and body are linked.

When financial stress is reduced, many people find it easier to solve financial problems, as stress levels affect cognitive capacity. Problem-solving ability creates a powerful sense of financial agency—the confidence that you can both handle current challenges and actively shape a better financial future. It is therefore a kind of ascending mental health spiral. Long-term financial difficulties, on the other hand, can be accompanied by a learned experience of helplessness, whereby people become easily discouraged, expect someone else to come to their aid, and eventually stop trying to solve their own problems. Discouragement and hopelessness increase the risk of depression and anxiety, creating a downward spiral.

If your own financial situation is stressful, the effects are never confined to one area of your life, as financial stress also predicts problems in relationships, both at work and in your leisure time. Mental health is also more prone to experiencing shocks, because it can be difficult for a person in financial distress to value themselves and their own actions.

Research shows that mental health problems, particularly severe disorders, are more common among people who also have financial problems.[4] Is it that mental health problems affect livelihoods, or is it that precarious livelihoods cause mental health problems? The answer to both questions is yes. Helen Uddy, director of the Money and Mental Health Institute, points out that there is a clear link between financial problems and suicide attempts, which should be taken into account in all decision-making. Suicide rates increase when financial security is threatened. When economic growth slows, it hits men's well-being particularly hard.[5]

Even for mental health issues that don't reach the severity of suicide risk, economic realities still have a significant impact. For example, few mental health professionals know anything about how clients cope financially and the financial risk factors in their daily lives that affect their mental health. Given the many ways in which financial security directly affects mental and physical health, one could envisage a future in which holistic healthcare includes financial counseling. This brings us back to basic needs: if you want to make a difference, sometimes you have to start with basic needs such as health, because it has a major impact on people's overall well-being.

A ROOF OVER YOUR HEAD

Living in a particular place, building a home either metaphorically or concretely, says a lot about who we are. Home has traditionally signaled more than shelter—it has been a marker of status and social position. A fine house has communicated to others one's financial status at the time, even if the appearance of the house does not indicate the debts incurred to build it. Moving from one place to another is also often seen as a step forward in life.

Studies have suggested that when home ownership is compared to renting a house, home ownership is associated with better well-being. This difference is probably due to the fact that owning a home is initially more expensive and requires resources that not everyone has access to. Indeed, it is often the case that if it is at all possible to buy a home, one is already in a reasonably good financial situation.

Homeowners are a very broad group of people in different life situations. Over a decade ago, Beverly Searle and colleagues published a survey and interview study examining the links between home ownership and well-being.[6] Surprisingly, the people who had the largest investments in real estate and who had benefited financially from the purchase of real estate perceived their psychological well-being to be worse than many others.

Interviews shed light on this surprising finding. Those who perceived their well-being as worse than others considered the properties they acquired (whether one or many) to be primarily investments. They were therefore concerned about how their value would develop. They did not attach as much sentimental value or memories to their properties as non-investors; they did not renovate them much to their liking and were prepared to consider moving to a better investment as soon as possible. Market developments, the constant work of maintaining properties, and the need to get better returns or move up the housing market ladder made them insecure. In contrast, people who owned their homes and felt that they owned a home that was suitable for them, renovated to suit their needs and reflected their values and needs, felt that their psychological well-being was better than average. They were less concerned about the development of their home's value, believing they would live in their home for as long as possible. They also described their home in very positive terms.

So is it the case that, from a well-being perspective, owning your own home is worthwhile? Very few people can buy a house or property without debt, so a loan should be factored into the welfare equation. There is very clear evidence from research that debt has a high potential to undermine well-being.[7] Does this then also apply to mortgages? The answer seems to be yes and no. Some people find themselves struggling with a (too) large mortgage, increasing their worry and stress about managing the mortgage and their paycheck. In such cases, a home mortgage can cause financial stress, the effects of which we have discovered. Even if the loan is large, some people are still happy with their share, as they feel they have spent their money wisely and take pride in the home they own. This is particularly true when people are able to use their wealth to fulfill their own values and goals. If family is an important value in your life, it is important that after mortgage repayments you can still afford to look after your children or limit your working hours so that you can get home for an evening meal together.

Smart Housing for Well-Being

- Live in a home that feels like your own—whether you rent or buy.
- Enjoy your home as a home. If you own your home, avoid paying too much attention to its market value. If you rent, don't let it bother you. In terms of happiness in housing, ownership is not the most important issue.
- The role of a mortgage is to enable you to live in your home. Instead of just numbers, consider whether this home matches your life values. Will you have money left over after the loan repayments to pursue other goals that are important to your well-being?
- If you invest in real estate, consider what brings you joy in investing and try to focus on them. Also note that there are stressors associated with investing, and it is worth weighing the impact of these on your well-being. Do you want to be involved in managing everything yourself or delegate it to others? Do you want to be aware of market developments on a daily basis, or is it enough to monitor the situation less frequently?

SAVING UP

Christian accompanied me on the train from Hamburg to Rotterdam on a rainy and chilly evening in late October. The train was five minutes away and I was ready to jump into the first carriage. However, Christian continued toward the rear of the train. "I always try to postpone the feeling of happiness," he said. "Once you're there, you can go straight into the station building." As a student in my twenties, I accepted his point of view with a shrug, myself being more of a person who lives in the now. In hindsight, I realized that I had stumbled upon a theme that distinguishes people regardless of culture or language: the ability to exercise self-control to have better consequences later.

The most famous research setting for this is probably Walter Mischel's marshmallow experiments at a Stanford University preschool in the 1960s.[8] Children were offered a marshmallow but were also told that if they left it waiting, they would receive two marshmallows at the end of the experiment. Interestingly, when these children were followed up years later, it was found that the ability to wait until the end of the test for two marshmallows was later associated with better performance in both education and working life.

The experiment has been repeated over the decades in many different countries and settings, and the results are still very similar. The marshmallow test is probably one of the most famous experiments in the history of psychology. That said, later studies showed that the context is the key. For some children, they should never leave the marshmallow uneaten, as it can be snatched away anytime. You cannot beat life experience in a lab environment.

Still, it seems that both self-awareness and self-control play a role in saving behavior. Even if we ignore the research, most of us would say that we know both people who put money aside and people who don't. Most people think they are saving too little, whether it is for retirement or other goals, whereas the risk of saving too much is relatively low. It is usually not a question of whether saving is financially feasible, because even a very small amount can get you started. Saving just seems to be a personal trait that some people have more of.

But is this really the case? Or is frugality a combination of external motivation and necessity? One of the ways to answer this question is to compare the culture of saving globally. In March 2025, the US household savings rate was 3.9 percent, in the European Union it was 14.6 percent, and in South Korea 35.7 percent. In some countries savings are a form of social security, and in others people invest more in real estate or other commodities. The US economy is heavily dependent on consumer spending, which accounts for approximately 70 percent of GDP. This creates a system where consumption is structurally and culturally encouraged. Easy access to credit cards, personal loans, and mortgage refinancing makes it simpler to borrow than save, creating a "spend now, pay later" mentality. The privatized healthcare system creates financial uncertainty that paradoxically discourages saving by making it feel insufficient against potentially catastrophic costs.

Saving is one way to strengthen financial security, but does it have a direct impact on well-being? While neither income nor wealth per se makes us happy, somewhat surprisingly, many researchers have found that saving improves people's perceived financial well-being.[9] In other words, a saver's own assessment of their personal financial situation is better than someone who does not put money aside. As already noted, perceived financial well-being has a major impact on mental and physical well-being. Saving increases our sense of security and self-reliance, and influences how positively we think about the future. It's not necessarily about money but about feeling able to make smart, voluntary decisions about our future finances.

Let's come back to the marshmallows. When the experiment has been replicated in different settings, it has been found that the outcome can be influenced. The first factor is visibility: if a marshmallow is placed in plain sight and within reach, it is much more attractive than if it is placed in a cupboard. The second factor is design. If the child taking part in the experiment has a plan about what he or she is going to do, it will be easier to resist the temptation. The third factor is functionality. If the child has the opportunity to do something while waiting for the experiment to end, it is easier to resist the temptation. Many children get active, for example, by singing, jumping, or talking to themselves. Walter Mischel believes that these strategies can also be applied to saving money. He suggests a few strategies that can help improve financial security in the future:

Focus on the feelings of the future. Instead of thinking about all the things you could get by spending your salary this month, create a clear picture of what you would like to be able to afford in the future. Visualize, plan, make your goal as attractive as possible. In other words, push away the temptation and move it further back in time. If you want to spend your retirement in a sunny villa in an Italian wine region, learn to say it in Italian and give yourself a moment to daydream about the perfect handmade pasta dish. If you want to extend the family cottage for future generations and finally build that greenhouse, start by drawing a floor plan and share the plan with those around you.

The journey may be more important than the goal itself, but the stronger the feelings of joy and excitement your goal evokes in you, the more it will motivate you to make decisions toward it in the moment. What you feel in the present moment best predicts what you may feel in the future. If you dream of a trip to a paradise island, imagine how you would feel if you were leaving next week.

If you are planning to buy a new home in another place, imagine how you would feel if you were moving right now. This will also help you weigh your own goals and how they affect your happiness.

Make a "what if" plan. Most of us know our own way of reacting to temptations. What if you've decided to save a certain amount a month toward your goal, but you discover that a nearby department store is having a 70 percent discount just for this weekend? It's very tempting to go and see what you can get at a huge discount, but the amount is out of your savings. You could prepare in advance by, say, making a list of the things you'll need to buy in the next six months. If these things aren't on sale at the department store, you've already made the assessment that they're not necessary. This is self-control automation: you don't need to make decisions; you can rely on your pre-rehearsed what-if plan. The more consistently you implement the plan, the more routine it becomes.

Identify what makes you slip up. Most of us are good at acting in a planned way in some things, but in other things or environments we are much more impulsive. For example, it's very easy for me not to do any impulse shopping because I don't have much time to spend in shopping malls and online stores. On the other hand, it's very easy for me to empty a whole packet of cookies in the evening when I'm relaxing after the kids have gone to bed and watching my favorite TV show. The only cure for this impulsiveness has been the fact that cookies are a forbidden purchase in our family. My husband even sometimes buys them for others and hides them from me at night (because the problem is real, believe it or not). We all have situations or influences that break our self-control more easily than usual. Once you recognize yours, you can prepare for them and remove them from your environment where possible.

Another approach is to try to understand why these situations or things are particularly powerful. Often, they trigger an emotional response; for me, cookies are strongly associated with childhood bedtime stories, a sense of security, and the experience of being cared for. As an adult, they make me feel good, which is probably linked to the memories evoked by the sensory experience. Understanding can be comforting, but it doesn't necessarily affect behavior—and it's not always necessary. The most effective way to avoid impulsivity is to remove the lure from the vicinity.

Look to the future with an open mind. Imagining the implications of the future and making choices based on them is a very popular and quite logical way to exercise self-control. Unfortunately, it is also often surprisingly ineffective. This strategy works best when it involves the near future, when expectations are clearly defined and when we can anticipate changes in the environment. This is because of a characteristic already noted: people have a very limited ability to imagine a realistic future. When it comes to the economy, we are more inclined to think more positively about the future than about the present. The more distant the future, the more vague our perception of it.

This optimism, both in the present and when we imagine the future, is good for our health, as many studies show that it maintains both mental and physical well-being. However, optimism is not necessarily based on reality. One of the most surprising findings in psychology has been that people with depression have a very accurate view of themselves and their environment. In other words, people need rose-tinted glasses—a healthy dose of unrealistic optimism. It could be considered a human trait that is not worth getting rid of.

At the same time, however, we end up finding it very difficult to imagine, for example, a future in which our current lifestyle makes us ill. Smokers do not ponder the state of their lungs in a couple of decades' time, those on the crest of a boom do not worry about economic decline and dwindling pension savings, those enjoying warm summer weather do not measure global warming. If we could objectively assess all the possible threats to life, it would be very difficult to live and feel well. Such a state of affairs is recognized by many people who live with constant anxiety. That is why carefreeness and spontaneity play such an important role in human life. Yet there are some things that should not only be left for a bright future but should also be saved for the future. The methods outlined in this chapter can also have positive effects in themselves.

Once you have made the decision to save, there are countless savings and budgeting strategies to choose from. It's worth exploring them and choosing the concrete way to manage your finances that works best for you. If you want to make saving easier, here are a few more practical suggestions.

Gratitude Diary

Cultivating gratitude is a strategy for strengthening patience, which has a research background.[10] Patience in managing one's finances is linked to one's emotional states and long-term well-being. Being mindful of where we spend our money allows us to increase feelings of gratitude and community in our own lives. Then, being mindful of your finances also helps you resist impulsive spending.

But how does gratitude affect the choices we make when spending money? Researchers tackled this question by designing an experimental setup for adults similar to a marshmallow experiment. The study offered participants either $54 immediately or $80 a month later. They were also asked to think of an event in their past that made them feel either grateful, happy, or neutral. Participants who focused on gratitude were more willing to wait a month to receive an $80 reward, while those who focused on happiness or neutral feelings were more likely to choose a small, immediate reward. Gratitude thus appears to increase patience when dealing with money, a conclusion that has been confirmed by subsequent studies.[11] Gratitude reinforces the feeling that we have enough of what we want. Keeping a gratitude diary is a way to increase feelings of happiness and satisfaction in life, so it is a strategy worth trying.

Save More Tomorrow

Richard Thaler and Shlomo Benartzi's "Save More Tomorrow" program is based on well-known traits of human nature. A large proportion of people plan to save in the future but never act on their intentions. It is the same thing as thinking we will start eating healthily and exercising in the future, ideally tomorrow. It is easy to limit yourself if the constraints don't kick in until later. Researchers have also noticed another tendency: people would rather give up a win than accept a loss—in effect, they don't want to lose part of the reward to which they are already accustomed.

The Save More Tomorrow program is all about these psychological laws. Participants pledge to increase their savings amount with each pay raise. The genius of the program lies in the fact that participants don't have to do anything. Very few participants stop the program once it has been started. They prove that perhaps the most effective way to approach saving is to set up automatic withdrawals from the account to a savings account and then forget about it.

Make Saving Public
Technology can also be harnessed to help you save. Dean Kartan and Jan Ayres of Yale University have developed a web-based goal-setting app called stickK, where people commit to a goal either by investing a certain amount of money or otherwise making the goal public. If the goal is not met, the money goes to charity. This kind of nudging is often more effective than relying on willpower alone.

OTHER FINANCIAL SKILLS

Saving is just one financial skill among others. Other financial behaviors include paying bills, investing, managing a budget, limiting spending, and managing debt. Financial management can be defined as all these activities that influence what we can afford and what we cannot afford. Our own behavior can be either positive and balancing or damaging and risky. Financial management requires rational economic behavior but also capability. Financial capability means being able to manage your finances in a way that increases your financial security. It is also self-nurturing: when I feel financially savvy, I am more comfortable with my own actions and have the courage to take responsibility for difficult decisions.

When programs and policies are made to improve economic well-being, they usually try to influence some form of economic behavior. However, there is no such thing as behavior that works everywhere and all the time, because the environment influences the consequences of actions. Researchers have also debated the role of economic literacy or basic economic skills and how they are transmitted through schooling and education. Of course, basic skills are needed, but another question is whether these basic skills and knowledge have an impact on economic behavior. In other words, even if you know how to manage your finances well, it does not lead to any more action than knowing what healthy food is. Accurate information enables you to do well, but it is often behavior that influences people's lives. Behaving in a financially sound way is often not easy, as it requires giving up things, self-discipline, careful budgeting, and realistic goals.[12]

PRACTICAL NUDGES

A few years ago, the Wellcome Foundation built an exhibition on psychology and magic. The psychological study of sensory information processing and our ability to perceive magic are surprisingly aligned. As a part of the exhibition, a screen showed a short video of a magician juggling in front of an audience and magically one of the balls disappears. When this video clip was shown to the test audience, about half of the audience thought they saw the ball fly upward and out of the frame, when in fact the ball was hidden in the magician's sleeve.

Magic is a dialogue between performer and audience, and fortunately we are not too familiar with the techniques of magic to maintain the illusion of wonder. Our brains have a strong need to find explanations for phenomena we do not understand. Our brains tell us that we saw things happen as we believe they could have happened. Imagination provides links between real things to help us better understand the world we live in. The way our thinking works affects not only the way we see the ball fly upward, but also everything around us.

Money is also a subject of our cognitive processes. Money is not just matter—paper and metal and plastic—nor just numbers or bank statements. It influences us, and, as you will have noticed, we all tell our own stories about it.

Behavioral economics is based on the idea that people's choices are influenced by social and psychological factors in addition to rational utility analyses. Psychologist Herbert Simon, a Nobel laureate and pioneer in the field, saw economic decision-making as rational but constrained. Because of our limited information-processing abilities, we must act partly on good guesses. Sometimes we may also choose a less rational approach, because it is not possible to concentrate on everything and energy must be directed toward decisions that are important to us.

Focusing attention is very relevant to our thinking. We tend to focus our attention on the things that are relevant now and ignore others. If you are planning to buy a new bicycle, you suddenly find that your surroundings are full of cyclists to whom you have not paid any attention before. If you read in this morning's paper that public transport congestion affects people's well-being, you will now find your irritation particularly acute when you are standing in a full bus for most of the journey to work.

Focusing your attention can also be a choice: you can concentrate on the feedback from people you value and are close to you, while you ignore the input from a stranger who grumpily criticizes your slowness on the subway escalator. Focusing attention on securing our own financial livelihood is a positive choice because it helps us set goals and move toward them. If you focus on, say, your monthly budget, you'll have more information available to you next month when you're deciding whether to buy lunch at your favorite diner or pack a lunch in the morning.

Attentional orientation affects the kind of sensory information we process during the day. Some of this information is perceived, but it doesn't leave much of an impression because it is not relevant to us. That means you may not be able to tell us what you had for lunch on Thursday last week. Some of the information is important to us; it evokes emotions and thoughts, which in turn create new paths of thought and brain connectivity. Many of our memories are vivid, their colors are deep and strong, and they are easily retrievable from our brain networks—in short, the memory trace is permanent. Other memories can be fuzzy, easily mixed up, or even transformed over time to match hearsay or another person's memories.

Strong imprints are often accompanied by a feeling that may be reactivated when the situation or event is recalled. Strong memories can also trigger strong emotional reactions and speed up decision-making on issues that are important to us. A positive memory of, for example, the freedom and joy of buying your first car with your summer job money can help motivate the opening of a savings account. On the other hand, a disparaging and derisive comment from a family member about how money is always slipping through your fingers can still grate years later and cause you to avoid all money-related decision-making.

For most people, financial well-being is an important issue that also requires a lot of work. Our upbringing and our personalities influence whether we value saving, investing, entrepreneurship, or using our money to buy lottery tickets. These are all personal choices, and we are likely to bear a great deal of responsibility for them. We may regret our lack of willpower or discipline when we indulge in expensive impulse buying. We may lament the fact that we were not better educated in our youth about the virtues of investing. We feel proud of a smart financial decision—perhaps we were on the cutting edge of a trend and stocked up on Spiderman costumes just when millions of kids wanted one. It is wise to feel a sense of responsibility and control over our finances, but not everything is up to us.

We all have individual ways of processing information that influence the choices we make in our everyday lives. Some of our thinking and behavior, on the other hand, follow psychological laws. These common traits have been the subject of much research in cognitive science, and understanding them helps us to be a little more aware of our common humanity.[13]

Some people feel that managing their finances is compulsory and boring. Others find it inspiring and motivating, which usually leads to better results. If you fall into the latter category, congratulations! You can skip the rest of the paragraph with a clear conscience. But if you are an average person who grinds their teeth over a tax return and sighs as they scroll through their bank statements, I am writing this for you.

When we focus on tasks that are uninteresting, monotonous, and uninspiring, our stamina, our ability to process information, and our creativity are limited. If we use this limited resource intensively during the working day, for example, and our motivation level is low, there is little willpower left at the end of the day. Comfort eating, impulse shopping, and channel surfing are common ways to unwind after a demanding and concentration-sapping day. There's no point in beating yourself up for brain fatigue, because you might as well be grumbling about shaking calf muscles after a run. By recognizing the need to relax and rest, you can prevent harmful relaxation habits that cause you problems afterward.

We are also guided, almost imperceptibly, by cues from our environment. The term *nudging*, coined by economics Nobel laureate Richard Thaler and law professor Cass Sunstein, refers to precisely these environmental triggers and characteristics. If you want to benefit from the leverage of nudging in your daily life, you should learn to recognize its laws.

In general, it seems that people are lazy to make changes, decisions, and choices that require information; perhaps their energy reserved for cognitive processing is out of the quota for the day. Most people avoid making extra decisions, whether it's choosing a phone ringtone or saving money. This is also true in situations where the default choice—the way things are—is not in your favor. We are more likely to make decisions that don't require explanation or reflection. Our electricity supplier or internet service provider may stay the same for years, while we wonder about rising costs. Finding out—that is, putting service providers out to tender—would require an informed decision, time, and reflection.

Most people also make choices that only have a short-term effect in the desired direction. For example, it can be difficult for us to realize how much more expensive life is when it is based on credit instead of savings. Paying the minimum amount on a credit card may seem like a good idea when money is tight, even if the consequences are undoubtedly bad for the financial balance of the following month.

Often it may be better that the big financial issues in life—such as social security, access to healthcare, or saving for retirement—are not just a matter of personal choice. In Nordic countries, many of these decisions are part of the social contract, where responsibility for looking after citizens is delegated to the government and members of parliament. In many other countries, personal freedom is highly respected. Freedom also often means more to do, and it is up to each individual to decide whether this is a good thing. In Finland, my native country, we live in a realm of limited responsibility, which at best safeguards the interests of citizens but at worst makes us lazy to deal with things that happen automatically.

However, the effect of the windfall can also be used in everyday life to help manage finances. The idea is to influence the environment in a way that encourages good choices and reduces the likelihood of bad choices. If you are mindful of human cognitive tendencies, you can give in to the power of nudge and forget all about it.

- Set up a permanent and automatic transfer to your savings account immediately after your payday. Make it as difficult as possible to access your savings account.
- Delete direct debits and regular subscriptions unless you want to forget they exist.

- Spend an hour a week paying bills and managing your account. Make this time as comfortable as possible for yourself and get yourself in control of your spending.
- Identify your goals, focus on them, and forget about the rest. Not everything has to be mastered, not everything has to be fun. Delegate the tasks you always get stuck on.
- Be realistic and set yourself an impulse shopping budget or a separate account. You can use it however you like. Once you give yourself permission to do something, the allure of it loses its luster.

Your own knowledge and skills are not always enough, which means that sometimes you need to bring in some extra resources to help you make decisions. These include situations where decision-making is difficult, one-off, or infrequent; when the situation is complex and difficult to assess; and when it does not provide direct feedback. For example, it is difficult to assess how much should be saved for retirement, considering the age structure of the population, the economic realities, and one's own state of health. In the housing market, we may seek additional information from trends, interest rates, and home condition surveys, but we are also forced to accept existing risks.

Despite life's challenges, we should remain hopeful because we possess the ability to accomplish remarkable things, find creative solutions to problems, and show compassion toward others. By recognizing the difference between our essential needs and wants, we can lead a life guided by our values. Although we may not have the financial means to afford our dream home, we might still be able to secure a comfortable living space and pursue a meaningful hobby. Even setting aside a small amount for retirement can make a significant difference and give us confidence in our future.

The juggler's lost ball is a good example of how many different things influence our interpretation of reality and therefore our decision-making. We assume that people think freely, but, in fact, it is rare for humans to do so. Our thinking is influenced by shortcuts, models, generalizations, distortions, optimism and pessimism, misinformation, or misinterpretation. If you look at our brain activity in terms of all these peculiarities, it is a wonder that we ever arrive at the right or useful conclusions. Our brains, after all, have evolved to sift through the vast amount of sensory information to the tidbits that matter to us at that very moment. The most cited example of this is the cocktail-party phenomenon, where, in the middle of a chorus of speech, we can distinguish with confusing accuracy if someone is saying our name. Our attention is immediately drawn to this potentially important piece of information.

Because we live at the mercy of our attention, one of the easiest and most recommended ways to manage our finances is to build patterns and financially sustainable habits. Structures can be relied upon, and living by them does not require constant evaluation or stretching of willpower, but once established, a routine that works for you will help you manage your finances almost automatically. Following are some common, psychologically smart approaches for people to try when considering how to reconcile finances and life.

Follow Up
It's easier to get things done when you regularly monitor their impact. Measuring is caring. As you implement your new approach, ask yourself a few questions and answer them on a scale of 1 to 10 (1 = I am very dissatisfied, 10 = could not be better). Carry out this same survey with yourself every three months and monitor progress.

Your own questions may mirror your own goals, but they could be, for example:

- How well am I aware of my financial situation at the moment?
- How satisfied am I with my financial choices in the last two weeks?
- Am I any closer to my own value-based economic goals?

Take Care of Yourself
All purposeful action benefits from taking care of our own well-being—respecting the basic needs that come first. Fatigue, boredom, self-reproach, and anxiety are looking for the easiest way to relieve discomfort. We end up making impulsive choices because we just don't have the energy to do anything else. If you're stuck—financially or otherwise—the first thing to do is to make sure of the following:

- You still remember when you last slept well.
- You eat and drink in moderation and often enough.
- You move around a bit.

If you're in a particularly stressful life situation, it's not the best time to make big life changes. Such stressful situations can include occupational burnout, having a child, divorce, bankruptcy, or the loss of a loved one. Take time to recover and recuperate when you need it, and make changes when you have the strength to do so. You will also need the strength to sustain the change. When you are tired, your resilience and perseverance suffer, and if you don't have the energy to go on, disappointment can undermine your confidence and faith in the future.

Set a Date in Your Calendar
One of the most challenging things in life for me has been to understand that important things take time, and I need to make time for them. As a time-optimist, I often do many things at the same time and underestimate how much time even just thinking can take. Set aside a regular time in your calendar to focus on your finances. Protect this time you've reserved, don't give it up too easily. Use the time you set aside even if you think nothing special is going on right now. New ideas and applications are sparked by these moments when you let your brain tinker with the subject. Once a week is necessary to make it easier to catch up with what you were doing and keep the memory fresh.

Accountability to Others
When the goal is known only to you, there is no need to explain to anyone why you gave it up. Once you've talked openly about your goals to others, they become public, and you have to answer questions from others about what your goal is. Many people want to show that they can commit to the decisions they have made, and at the very least, commitment is something that needs to be considered regularly if someone else is aware of the goals. External monitoring is provided by coaches, nutritionists, physiotherapists, and financial advisers. It is also easier to go for a run when you have arranged it with a neighbor. We don't want to disappoint other people's expectations, and that also helps us to manage our finances.

Start Now Rather Than Tomorrow
Tomorrow is by far the most popular time to start anything new. Today I can imagine waking up at 6:00 a.m. (without an alarm clock), working out, making green smoothies, writing a blog, and planning a weekend hike. If I think about these things first thing in the morning when I wake up (to the sound of the alarm clock at 7:30 a.m.), I'm already exhausted and decide to gently ease into it with making a cup of coffee instead.

This feature of the human mind does not mean that you cannot achieve a wide range of things and commit to making choices that support well-being. But it does mean that if you don't feel you can do them now, it will be difficult for you to do them tomorrow. So why not start now, and realistically assess whether it's possible to do everything you want to achieve. The Save More Tomorrow program mentioned earlier in the chapter is built around this principle. It's easy for us to commit to saving tomorrow, but then it's worth automating the actual saving activities.

+ + +

When combined, mindfulness and nudges create a powerful toolkit for effective financial management. One is not better than the other. Being mindful helps people become more self-aware and deliberate in their financial decision-making, while nudges provide the structure and guidance needed to encourage positive financial behaviors and overcome common pitfalls. By incorporating both approaches, we can develop healthier relationships with money and make more informed, purposeful financial choices.

LIFELONG PLANNING

I take the elevator to the sunny yellow floor, where nachos and glasses of wine greet a motley crew of women aged around twenty-five to forty. The dress code is "Christmas outfit or sweater." The atmosphere is expectant, and the friendly staff quickly relieve the anxiety of those arriving alone. A cheerful buzz fills the space. It could be any networking event, but today the topic is retirement savings. There is no official-looking representative of an insurance company to be seen, as this casual event is from women to women.

To start the event, we are tasked with setting our financial goals for the coming year. I say something bland and noncommittal about saving to my neighbor Veronica, who in turn tells me that she is raising a second round of investments for her company, which aims to make dancing part of everyday life, training teachers for different communities and giving us the chance to express ourselves, not unlike Beyoncé. I nod enthusiastically because Veronica's plan fits in well with the theme of the evening: you can do something new, even downright topical and interesting, with retirement savings.

It's also in line with all I have witnessed happening in this group lately. Men and women of all ages are freelancers, entrepreneurs in their own right, bold branders—and increasingly alone with the big questions of their own finances. How do I secure my life when I am responsible for my income, taxes, financial downturns, and ultimately my pension? Numerous communities online and in offices have sprung up to counteract this loneliness, and the corporate HR department has been replaced by a tribe or entrepreneurial hub.

This event is organized by PensionBee, an innovative company that makes retirement saving attractive. Pension saving is a special case of saving because it is many things at once: a way to manage your finances, take advantage of tax benefits, invest at a low cost, secure your future, and ensure a stable return. The most important thing is to know what you want to achieve by saving for retirement. There are many ways to invest your savings, including ethically, while taking care of the environment.

The women listen intently, sometimes nodding, and the atmosphere is warm. "I would like to work a four-day week." "I would like to coach people on money." "I would like to raise seed money for my business." PensionBee cofounder Romi Savova jumped from a political science student to a risk analyst at Goldman Sachs and went on to earn an MBA from the Harvard Business School. Her start as an entrepreneur was daunting, but the company has grown rapidly and now has over two hundred employees.

Romi based her business idea on her own confusion in the retirement savings jungle. She found she was not alone in feeling uncertain about the choices she was making. When people hear the words *pension, retirement savings*, and *taxation*, many immediately give up. Many also have a very vague idea of their own pension savings and what they are worth. Most of Romi's listeners are in their thirties, but a large number of them have never heard two young, dynamic women talking about finances and pension saving directly to women. In the age of automated contact, Romi has invested in customer service and face-to-face encounters.

One of the cornerstones of economic prosperity is financial freedom. Freedom to make reasonably independent, free, and low-stress decisions about our finances and our lives more broadly. We want to make such decisions even after we are no longer in the workforce. Although the retirement age is rising in many countries, life expectancy has also increased, so we are spending longer in retirement after working life. Many older people are also healthier and lead active lives.

An interesting study asked a group of people how they perceived themselves in the future—whether their vision of themselves in the future was very similar to or different from how they see themselves in the present. The more similar and close the image of themselves in the future was to the present, the more motivated people were to save for retirement. If they thought they would be a completely different person in the future, they were also less likely to get excited about saving.[14]

Planning for the future therefore requires not only the optimism discussed earlier but also a kind of vision of continuity and possibility. It also requires confidence that it is possible to live a life of value and meaning. If you would like to explore further, have a look at the MIT Future You project,[15] where you can chat with an AI-generated version of yourself in your sixties, to cultivate self-reflection and long-term thinking.

Although in many countries pension saving is regulated by the state, either through automatic pension accumulation or through the workplace pension fund, it is still a headache for pension savers. It is difficult to know how and when to save, what is a sensible investment, whether one's own savings plan is fit for its purpose, and what is a reasonable cost for private pension insurance. And how will the changing age distribution of the population affect pensions? Is it better to make independent decisions or to rely on the pension system in your country? There are more questions than answers, but we should still plan for the years ahead.

Lynda Gratton and Andrew Scott, in their book *The 100-Year Life*, raise timely questions about how we see the different eras of our lives.[16] Life expectancy has increased by two to three years over the last decade and is likely to continue to do so in the future. More and more people will live to be one hundred years old. It is therefore very likely that working lives will lengthen and that correspondingly more pension savings will be needed to last for the rest of our lives. However, the idea that we should be able to hold on to our careers as long as possible, even at the expense of our own well-being, demands alternatives.

I would suggest that it is worth challenging the idea of working life as a straightforward continuum. Instead, we could consider what is meaningful and motivating at different ages. Aging means accumulation of experience, accumulated life wisdom, and possibly also the motivation to work in socially relevant roles. It is also a time to benefit from those aspects of work that generate social well-being. As we get older, we may be good at exploring, delegating, leading, encouraging, coaching, and meeting people, or at least we may have had time to get to know ourselves and know our own strengths. The size of the salary may no longer be the first motivator, and volunteering can also feel attractive. Regular upskilling is increasingly important for people of all ages, and today moving from one sector to another can be more flexible than in the past, providing unexpected insights and benefiting both employer and employee. Rather than spending the latter stages of a career cooling down, it is possible to move into roles that have something to offer at the right age.

The same economic laws apply to retirement as to the rest of our lives: financial freedom gives freedom to make other decisions. The more you have planned well into the future and saved for retirement, the better your chances of doing things that feel meaningful—whether in your free time or at work. The main insight I took away from the retirement event for young women was that saving for retirement is a recommended, versatile way to manage your finances and something you can be interested in, regardless of your age or financial status. The goals of retirement saving may be far away, but the savings decisions and their implications are here and now.

My personal hero is the eighty-five-year-old Nobel Prize–winning author Margaret Atwood. She has written poignantly about growing old: "I believe that . . . everyone else my age is an adult, while I myself am just in a disguise."[17] I know exactly what she means. Getting older doesn't actually make us better or wiser as human beings, although it is undeniably felt in the body. Age feels a role of its own that we eventually will have taken on, but no one knows how little we may feel according to our age. As an adult I have learned to regulate my own behavior and emotional expressions, but I often wish I could do more things out of free will, with spontaneous joy, just because I can. When young we often think that adults can do whatever they want, but most of the time adulthood doesn't feel like freedom at all. Maybe it's that lightness and carefreeness requires enough age and wisdom.

When we still lived in a predominantly agricultural society, older people were important labor resources. Who else would have looked after the children and the house while the rest of the family worked at the farm? The experience and wisdom of older people was valued because it was largely what the young people themselves also needed to secure their work and livelihood. Today, in industrialized societies, the role of the elderly has changed. The principles of the market economy have increased mobility and reduced the dependence of young people on the resources of their parents. Inheritances are no longer the most likely basis of wealth or the family a source of financial stability.

This has also contributed to the fact that age no longer automatically brings respect in the community, and younger generations may leave their parents behind them in pursuit of success elsewhere. Of course, retired people are also moving around more than before and may be living a new era of freedom, without the responsibilities and worries of the rest of the family. Many are also moving into retirement communities or houses where they can build new relationships and get support and help from their environment.

Age therefore no longer offers a predefined role, any more than of the wise village elder or the elderly person living a new youth. Although physical limitations come in many forms, we are generation by generation becoming healthier and more aware of what a healthy life is. Research shows that confidence in our own abilities also plays a role—if you believe you can do something, you probably can. Little stress and strain can even be beneficial. Getting older can change the way we do things, have adventures, and try something new. Some things have to be done differently, but nothing is impossible to start with. Personal freedom can be at its strongest for older people who are not content to stop living their lives and take new steps in a direction that does not have to be clear. Many can leave their footprint on the world in later years.

Here is a quote from Simone de Beauvoir that I particularly like: "There is only one solution if old age is not to be an absurd parody of our former life, and that is to go on pursuing ends that give our existence a meaning—devotion to individuals, to groups or to causes, social, political, intellectual or creative work.... One's life has value so long as one attributes value to the life of others, by means of love, friendship, indignation, compassion."[18] The same could be said for every stage of life. It is necessary to be interested in and care about things outside ourselves. To ask questions, to make meaningful choices, and to dare to take risks from time to time. A new phase of life is always an opportunity to discover something new about yourself. The expectations of aging are in many ways imaginary.

INVESTING FOR IMPACT

Investing is not my area of expertise. Most people are like me—they think about investing at certain points in their lives when the future seems particularly close (like when you have kids or plan for your pension). I have had good advice and bad advice; I have invested with enthusiasm and lost faith, ups and downs have followed. This section is not about where you should be investing and how (there are other excellent sources for that), although my free tip would be index funds and long-term investment plans. (Index funds follow the market and deliver steady, predictable returns. Actively managed funds try to beat the market, but their results are less predictable and depend on the manager's skill and market conditions.) This section is more about the kind of investing that relies heavily on values, investing for impact. Bear with me, in the following paragraphs I am going to use many terms that I don't use in everyday life and that are truly opaque for people outside financial professions, but I believe the journey is worth it.

Evita Chiang Zanuso is the COO of the Katapult Foundation, a group of companies investing in and scaling sustainable impact-focused tech start-ups. She captures my thoughts when she says: "At times you wonder, is it making a difference? But I would follow the thinking of Stoic philosophers: there are many things that we cannot control. What we can control are our own actions, how we show up in the world. All our actions matter, impact investing is just a part of them."

Besides talking to Evita, I had the opportunity to meet with coauthor of *Sustainable Investing* Tiina Landau and the founder of Grounded Investment Company, Thekla Teunis. I was hoping to understand better what we mean by sustainable investing or investing for impact, and why people should know what they are investing in. We can be reasonably sure that default banking does not automatically direct our money to sustainable causes, and the same could be said about our pension investments. In fact, people are rarely aware how their finances are working in the global arena.

Evita has been working in the impact investing sector for thirteen years. She pivoted her career from mainstream investing, as she wanted to have a more positive impact on society. Thekla's work is focused on regenerative agriculture in sub-Saharan Africa, but she too has worked for big companies like Shell and initially wanted to change the industry from within. Tiina worked for banks and investment companies before becoming a leading expert in sustainable investing. Since I am having difficulties in navigating with the terminology, they explain to me that in sustainable investing, environmental, social, and governance (ESG) factors are integrated into investment decisions. Sustainable investing is often focused on companies and their products, services, and practices (e.g., whistleblower protections), and these companies are committed to sustainable processes. Responsible investing means essentially the same thing, while ethical investing focuses on choices based on personal ethical values, such as excluding certain industries.

Impact investing, on the other hand, is focused on solutions and seeks both measurable social and environmental impact and financial returns. Impact investing may incorporate higher return and failure rates (depending on how they are managed), e.g., social lending, social enterprises, or investing in opportunities where government is involved, for example social bonds. However, the definition of impact can be subjective and context-dependent; how we determine the impact is also linked to the values we hold.

Is impact investing profitable? It seems that nobody can give an exact answer to this. There is no universal relationship between impact investing and financial returns—it varies greatly by case. Some impact investments can deliver high returns, while others may require accepting lower returns for greater impact. Impact funds also tend to be actively managed, and most actively managed funds tend to underperform.

Buying and selling shares on the secondary market does not in itself have a direct impact on companies. Real impact is achieved through active ownership, where investors influence the activities of companies. In some countries small investors can only get involved by investing in a fund that engages in active influence. According to Tiina, the field has developed significantly: previously, responsible investing was based on voluntary self-regulation, but now legislation defines sustainability criteria. This has increased standardization and helped prevent greenwashing.

The easiest way for private investors to start responsible investing is to choose an ESG investment fund or a fund that takes responsibility into account. When moving into direct equity investments, they have sustainability ratings such as MSCI or Morningstar's assessments of companies' sustainability. That said, ESG is under a lot of pressure and many have questioned if the existing metrics and frameworks are useful, and it is sometimes regarded as a less ambitious and compliance-focused approach. Many sustainable funds just use basic automated scoring systems that can be easily gamed—this has led to ridiculous situations where oil companies get better ESG ratings than clean energy companies. Most of these funds simply exclude certain industries (like tobacco or weapons) or rely on box-ticking exercises rather than doing real analysis.

More direct impact can be achieved by participating in the financing of early-stage companies, including share issues and crowdfunding, where the money allows companies and people to develop new, useful products and services. In some countries, like the United States, there are also mobile applications you can use to facilitate the process. Investment frauds can be a risk factor in these kinds of retail investor solutions, so careful consideration is needed. In its simplest form, impact can be achieved by direct investment in local businesses or friends' ventures. There are investment syndicates that pool smaller amounts ($500 to $1,000) to meet minimum thresholds and regulated impact investment funds with smaller minimum investments ($100 to $1,000).

Tiina also highlights the potential of community-based investment models and crowdfunding platforms for responsible investing, bonds for social enterprises and charities, and investment trusts that have floated on stock exchange investing only in high-impact market options. Interesting examples include Schroder BSC Social Impact Trust (United Kingdom) investment crowdfunding on Triodos (United Kingdom), and Calvert Impact–Community Investment Note and Cut Carbon Note (United States).

Investing is only one tool of many. Sustainable economic choices can be made, for example, by applying for green mortgages for energy-efficient homes, choosing sustainable places to live near public transport, and taking sustainability into account when investing in residential properties or land. Pensions are also being invested, and if we have any pension coming to us, it would be good to know how. Since pension funds control most of the investment money, they have the real power. When pension funds make demands, investment companies actually listen and respond.

Still, there are psychological barriers: it is difficult to get started, it can be overwhelming to think for ourselves when we have been relying on financial advisers, and often the main barrier to values-aligned investing is fear of losing security. There is also a difference between earned and inherited wealth; people tend to think that earned wealth—for example, in the technology start-ups—should be distributed, whereas inherited wealth has been accumulated by many generations and is seen more as a responsibility to maintain and grow. Impact investing is the opposite of being passive. It forces us to find out what our values are, which will take time and self-reflection. How do these values align with our community or even society?

Evita and Tiina seem reasonably optimistic about the benefits of technologies. Technology if used properly is a great way to democratize knowledge. Until now, investing in projects that do good for the world (like renewable energy or affordable housing) was mostly for big banks and wealthy people. But new technology, such as blockchain and impact tokens, is changing this. One example is Kiva, a leading microfinance organization in the United States, raising funds from individuals and distributing them to organizations operating in underserved communities.

Blockchain simplified means that you buy a small piece of the pie; you can sell when you want and you can see the permanent, public record of how your money is used. For example, blockchain could potentially have an impact on how disaster relief and humanitarian aid relying on individual donors works. Money could be directed to emergency relief, refugee assistance, and community rebuilding efforts. Donations become transparent transactions that can be followed from donor to recipient, with each step recorded permanently. More money could reach people in need because there's less fraud and waste, and donors can see exactly how their contribution has helped.

Thekla admits that she is more skeptical about the transformative power of blockchain solutions—she suggests that the real challenge is in ground-level data collection, not in how the data is stored or published. Impact measurement is complex; for example, how we measure the increase in farmer income involves many variables. Independent auditing should be available when claims of impact are made, and we should not focus too heavily on measurable short-term outcomes when long-term impact is really what we need. And to be honest, infrastructure investments like roads may have greater long-term impact but are harder to measure and perhaps less appealing for investors. Finding genuine impact investments requires significant research effort, but it can be a rewarding way to understand how our financial markets work.

If you are interested in the future of impact investing—a future where every investor, regardless of size, can contribute to and benefit from solutions to our world's most pressing challenges—consider at the same time that there may well be regulatory and quality-control challenges that you need to be aware of. You may want to start with these steps:

- Education first: Begin by understanding the fundamentals of impact investing.
- Start small: Test the waters with causes you care about and see how their impact is evaluated.
- Diversify impact: Just as with traditional investments, diversification across different types of impact assets can help manage risk.

SOCIAL MEDIA ECONOMY

The phenomena and effects of social media have been a favorite topic of researchers and journalists for a long time: how the changes that have taken place over the last two decades and the emergence of social media as a whole affect us, people who have never experienced anything like it before. Social media interests almost everyone, whether they are involved in it in some way or not—the threats of social media, the opportunities it offers, how it changes the way we connect with others.

During my brief time on social media, I have noticed that I am particularly sensitive to approval, attention, and lack of attention. I feel restless, I check and doubt my own words and their impact, I write platitudes, and I am completely devoid of any sensible opinions that could be summarized in the given number of characters. Social media does not reinforce my strengths and seems to highlight my weaknesses. But what I often fail to consider is that I am dealing with an economy and making trade-offs day to day.

People create posts on social media for different reasons. Getting likes and comments motivates many users to post more. For creators who can earn money (like YouTubers), financial rewards have an even stronger effect on how much content they make. Social media gives us an opportunity, a stage, and a voice to present ourselves in the light we want, whenever and to whomever we want. Connections with others are created through global platforms whose interests go far beyond simply offering us the opportunity to connect with friends and family. I myself have benefited from the opportunities these platforms offer for marketing and for presenting my own thoughts and messages, especially to selected target groups.

Social media has also fundamentally transformed how young people approach money and investing, creating new psychological challenges. Research shows that half of the Generation Z investors get their financial advice primarily from social media,[19] where algorithmic feeds constantly expose users to curated success stories while hiding failures, leading them to overestimate their chances of financial success. The platforms have gamified investing through features like trading competitions and real-time sharing, triggering the same psychological rewards as gaming and encouraging gambling-like trading behaviors. The constant exposure to wealth displays can also create an illusion of normality and fear of missing out. Many young people are taking on significant debt to fund lifestyle purchases that will photograph well, and heavy social media users are more likely to accumulate debt for appearances.[20]

I belong to the last generation that grew up without social media, which is why it has never felt a natural place for me to be in but rather an arena I learned as an adult, whose rules I still have to think about from time to time. Fortunately I am surrounded by the much-talked-about digital natives who are active on social media every day, producing, editing, evaluating, and counting followers before they even learn to read. One of them is fifteen-year-old Mila, who runs a successful social media channel focused on horses and riding. She updates her social media content daily and posts three videos a week, which take a long time to compose, edit, and organize. In total, Mila spends about seven hours a week in this work.

Two main things determine what appears in your feed: whom you're connected with and the platform's algorithm. Your friends and accounts you follow provide the initial pool of content. The algorithm then picks from this pool, often favoring posts similar to what you've engaged with before. Internet activist Eli Pariser's book that changed our thinking permanently, *The Filter Bubble*, was published in 2011.[21] Pariser argues in his book that personalized search results and algorithms that aim to show users content they are interested in also limit users' exposure to different opinions, diverse information, or conflicting information. People end up in their own information bubbles, which reinforce their existing views and prevent them from encountering opposing perspectives.

Technology allows us to achieve comfort and security without having to make conscious choices about it. Each bubble looks slightly different, but when I look at my own, it is disconcerting to see how harmonious it is. It is difficult to find anything I would strongly disagree with, as I have not actively chosen to follow people or organizations that would offer a different perspective. However, more and more people, especially young people, are seeking most of their information from social media groups and forums.

Although social media was created to generate discussion, a significant proportion of people follow it without contributing input. Two-way communication has become one-way information absorption for many. Even when we do not believe the information is accurate, it leaves a mark. Ads on social media are also highly targeted based on your personal data. Platforms collect information about what you do both on their site and across the internet. This helps advertisers show you products you might actually want, but raises privacy concerns for many users.

When Mila tells me about her hobby, she comes across as professional, articulate, and experienced. She describes herself as cheerful, enterprising, and determined. Mila wants to see things through, to develop in her field, and at the same time increase her self-awareness. She writes about her everyday life, answers questions, and sees the content she produces as a diary, authentic and honest. She also publishes stories about difficult moments and mistakes she has made. However, Mila is not immune to self-doubt; sometimes she wonders whether it is worth writing about difficult experiences or problems publicly when her own emotional work is still in progress. On the other hand, encouragement and support can help her move forward, and many people seem to appreciate raw honesty.

As a social media novice, I often wonder what it would be like to be braver and more open when the response is not always what you hope for. Would I be able to handle it, and what would I like to see and read about myself? Mila has seen unpleasant gossip about herself on various channels and forums, which she has often responded to with a private message stating her own opinion. Sometimes this has helped, and the writer has deleted their previous comments, but sometimes responding only fuels the smoldering flame of hatred. The more you use social media, the more negativity you encounter.

Mila's own social media strategy is to always comment positively. She strives to be who she really is and says she easily notices when someone on a channel is being inauthentic, copying others, or inconsistent, in which case she loses interest. It seems to suggest that a certain kind of consistency in identity, understandability, and narrative coherence is a guarantee of quality. In other words, social media is not a mirror for change and variation but rather a platform for reliable storytelling, where the style remains at least reasonably consistent. Mila herself follows familiar riders, coaches, and inspiring accounts. In Mila's view, very few people dare to express their opinions unless they are anonymous. A single wrong comment can trigger a storm of criticism, and the most hurtful comments are always anonymous.

Mila's experiences bring to mind the spiral of silence theory. German opinion poll pioneer Elisabeth Noelle-Neumann developed a communication theory in the 1970s according to which people are likely to remain silent about their opinions if they think that their views are contrary to the general opinion or socially accepted views, which can lead to their voices being absent from public debate.[22] Spirals of silence are contagious and often lead to one opinion rising above others. According to Noelle-Neumann, what we fear most is being isolated from others.

Back in the 1950s, Leon Festinger asked: "What happens to a person's personal opinion if they are forced to say or do something that goes against their opinion?" The answer is that something has to change, because we find it difficult to tolerate such internal conflict. Social groups are dominated by a "climate of public opinion" that influences which opinions are expressed and which remain unspoken. When people realize that their opinions are contrary to public opinion, they withdraw and conform, which further reinforces the prevailing view. They may not even notice that they are withdrawing; it can happen unconsciously and without any actual decision-making. The human mind is accustomed to making small adjustments in behavior that are aimed at social acceptance almost automatically.

Social media environments have given this theory a new relevance. Many researchers believe that anonymity can mitigate the effects of the spiral of silence. Others have argued that the spiral of silence is reinforced when we increasingly move within our own bubble, where prevailing and generally accepted ideas are echoed.

Renee Engeln, a psychology professor at Northwestern University, has studied how cultural ideals affect the well-being of women and girls and has also written a book on the subject.[23] According to Engeln, there is an obsession with beauty and appearance, which has a negative impact on the lives of women and girls: it limits their time, energy, and financial resources. Constant concern about appearance can lead to "beauty sickness," which causes constant worry and stress and distracts attention from other aspects of life. Researchers have found that the more time young women spend on social media, the more they compare themselves to others, feel insecure, and have negative feelings about themselves.

Beauty also comes at a price. Investing time, money, and mental resources in beauty often takes away from other areas of life, such as personal growth, education, and career. In other words, social pressure and the emphasis on appearance influence decision-making and behavior in the longer term as well.

"Beauty addiction" is not limited to girls, although there is significantly more information. The impact of social media on boys' appearance pressures is a growing area of research, and it appears that in addition to many shared pressures, there are also some gender-specific characteristics. Boys are often exposed to images in social media that emphasize muscular, athletic, and "ideal" male body types. Body image problems have been observed particularly among boys who spend a lot of time on social media platforms that focus on appearance and physical performance. Social media also often reinforces narrow gender roles, according to which a man should be strong, have leadership skills, and be physically capable.

Social media is habit-forming. Research shows that about one-third of social media use comes from habits and self-control problems rather than conscious choice. This is why many people use it more than they intend to. The effect on your well-being isn't straightforward. Some studies show taking breaks from platforms like Facebook can improve mental health and reduce anxiety,[24] while other research finds smaller or no effects.[25]

Despite the potential downsides, people highly value social media. When researchers asked how much money people would need to give up Facebook for a month, answers were around $48 on average.[26] Social media also affects society more broadly by influencing our political knowledge, how divided we become, and even how we participate in democracy.

The exploration of social media's psychological and social effects reveals a profound economic reality: we are constantly making invisible financial trades with our attention, time, and emotional well-being. Like investors in a volatile market, we exchange our most precious resources—hours of our day, mental energy, and authentic self-expression—for the uncertain returns of likes, followers, and social validation. The "beauty sickness" and comparison culture that platforms foster create what economists might call negative externalities, where the true costs (anxiety, self-doubt, financial pressure to maintain appearances) are hidden from the initial transaction of scrolling and posting.

Just as Mila spends seven hours weekly creating content, millions of users unknowingly budget significant portions of their lives to feed algorithms designed to capture and monetize their attention. This represents a fundamental misalignment between our stated values—authentic connection, meaningful relationships, personal growth—and where we actually invest our time and energy. Understanding social media through this economic lens reveals that our digital choices are ultimately financial choices. Recognizing the consequences of this trade-off is the first step toward making more intentional decisions about how we want to spend the currency of our attention.

PART IV
THE NEW STORY

CHAPTER 12

BUILDING A VISION

How we spend our days, is of course how we spend our lives.
—ANNIE DILLARD[1]

ASK QUESTIONS

Some questions that not many people remember to ask are: What kind of person will I become through the work (paid or unpaid) I do every day? What traits or qualities will it strengthen in me? What opportunities will it give me? What will I learn through my daily activities and responsibilities? Does my role—whether as an employee, caregiver, volunteer, student, entrepreneur, or community member—feel like something I can identify with while appreciating my own contribution to the world? How do I spend the money and resources available to me, whether earned through employment, received through support systems, generated through creative endeavors, or allocated through family responsibilities?

A job with high status does not necessarily feel better than a job with lower status. The salary may also be insufficient when compared to the amount of work involved. That is why it is important to look at working life from a perspective other than that of individual economic gain. If we asked people what benefits their work brings to their fellow human beings and society, we could stimulate thought and discussion about the meaning and future of work in a broader sense.

The pandemic and subsequent economic upheaval have sparked a fundamental reevaluation of what work means in our lives. Books like Tim Ferriss's *The 4-Hour Work Week* and other explorations of our misplaced priorities have found increasingly receptive audiences, prompting many to question whether endless striving and self-sacrifice truly serve our best interests. A growing number of workers are prioritizing work-life balance, mental well-being, and meaningful contribution over traditional markers of career success. The phenomenon of "quiet quitting"—doing only what's required rather than going above and beyond—may reflect a collective response to chronic overwork and burnout. Even those who previously embraced demanding work cultures are beginning to admit, often privately, that stepping back from excessive professional demands holds genuine appeal. This shift suggests a broader cultural awakening to the hidden costs of treating work as life's primary organizing principle.

"Quiet quitting" is part of a trend in which employees are looking for more meaningful or rewarding career paths. This way of thinking is based on a philosophy of sufficiency: there is no need to strive or perform beyond your own capabilities; it is possible to set limits and determine what is enough. Younger generations in particular, such as millennials and Generation Z, have brought different expectations and values to the workplace, including flexibility, meaning, and balance. However, flexibility is often a double-edged sword. Whereas previous generations formed close, long-lasting relationships with their employers for decades, today many consider it a point of honor to move on every couple of years and renew their role. Rapid change and the constant competition it brings can also be stressful. The life of a freelancer is demanding, and a permanent job can feel like winning the lottery.

Ultimately, it is not so much about quitting as it is about questioning what is meaningful and where we want to invest our energy. If we give ourselves time to think, changes are also more likely to happen. When we stop listening to others, we have more time to listen to ourselves, and then the quality of our voice matters. Our inner critic may say that it's too late or that we don't have the necessary skills to start a new career. If we manage to forget for a moment who we have been up to now, the world seems almost unbelievably open. At its best, a job interview is a reasonably good way to find a suitable job, especially if you are prepared to really ask questions and listen to what the job will be like. A job can also be suitable because it allows you to do other things besides work, and money gives you the freedom to do so.

STEP ONE: MAKE SPACE TO LISTEN AND OBSERVE

The biggest problem I always encounter when I want to think about something in peace is that I don't have the space or time to do so. Or at least that's what I tell myself. In reality, I often have the space and time, which I fill by making myself busy or, alternatively, immersing myself in something that entertains and, in my opinion, relaxes me (social media, TV series, books, magazines, stretching, messaging friends). Over the years, during conversations in psychotherapy, I have come to realize that for most people (myself included), it is incredibly difficult to do nothing and listen to what the experience has to say. You can think about this for yourself: how easy is it for you to be alone with yourself and do nothing useful for a moment? It may sound strange, but give it a try. Take some time today to watch the grass grow, the snow fall, or a candle flicker, and let your thoughts come and go. Half an hour is enough to begin with.

If the above challenge ends after five minutes with frustration, anxiety, or restlessness, don't worry. This is usually the case. The ability to just be is also a result of practice. When we are busy and active, it is also easier for us to ignore what our body and mind are telling us. I recently talked to a friend who works in occupational health services. She told me how people come to the clinic with various vague symptoms that have persisted for months, sometimes even years. Typical observations (but by no means the only ones) include a high pulse, skin symptoms, various pains and aches, sleep disturbances, memory lapses, difficulty making decisions, digestive problems, headaches, and persistent minor infections or colds. When the combination of symptoms cannot be explained by any physical illness, the question arises as to whether it might be a case of chronic stress or emotional overload.

This is a completely new idea for many people, and it is also difficult to accept. They have lived a productive and fulfilling life with many good things, often including conscientious care for their own health and well-being. One could say that they have successfully adapted to society and its expectations. However, the body adapts to a limit, as it senses firsthand all our experiences and their effects. Stopping to consider the matter requires listening to oneself and one's experiences, which does not happen automatically. It often has to be practiced again and again. If a change in life is necessary, it also requires us to take a moment to come to terms with our reality.

Musician and composer Pauline Oliveros organized the first "deep listening" retreat in 1991 and has since developed this practice for new generations of artists, in addition to art lovers and people who want to be more fully connected to their environment and experiences.[2] According to Oliveros, it is important to distinguish between hearing and listening. Listening is always a conscious choice to pay our attention to what we hear and to what it evokes in us. Many teachers of conscious presence and interaction also consider deep listening to be the basis for consciously interacting with another person, truly striving to understand what they want to tell us.

Deep listening is also a way of perceiving what is going on within ourselves and striving to understand, with the same commitment, what our body and mind are telling us. Exploring our feelings and experiences is important because it helps us to distinguish between habits and the self behind them. Especially when we have to work with strong emotions, whether they are our own or those of others, it is good to be able to stop and listen without rushing.

Ask yourself:

- What experiences and choices have brought me to this point in my life?
- What internal and external barriers are limiting my progress, and what strengths and resources are available to move me forward?
- Who believes in me and stands ready to encourage my next steps?

Life changes are most difficult when our resources are at their weakest and our thinking is at its narrowest. One of the most insidious effects of stress and mental strain is that we are unable to see alternatives to our actions. Our thinking becomes locked into apparent self-evident truths and assumptions about what is possible or probable. Sometimes we need to change our current habits and ways of doing things in order to move forward.

Life changes can be necessary for many reasons. When we allow ourselves to change, we open the door to new experiences in life. Change can mean trying a new career path, moving to a new city, taking up a new hobby, or meeting new people. Change can bring something surprisingly valuable and meaningful. Through new experiences, challenges, and learning, we gain knowledge, skills, and perspectives. Change often increases self-confidence and helps us discover new strengths and abilities within ourselves. Sometimes it is necessary to change something in order to feel happier and more satisfied. Change can help us remove toxic factors, such as bad relationships or unsatisfying work, and create space for new positive things and experiences. Change may be the only way to feel better.

When I create space for solitude—moments uncluttered by daily demands—I can better observe the narratives my mind constructs. This intentional pause often reveals insights that would otherwise remain buried beneath the surface of busy living. What emotions and thoughts emerge in this stillness? How do they arise and fade? Are there recurring patterns that consistently claim mental space? Learning to articulate these inner experiences takes both time and practice, but it allows for greater precision in understanding ourselves.

Travel offers another pathway to this kind of clarity. What I like most about being a stranger in a new country or city is the temporary suspension of familiar roles and identities. Everything becomes fluid—how I live, eat, move through streets, connect with others, and navigate expectations. There's a unique freedom in adjusting to unfamiliarity, where the usual constraints of identity loosen their grip. From this distance, I can see my habitual routines and behavioral patterns with fresh eyes, questioning their necessity and permanence. A different environment can dramatically shift how we experience and perceive ourselves.

When I talk about change in this chapter, I am mostly talking about how it looks from the outside. I often ask people what it looks like when they do things that correspond to their values and goals. If you can see yourself in motion, it is easier to understand what you actually want to change in your life. If there was a fly on your ceiling observing your daily life 24/7, what would it see? Studying and mapping behavior has been a big part of my working life. In the early years, I thought about what children do, why they do it, and how I could influence them. Children are excellent collaborators because they find it easier to understand what happens in everyday life. Then I moved on to working with adults whose heads are a whirlwind of emotions, thoughts, reasons, and explanations.

Adults often find it more difficult to understand their own actions, and they often need help with this.

Eventually, I moved from working with individuals to working with groups of people who behave in similar ways and change their behavior according to the same principles. Nothing is as interesting as noticing how people change the world by changing their own behavior, and sometimes we can even help others to change theirs.

Behavior transforms through the interplay of three key forces: our environment, our knowledge and skills, and our motivation. Sometimes change is thrust upon us, as during COVID-19. In such cases, mandatory new routines gradually reshape our mental landscape, altering how we think about ourselves and our world. Our attitudes, opinions, and beliefs often follow our actions rather than precede them—we may discover that acting differently leads us to think differently. This suggests a powerful strategy: sometimes it's worth simply beginning a new behavior and observing how our mindset shifts in response. Like a feedback loop, action can generate the very motivation and perspective we thought we needed before starting. Other times, sustainable change requires us to first build the necessary motivation, develop relevant skills, or cultivate environmental support. The key is recognizing which approach serves us best in any given situation—whether to act our way into new thinking or prepare our way into new action.

STEP TWO: ACCEPT YOURSELF AND OTHERS

Life stories and biographies are fascinating not only because they are often surprising and even unbelievable but also because they are curated, a collection of experiences selected from one person's life that fit together like pieces of a puzzle. Everything fits together and forms a whole that is greater than the sum of its parts. In reality, life is full of contradictions, rough edges that have not been smoothed out, and strokes of luck or misfortune that once again disrupt the carefully constructed fabric. Yet it is the incompatible pieces of life that can be the most interesting—individual, strange, inexplicable, and revealing. Accepting the contradiction and imperfection of one's own life story is one of the most difficult tasks in human life.

Sometimes our memory tries to erase these events, as they are not supported by other experiences and are difficult to understand. Memory acts as a repository for stories and strong emotional experiences. It is best at dealing with things that it can connect together, like a string of pearls. We gravitate toward narratives that reinforce our perception of life as a coherent story—complete with beginning, middle, and end, following familiar rhythms within recognizable boundaries. These mental frameworks become so entrenched that seeing beyond them requires us to embrace contradiction and possibility where we once saw only limitation.

Paradoxically, while we struggle to imagine new possibilities, we readily accept statistical probabilities, concluding that past patterns will inevitably repeat themselves in the future. This creates a curious blind spot: we underestimate our capacity for transformation while overestimating the permanence of current circumstances. Breaking free from this cognitive trap means learning to hold two truths simultaneously—that patterns matter and that change is always possible, that our stories shape us and that we can rewrite them.

Statistical probabilities are almost impossible to understand by mere deduction, because our brains are designed for a completely different task. They have a tendency to notice and exaggerate threats and their probability, because this has been essential for survival. A sufficient amount of fear prevents us from taking risks. One of the most important human abilities is to accept one's own fear and face it calmly, as Michelle Obama describes in her book *Becoming*, or less calmly, as almost all of us do in some situations. The armor of calmness is created gradually but often consists of small pieces of fear that a person has experienced over and over again. They have been polished and cared for; fear is present in everything we do, but it never permanently takes control.

What does facing fear and uncertainty require from a person? I believe that one of the most important things is what surrounds us. People who encourage us and at the same time create a sense of psychological security. Fear does not prevent us from being accepted as we are—imperfect, human, and constantly changing organisms. Our greatest fear is often being left out, as members of the herd cannot survive outside the herd. Unfortunately, one of the most clearly unifying characteristics of a herd is sufficient similarity, and accepting differences also requires recognizing that each of us is in some way different and an outsider. Accepting ourselves helps us accept differences in others as well.

The consequences of a worldview that rejects differences are harmful not only for ourselves but also for others. When we cling to roles, characteristics, and beliefs rooted in childhood, we easily create expectations for those around us. It is easy for parents to think that they know from experience how their children should live their lives. Of course, the opposite is also true: at some stage, many people start to think that they could suggest better ways of living to their parents. It is easy to sell your own lifestyle and values to your partner. At work, it may be easier to hire someone who is ethnically, culturally, and socially similar to the other members of the team.

When was the last time you actively tried to meet someone who was completely different from you in terms of their personality, characteristics, or background? If you can tap into this sense of interest and curiosity, you are lucky. On the other hand, it is also something you can practice. I often think that I am open and genuinely interested in new and different things, but in reality I am only receptive to a certain kind of difference, one that I can relate to or that I appreciate and understand. Even the slightest challenge to my otherwise open and curious mind leads to discomfort and a vague desire to avoid anything strange or threatening.

Resistance to diversity often stems from fear of the unfamiliar—a defensive stance against anything that challenges our established worldview. We tend to see ordinariness as the default lens through which we interpret the world, yet this assumed normalcy can be fragile, cracking apart in the small moments when difference reveals itself through unexpected words, gestures, or expressions. I recognize this dynamic in my own behavior when I withhold my perspective in conversations, convinced that my experiences are too foreign to be understood or valued. Other times, I swing to the opposite extreme—boldly placing my truth on the table like dropping a Walmart bag on an antique mahogany sideboard. Take it or leave it, here it is! And more often than not, it is left there untouched.

Despite our genuine desire to connect, we are only human, and we often need guidance to do so. None of us are always ready to accept everything that comes our way. That is why we have the ability to regulate and diminish, sometimes even ignore, the emotions we experience.

STEP THREE: BE AMBITIOUS

How many "new lives" have supposedly begun with the turn of the year or the start of a fresh semester? Until that magical date arrives, we give ourselves permission to coast—relaxing, avoiding difficult decisions, simply going with the flow. Yet the fundamental obstacle to lasting change often remains unchanged: our environment still doesn't encourage the exercise we claim to want, our motivation hasn't meaningfully improved, and we haven't developed new skills to sustain cycles of success and satisfaction. Nothing has actually shifted except the dark numbers on a calendar page.

Instead of repeatedly resolving to become better people, what if we took a different approach? What if we examined our environment and daily life with curiosity: How do they shape our being, routines, and roles? Do they perpetuate patterns we claim to want to escape? What specific encouragement and support do we actually need? Are there concrete skills we could begin developing, taking just one small step forward? Sometimes I notice that habits meant to be temporary have become default settings simply because they require no effort to maintain. When I genuinely want change, I've learned to ask: Does this desire come from within me, or is someone else wanting me to change? What does this transformation actually feel like when I imagine it?

When I began writing this book, I focused on people navigating major life transitions and what they might need to redirect their paths. I soon realized, however, that even dramatic external changes—new jobs, relationships, countries—often leave us acting exactly as we did before. We may find ourselves on the other side of the world, yet operating with the same internal patterns and responses. Despite every opportunity to transform our existence, we navigate new terrain with the confidence of an old hand, following familiar neural pathways. This happens partly because our brains naturally gravitate toward safety and familiarity. The brain prefers well-established neural networks—synaptic highways that avoid traffic jams of conflict and uncertainty. Learning to tolerate ambiguity and insecurity goes against this natural tendency, even though such tolerance often serves us better than our instinct for comfort.

One of our pitfalls in securing our existence is the pursuit of perfection. This strategy has been proven ineffective time and again, both in working life and in leisure time. Very often, however, people cling to it and do everything they can to be closer to flawless, consuming all attention and energy. I myself notice that there are areas of life where accepting my own imperfections is not a problem. Then there are areas of life where I try to be good at everything, all the time. Most of the time, this backfires when I tense up, get stressed, and find it difficult to admit my mistakes. And yet I never learn! At certain stages of life, humor prevents any kind of excessive nitpicking, because there are so many areas where we can fail. When we do a lot of different things and don't have time to be meticulous, our thresholds are lowered and we realize that this is actually how most people function.

Being ambitious can also mean surrounding ourselves with sources and people that have a positive influence on us. Sometimes they can challenge us to grow and change our thoughts about life. Sometimes they keep our hope and curiosity alive. To quote Charles Bukowski: "The free soul is rare but you know it when you see it—basically because you feel good, very good when you are near or with them."[3] It is worth holding on to them and giving yourself the opportunity to do better.

SETBACKS AND SURVIVING THE DARKNESS

Let me share a true story that still makes me wince. I suspect I'm not alone in harboring such tales in the hidden corners of memory. As a young adult, my grandparents presented me with a substantial banknote to celebrate an academic achievement. For a student living on a shoestring budget, this wasn't just generous—it was transformative. I felt a rush of happiness, relief, and deep gratitude. For reasons I can no longer fathom, I tucked that precious note inside a magazine and carried it in my lunch bag during a short domestic flight back to university. During the flight, I contentedly ate my meal, read through the magazine, and carefully bookmarked my place—unknowingly sealing the banknote inside those pages. When the plane landed, I gathered my belongings and walked off, leaving the magazine behind on my seat. I never saw my grandparents' gift again.

If you can identify, even for a moment, with the feelings I went through after this event, I will be grateful. You may have much more difficult experiences or longer-term money-related problems. You may think I got upset for nothing. That's okay, because this is not a competition. Emotions are born in the growth environment we have lived in and they are always relative. If I asked you to reflect on the most difficult money-related experience in your life, what would you say and more importantly, how would you feel? Is the memory uncomfortably powerful for you? Often these memories are stored on the hard drive of our brains with the greatest possible accuracy.

Perhaps you have experienced, as I have, the profound relief of finally being heard—of being able to simply say "I am sad" and have that sadness acknowledged. Too often, grief is met with well-intentioned but elegant evasions. We tell ourselves that everything is fine and throw ourselves into frantic cleaning, intense exercise, endless work, or mindless online shopping. Humans possess remarkable ingenuity when it comes to circumventing difficult emotions.

What does this emotional avoidance have to do with money? Nothing connects more directly to financial well-being than the emotions that money triggers within us. While researchers have established that money doesn't increase the frequency or intensity of positive emotions—as discussed earlier in this book—our lived experience often tells us otherwise. We reach for purchases when we're sad, celebrate successes with spending, or use financial control as a buffer against uncertainty. Understanding this emotional dimension of money is crucial because our financial decisions are rarely purely rational—they're deeply intertwined with how we process and cope with the full spectrum of human feeling.

Emotions are our inner world and help us interpret our environment, but they do not provide simple and objective answers about the nature of reality. Be curious, be open, and ask questions. Name your feelings as accurately as possible. When it comes to money, be particularly interested in the emotions it evokes and how they guide your actions. Identifying your emotions will help you make better financial decisions, because without them, your choices would also be meaningless. Be aware that emotions can lead you into addiction or long-term stress, making it almost impossible to be open to emotional experiences. Take care of yourself, as emotions are easiest to deal with when you are not overwhelmed or tired.

People who feel happy tend to experience more positive emotions. If we look at people in general, we tend to be overoptimistic. This is useful, because optimistic people live longer than pessimistic people. However, happiness is not the same as cheerfulness. The difference between the two is that happiness is also about giving space to the range of emotions and the ups and downs of life. If your feelings and experiences are very intense, repetitive, and causing you distress, consider talking to a trusted loved one or health professional. Help is available and should be sought.

WORKING WITH ADDICTION

Shopping addiction involves the intersection of money and emotions. The following exercises can be applied to working with addiction. Breaking the cycle of addiction takes work, repetition, and regularity. Working in a group is also often helpful.

Explore the Feeling of Need

Choose a quiet place where you can sit in a chair or lie down on the floor. Become aware of your body touching the floor where you can feel it. Focus your attention on the feeling of neediness that fuels addiction. How does it feel and where in your body? The source of the addiction, whatever it is, is not the object of your attention but the feeling of longing and need in your body. Avoid telling stories of addiction in your mind, and if you find your mind wandering, keep returning to the sensations. These feelings are the focus of the practice, like a candle flame or a breath. As you explore the feeling, you may notice it changing in quality or intensity.

Explore the Pleasure of Novelty

This exercise can be done sitting in a central square in a shopping mall. The mall as a building, the sounds, the advertisements, the architecture, all tempt us to buy something new. The brain gets a sense of satisfaction from the sheer novelty of the novelty, which lasts for a moment and then demands something newer and better the next. Take a bottle of water with you, for example, and open it while you sit down. Concentrate on the water bottle with all your senses: smell, taste, listen, feel, look, notice all the little details in this water bottle that you have never noticed before. Exercise your curiosity. Redirect your attention away from the feelings of boredom and restlessness that often trigger the need to buy something new. In what way is this a new experience? How is it different from, say, buying a new jacket, and how is it similar?

FINANCIAL SETBACKS—IT HURTS!

Joanna is a thirty-year-old café owner who has been running her business for several years. She started her own venture out of necessity after losing her first job when her employer faced financial difficulties. Growing up in a low-income household, Joanna's family of four children faced even greater hardship after her mother's death when she was sixteen. From an early age, she learned that anything she wanted required her own effort—while still in high school, she began working part-time at a coffee shop.

Now determined to achieve financial independence, Joanna is methodically saving for her own apartment while watching her friends buy homes and start families. She maintains a disciplined approach to money, living in affordable shared accommodation with students despite the occasional friction that arises from their different life circumstances. Joanna prides herself on being goal-oriented and realistic about her finances, refusing to spend her hard-earned money carelessly.

Yet this financial discipline has come at a cost. Joanna has noticed that joy seems to have drained from her life—she rarely does things she enjoys because they require money she's determined to save. She carries anger toward a society that has dealt her financial setbacks beyond her control, and even minor disappointments trigger disproportionate self-criticism. When an expensive lunch proves disappointing, she berates herself for being foolish. When friends suggest she should "live a little" instead of constantly saving, she bristles with frustration—no one else seems to understand the struggle behind her goals or how much harder everything feels for her than for others.

In a perfect world, we have limitless choices and possibilities when it comes to managing our finances. In the real world, we have a limited number of choices and opportunities in the present moment, and the right to fail, to screw up, to financially bankrupt ourselves—or whatever financial backlash means to us. For many of us, financial failures are the very failures that are difficult to talk about with friends and family. It's hard to admit you need help in a really tough situation. If you've ever been in a real money crunch, you might recognize a whole rush of emotions. Shame, hopelessness, helplessness, body alert, disappointment, anger ... any number of emotions can be associated with the situation.

Financial difficulties also increase your body's pain levels, which I think is a good illustration of how significant the issues are. Eileen Chou from the University of Virginia has done a pilot study on these connections. In her research, she found that in addition to personal economic insecurity (in the case of the study, unemployment), job insecurity and simply *thinking about* economic insecurity increased the experience of physical pain or decreased the ability to tolerate pain.[4] The explanatory factor was a sense of control: when we feel our economic future is sailing on a stormy sea without an anchor, we are particularly vulnerable to experiencing pain. It is possible that we are then sensitive to anything that threatens us, but there is not yet enough research on this topic.

What if you tell a colleague or partner that you are in pain or distress because you have experienced a significant financial setback? Several studies have shown that psychological distress and physical pain are caused by similar neural processes. Relationship disappointments and the threat of rejection also seem to activate the same brain areas as physical pain, so the same painkiller may even alleviate both symptoms.[5] These groundbreaking studies provide a new perspective on how our physical and psychological experiences are intertwined.

Joanna is trapped with feelings of anger and irritation. She doesn't talk about them and is ashamed of her own negativity and jealousy, but that doesn't make the feelings go away. The first step for her is to accept that it is natural to feel disappointment, sadness, and anger when faced with difficult life events. Talking about them is a relief. At the same time, it is a good moment to reflect on what she values, who she is as a person, and how she carries that out in her everyday life.

For Joanna, spending on things that are necessary and bring her joy can be important. She may find pleasure in setting aside a small amount of money each month from her salary to do nice things. The amount doesn't matter, but its existence does. If she wants to go for a coffee and an art exhibition on the weekend, the financial contribution is relatively small, but the psychological impact is big. Money can increase the degree of freedom in life, and sometimes it is important to realize that even a small increase in freedom is important.

In life, there is what is known as core emotional pain or "clean pain," which often follows loss or disappointment. Clean pain has been with me when I have had to leave a place I love, it has reared its head when I have received a polite rejection call after a tough job interview, and it has been at its worst when I have lost someone close. Clean pain is also a natural consequence of financial loss or business bankruptcy. It can be a step on the road to personal growth, but this trait does not take away the pain it causes. In fact, pain can be a prerequisite for growth. The pain is often most acute in the context of a related event and usually diminishes over time. Often, grief work is needed so that at some point after the loss, life can continue as it is offered.

Clean pain is different from so-called messy or dirty pain, which is a much more complex phenomenon. Messy pain is full of self-blame, doubt, anger at oneself and others, and "I wish I had done things differently" thoughts. This pain sustains itself, and with it it is hard to notice anything else in life. The financial setback is often followed by thoughts of guilt: if I had been better, more skilled, a different person, better prepared, wiser. . . . In fact, you can add any blaming thought to the list and be sure that the experience is human and many will recognize it. The blame is caused by the fact that adult people are thought to be responsible for their own lives. However, the truth is that random things happen in life too.

There are unforeseen changes, and things that are thought to be impossible. If we can identify the pain that follows financial loss, it opens up the possibility of asking for help where we need it. When faced with the experience of pain, I would hope that everyone would be met with understanding, appreciation, compassion, and listening attention. There could be less advice or exhortation to pull yourself together. When we lose the opportunity to follow the path we have chosen, it is okay to be sad. When a business in which we have invested our time and passion fails, it is natural to feel pain. Recovery from pain is possible, even though grief may surge unexpectedly when life's pressures return. If you've experienced loss, allow yourself space to heal without rushing. You don't need to fix everything immediately, nor should you let devastating thoughts cloud the natural grieving process. When pain is clean, let it exist without judgment.

REDEFINING SUCCESS

Pygmalion was a Cypriot king and sculptor who loved a statue he had carved so much that he prayed to the goddess Aphrodite to bring it to life. Aphrodite granted his request, and the statue, known as Galatea, came to life and became Pygmalion's wife.[6] This story gave rise to the idea of the Pygmalion effect, a phenomenon in which high expectations lead to better performance. As early as in 1968, a study found that learning outcomes are influenced by the teacher's perception of their students and their abilities;[7] in other words, strong beliefs and expectations can change reality. People tend to judge others quickly, focusing on a few characteristics that color their first impressions. Expectations we have of ourselves are also influential. It is particularly harmful for children and young people to be seen through a one-sided role, both as individuals and as members of a group. This reliance on heuristics, quick assessments, and shortcuts may be necessary in some situations, but it rarely, if ever, provides us with enough information.

Life is full of stories of how once upon a time there was a young person who lived happily ever after. If you take a look at social media, for example, these stories are remarkably common and very similar things happen. We are expected to be ambitious, financially successful, educated, married, starting a family, and generally be nice people with plenty of social contacts. Sometimes these things do make us happier, sometimes they don't. Parents often say that they wish their children would "succeed in life." This is especially true in cultures that traditionally value good performance in studies, work, and family life. In many Western countries, children are expected to be happy rather than successful, even though happiness may be defined by past generations' beliefs as, for example, a well-paying job. The pursuit of such success or happiness may also be strong within ourselves, at least if we do not question the contradictions inherent in the pursuit of it.

Very often, we adopt a culturally constructed view of people who are "successful in life," who are financially successful or are particularly good at managing their money. Financial success is often associated with personal qualities and character traits: willpower, thrift, prudence, materialism, determination, leadership, and self-confidence. Conversely, poor financial performance is associated with the opposite characteristics: weakness of willpower, impulsiveness, insecurity, and, surprisingly, positive qualities such as compassion, gentleness, kindness, and depth.[8] Could it be that the tradition of the poor but profound thinker lives on in the undercurrents of our culture? Our perceptions are also influenced by gender roles, as men are traditionally thought to be responsible for providing an economic livelihood and women for looking after the family. For men and women, "succeeding in life" has meant different things.

These images of financial success are common, but they are also so limited and stereotypical that they can be counterproductive. Hardly anyone thinks that low-income earners have chosen meditation as their life's goal, like the poor monks of the Middle Ages, or that women are incapable of creating wealth, but traditional images are slow to disappear.

In everyday life, it is very important to recognize how our own beliefs about economic success shape our opportunities and influence how we behave. If our own self-image does not match our ideal of a financially successful person, it may be that these images lead us to think that success is alien or impossible for our character. We avoid talking about the difficult subject or downplay its importance. If we think that economic success belongs only to people who are educated in, say, traditionally high-paying professions and who have a materialistic view of success, it will also have a direct impact on society. Economic resources provide both opportunities and the ability to make decisions and choices. If we exclude ourselves from the economy, we also leave decision-making to a like-minded and culturally homogenous group of people and lose the opportunity for a truly diverse and democratic society.

In contemporary Western society, economic success has become virtually synonymous with social status. *Status*—our position within society or specific communities—can stem from various sources including financial achievement, professional accomplishments, or accumulated expertise, and we often hold different status levels across different social circles. This equation of wealth with worth represents a relatively recent historical shift: in past centuries, society placed greater value on ancestry, heritage, or spiritual devotion. Just a few hundred years ago, rapid enrichment was often viewed with suspicion rather than admiration.

Recent research over the past decade has revealed a fascinating paradox about money's relationship to well-being. Studies show that people do indeed value money for its ability to elevate their social status, but when this status effect is isolated and removed from the equation, wealth itself may contribute surprisingly little to life satisfaction. This finding connects to the hierarchy of needs discussed earlier: money primarily addresses middle-tier concerns rather than our deepest sources of fulfillment. The implications become clearer when we consider our social environment. When we surround ourselves with people who are wealthier or who appear to hold higher social status, we inevitably fall into the comparison trap, experiencing dissatisfaction and stress regardless of our absolute level of prosperity. This suggests that our financial well-being is less about the actual numbers in our accounts and more about our relative position within our chosen reference groups.

Comparison itself is a source of dissatisfaction, because we then always see our lives through an external evaluation. The easiest point of comparison is the closest reference group, people in a similar position. "Beggars do not envy millionaires, though of course they will envy other beggars who are more successful," said the philosopher Bertrand Russell in the 1930s. But the comparisons never stop, because there is always someone who is better off, earns more, or is just luckier. It is through comparison that status also affects the experience of happiness: the wealthy are much more likely to encounter people who are less well off than they are, while those on low incomes are more likely to encounter people who are better off than they are. Such comparisons can lead to either satisfaction or dissatisfaction—whether conscious or unconscious.

Economic success and the traditional status it brings is one way of talking about economic well-being. However, a better picture emerges when the idea of overall balance and the use of limited resources is added to the mere amount of money. What if financial success did not mean the same thing as high status, but financial success meant less stress, fewer hours worked, less debt, less worry about possessions? Research based on the American Time Use Survey (ATUS) shows that commuting ranks among the least enjoyable daily activities, with high stress and fatigue but low meaning.[9] We also know that as incomes rise, people are forced to spend more time working and commuting.[10] If you look at the people you know with this idea in mind, you might find that you view financial success in a very different way.

Traditional definitions of personal success often overlook their relationship to broader societal well-being—rarely do they encompass goals like creating an egalitarian society, ensuring family security, or protecting the environment. Yet these collective outcomes profoundly shape our individual experience of happiness and fulfillment. This disconnect suggests we might need to fundamentally reframe what "success in life" means, shifting focus from personal achievements like high salaries and bank balances toward the positive impact we create in the world around us.

Sahil Bloom's *The 5 Types of Wealth*[11] offers one such reframing, challenging the narrow belief that money represents the only meaningful wealth. Instead, he proposes a holistic framework encompassing five interconnected dimensions of time, social connections, and mental and physical wealth, along with financial wealth. This approach resonates with me, particularly because it recognizes that true prosperity extends far beyond financial accumulation. I appreciate that this framework doesn't demand perfect balance across all five areas to qualify as a successful life. Rather than viewing them as a checklist requiring equal attention, we can understand them as interconnected elements where deficiency in one area often ripples through the others. This interconnectedness means that strengthening any single type of wealth can create positive momentum across our entire life experience. If anything would be missing, perhaps that would be community wealth—the purpose we have as a human being, being part of the life on this planet.

CHAPTER 13

BEING THE CHANGE

*Don't turn your head. Keep looking at the bandaged place.
That's where the light enters you.*

—RUMI[1]

WHAT WE KNOW

"The present moment is, in its own way, outside of time," wrote philosopher Hannah Arendt in the 1950s.[2] People live in a busy and fast-paced environment, where planning for the future or worrying about the past can seem like particularly necessary ways to keep on top of things. However, worrying about the future and the past prevents us from being present in the here and now. The present is the only moment in life when we can act, and we forget this almost every single day. If we want to influence our everyday lives, the time is now. Genuine encounters and conversations cannot be postponed to the future, nor can understanding the past replace interaction.

Throughout the writing of this book, I've encountered stories that have moved me deeply—some filled with heartbreak and disbelief, others brimming with hope. What emerges consistently is humanity's remarkable capacity for resilience and reinvention. We possess an inexplicable ability to adapt and believe in a brighter tomorrow, even when facing seemingly insurmountable obstacles.

As we've journeyed through the complexities of money and values, these discoveries have shaped our way:

Your money story is your inheritance—but not your destiny.
Each of us carries a financial narrative forged in childhood and

adolescence, shaped by family dynamics, cultural messages, and early experiences with scarcity or abundance. Like DNA, this story becomes part of our psychological makeup, influencing our adult financial behaviors in ways we rarely recognize. Yet unlike genetic inheritance, our money story can be rewritten through awareness and intentional change. Think of it as editing a manuscript—the original draft informs the work, but conscious revision can transform the ending. Your money story is also woven into the broader fabric of social and economic reality. Understanding your own financial patterns within this larger context builds both self-awareness and empathy for others facing different challenges.

Financial struggles can feel intensely personal and shameful, but they're often rooted in systemic issues beyond individual control. Everyone deserves access to financial education, emotional support around money anxiety, and practical tools for building security. Asking for help with money shouldn't be any more stigmatized than seeking support for health, relationships, or career development.

Emotions are the invisible hand guiding financial decisions. Far from being purely rational calculations, our financial choices emerge from a complex interplay of feelings—fear, hope, shame, pride, anxiety, and excitement. Learning to recognize and work with these emotional currents, rather than being swept away by them, transforms how we relate to money.

Avoidance creates the very problems we fear most. When anxiety about money becomes overwhelming, our natural response is often to look away—to avoid checking bank statements, delay financial planning, or postpone difficult money conversations. Yet this avoidance, like ignoring a small leak that eventually floods the house, typically amplifies our original fears and creates new complications. Breaking this cycle requires courage, but the relief and empowerment that follow make the initial discomfort worthwhile.

Money amplifies life but cannot create it. Money functions like a magnifying glass—it enhances what already exists but cannot conjure what isn't there. Beyond meeting our basic needs for food, shelter, and security, additional wealth yields diminishing returns on happiness and fulfillment. Money can purchase a larger home but cannot expand your circle of meaningful friendships. It can fund medical treatments but cannot guarantee robust health. It can provide comfort but cannot deepen intimate relationships or infuse your work with purpose. The seductive "If only I had more money, then . . ." thoughts often mask our reluctance to engage in the harder work of human connection and personal growth. Before reaching for the credit card as a solution, consider whether reconnecting with old friends, committing to regular exercise, or having difficult conversations might address the real need. When we already have enough to meet our genuine needs, waiting for money to solve life's deeper challenges keeps us perpetually stuck.

Saving is good for us. Here's genuinely good news: saving money benefits nearly everyone—ourselves, our communities, and our environment. The act of saving builds both psychological and practical resilience. It creates a buffer that transforms how we navigate life's inevitable challenges, allowing us to make decisions from a place of stability rather than desperation. Many problems become more manageable when you're not simultaneously scrambling to pay basic bills. The key is balance. When saving becomes compulsive or anxiety-driven, it loses its protective power and becomes another source of stress. Healthy saving feels like building a foundation, not hoarding against imagined catastrophes.

Money conversations shape the next generation. Money permeates family life whether we acknowledge it or not—through the choices we make, the tensions we carry, and the examples we set. Children absorb our financial attitudes like sponges, often learning more from our behavior than our words. The responsibility and opportunity to model healthy money relationships begins remarkably early. A five-year-old learning to make thoughtful choices with their allowance will internalize those lessons far more deeply than a teenager receiving lectures about budgeting. Financial education isn't about teaching complex investment strategies to preschoolers—it's about demonstrating values like gratitude, intentionality, and the connection between effort and reward through age-appropriate experiences.

Money is a mirror reflecting our deepest values. How we earn, spend, save, and share our resources reveals what we truly prioritize, often more clearly than our words ever could. When we align our financial choices with our authentic values, money becomes a tool for creating the world we want to live in—one that supports not just our individual well-being but the flourishing of our communities and planet. An equitable, sustainable society where everyone has access to adequate resources isn't just a moral imperative, it's a practical foundation for collective prosperity and peace of mind.

Talking about money openly and honestly is not always easy from the start, but it's worth practicing. Gradually, even the most difficult feelings will subside and the need to avoid them will diminish. When you want to make progress, step by step is a better tactic than going all out quickly. You can begin with social media: there are communities where you can start a conversation and get good advice at the same time. Once you've found your voice in these virtual spaces, bringing up money conversations with friends or partners becomes less daunting. Online financial communities can be your training wheels—they help you build confidence and find your language before navigating more personal terrain.

However, it's important to recognize that online wealth-building communities often attract people who are already comfortable discussing money, either because it comes naturally to them or because life circumstances have forced them to engage deeply with financial topics. Like any specialized community, these spaces can develop their own culture and assumptions that might feel foreign or overwhelming to newcomers. If you find yourself feeling out of place in these environments—perhaps the tone feels too confident, the focus too narrow, or the values misaligned with your own—pause and ask yourself what you're truly seeking. Are you looking for practical financial strategies or emotional support around money anxiety, or a community that shares your broader values about wealth and its role in society? Different online spaces serve different needs, and finding the right fit is important

It may be that you want to secure your own finances adequately, but you want to make your investments responsibly. Or you may be hoping for tips on how to reduce your consumption while reducing your own working hours. Or you just want to manage your finances as efficiently as possible so that you can concentrate on other things you value.

Financial freedom encompasses more than just having money—it's also the profound relief of not constantly worrying about it. Like a background hum we don't notice until it stops, financial anxiety can consume mental energy we didn't even realize we were spending.

The cultural silence surrounding money conversations serves powerful interests but rarely our own. In many societies, discussing finances occupies an uncomfortable middle ground—not quite taboo but socially delicate enough to discourage open dialogue. This silence, however, isn't neutral. While consumer protection laws require companies to disclose lending terms and investment risks, many people lack the confidence or knowledge to effectively evaluate these options. When money talk remains hushed, it benefits companies that operate within legal boundaries but employ predatory practices—like payday lenders targeting vulnerable communities or investment firms burying fees in complex documentation.

Salary transparency offers a powerful example of how breaking financial silence serves justice. When compensation criteria are open and consistently applied, it becomes much harder to perpetuate gender, racial, or other discriminatory pay gaps. Conversely, cultures of salary secrecy often protect unfair practices while leaving individual employees feeling isolated and powerless.

In the early 2000s, professor Ed Diener studied particularly happy students.[3] His subjects were not those who were slightly happier than average but those who actually rated themselves as being at the peak of happiness. He found that these students had no more pleasant events in their lives than anyone else. They did not play sports or exercise any more than anyone else. No single factor explained their happiness, but it turned out that strong social relationships were essential for happiness. Although Diener's study was small, I believe there is a grain of truth in it. It is not the level of wealth that matters for happiness but the people around us. Still, it pays to manage our finances in a reasonable way so that we have more time to strengthen our social relationships and enough freedom to be with the people we care about.

For me, financial freedom means having the capacity to make a meaningful difference—both in everyday moments and in the larger currents of change flowing through our world. It's about moving from financial survival to financial purpose. This freedom manifests in countless ways, from the beautifully simple to the transformatively complex. Money can ensure that a child has notebooks and pencils for the school year. It can fund programs that help recently divorced or widowed individuals reclaim their financial independence. It can support breakthrough environmental technologies that might reshape how we power our future. The possibilities are as varied as human need and imagination, limited only by our willingness to see beyond our immediate circumstances.

When I secure my own financial foundation, I create something more valuable than personal comfort—I build the capacity to stay engaged with what matters most, even when times get difficult. Financial stability becomes the platform from which I can continue advocating for change, supporting causes I believe in, and responding generously when others need help. It's the difference between being overwhelmed by immediate needs and having the bandwidth to think strategically about impact.

Understanding how money flows—where it comes from, where it goes, and what it accomplishes along the way—transforms it from a source of stress into a tool for intentional living. Everyone, regardless of their bank balance, has the opportunity to align their financial choices with their values. Whether that means supporting local businesses that reflect your principles, choosing investments that fund solutions to global challenges, or simply ensuring that your spending habits don't undermine the world you want to create, every financial decision becomes a vote for the future you envision.

Money can indeed create happiness, but only when it serves something larger than accumulation itself. When money becomes a bridge between our values and our actions, it transforms from a burden we carry into a current that carries us toward meaning.

WHAT WE SEEK

I always walk into the British Museum through the back door. It's a lesser-known entrance on a leafy side street that leads straight into a long gallery displaying achievements in various fields of science spanning hundreds of years. On quiet winter mornings, it is a haven of peace. A place where time seems to stand still with the comforting knowledge that inventions have indeed been made and because of them the world is a little better. I often find myself wandering up the stone and stark stairs to the Asian gallery, which somehow feels particularly peaceful and where the protagonists are not warlords, self-serving individuals, or despotic rulers. The Asian gallery is dominated by a bronze, gold-plated woman, her upper body naked and, judging by her physique, in the prime of her life. Her name is Tara, and her only superpower is the ability to fulfill wishes.

For thousands of years, people have sought help and safety in difficult times from symbols, spirits, deities, signs in the sky, and nature. If I had lived in Sri Lanka nearly three thousand years ago, I would probably have sought help from Tara, who was believed to be the spirit of generosity and compassion. Tara is one of the most impressive statues in the entire museum, at once calmly beautiful and comforting, her right hand in a position known as Varadamudra, the gesture of granting wishes. Tara is meant not to be worshipped but to inspire reflection and meditation on compassion and generosity.

In Sri Lanka, Tara was a messenger of Buddhism, but before that she was a mother goddess in Hinduism. Tara does not belong to any single religion, school of thought, or culture but is a universal reminder that compassion and help exist around us if we allow them to. Today, Tara is forgotten in Sri Lanka but remains a symbol of a living tradition in Nepal and Tibet.

The enduring psychological structure of humanity is the appreciation of fairness and equality and the condemnation of injustice. Almost everyone values generosity in some form or another. However, these permanent psychological constructs operate in a world that is constantly changing. Behavioral economics presents us with a human spectrum of desires, needs, and plans that are influenced not only by money but also by the social, economic, and psychological factors of the environment. Economic, political, and social change is driven forward like a force of nature, but it is not governed by natural laws. In the midst of this opaque and complex change, we often long for the sense of security that stability and predictability can offer. Security in the midst of change is an illusion, but we need to give ourselves time to understand what is happening.

In a changing world, financial security is an important survival tool, because if we can secure ourselves financially, we can take a breather and build a protective wall between ourselves and the ongoing turmoil. Throughout history, financial security has been the privilege of a select few, and even for them, security may have been fleeting; fortunes have been won and lost. Despite the safety nets of welfare states, global economic change and job insecurity are reaching people today at an ever-increasing rate. The future is open, with ever new and more complex technological and economic challenges ahead. While economic optimism is not always justified, it is a healthy way to approach the future. Optimism helps us to take an interest in the future and to plan for the long term.

One of the big economic issues now and in the future is ecology. Kirk Warren Brown and Tim Kasser have studied the links between ecologically sustainable behavior and perceived well-being.[4] Sometimes these are seen as opposites, because when individuals consider environment, it leads to restrictions on consumption and choices that can not only cost more but also make everyday life more difficult. For example, giving up the car means either being tied to public transport timetables or spending more time cycling or walking. In addition, consumption in general can lead to feelings of guilt and responsibility, as making environmentally positive choices requires a willingness to explore better alternatives. However, the researchers concluded that the more people made ecological choices, the better their well-being. Further analysis revealed that well-being was particularly enhanced by intrinsic motivation (doing things according to one's values and goals) and mindful presence (being aware of one's own feelings and thoughts in the present moment).

An interesting study among Chinese youth found that while materialistic values seem to decrease ecological behaviors, connection to nature helps to maintain a sustainable lifestyle.[5] These results have also been interpreted to mean that a green, ecological view of oneself is good for self-esteem and enhances communal experiences.[6] These results challenge the connection that we have traditionally seen between well-being and a money-based rational economy.

Statistics do not always provide a clear picture of what people really think. Laura Hyman and her colleagues have interviewed people in the British middle class about what money and work mean to them.[7] Although Western societies are very materialistic, most of the interviewed felt that having too much money is not good for well-being. This recurring theme is also very present in Scandinavian culture through proverbs and stories. When people are asked how happiness comes about, they often describe it as something that lies within the person and is difficult to influence by external means. The rich are believed to be in some ways more prone to heartbreak and other problems, especially if they rely too much on the surface glamour of life.

In the United States, similar ambivalence toward wealth has been documented by researchers at the University of California, Berkeley, who found that while Americans pursue financial success, there may be psychological costs of extreme wealth.[8] Robert Putnam's influential work on social capital and community connection has given us plenty to think about: he argues that poverty isn't just deprivation but also isolation, noting that excessive wealth can similarly isolate individuals from broader community bonds.[9] This paradoxical relationship with money is reflected in what sociologists call "the American Dream paradox":[10] while Americans value financial success highly, they simultaneously report that relationships and meaningful work contribute more to happiness than wealth accumulation alone.

The Empower "Financial Happiness" study[11] found that 65 percent of Americans define financial happiness as "living debt-free" rather than maximizing wealth. The same study found that Americans believe it would take a net worth of about $1.2 million on average to be happy, with significant generational differences: for millennials $1.7 million, Generation X around $1.2 million, baby boomers just under $1 million, and Generation Z about $487,000. This may well suggest a cultural shift away from pure materialism toward what researchers term "post-materialist values" and at the same time considerable headwind for younger generations in achieving financial security.

Of course, we may not always be ready to admit our less noble instincts. Many people think that other people are more materialistic than they are, and youth in general have been often seen as more materialistic than older generations.[12] To be fair, don't we just easily forget what it is like to be young and trying to fit in the society around us? The middle class does not want to see itself as materialistic, as its own values are seen as different from others, perhaps more focused on intellectual capital. The past is also often seen as less materialistic than the present, and the past is remembered as more communal: there was more environmental support and face-to-face encounters.

"Money can't buy happiness" is in many ways an ideological stance, reflected not only in politics, for example, but also in what people consider ethically acceptable. Perhaps advertisements and popular culture convey the image that a large number of people see possession and the acquisition of money as desirable. However, many of those interviewed for the surveys admit that buying new things, such as clothes, gives them pleasure.

There is a reasonable consensus among futurologists and trend followers that spending and the way we spend money will change radically. The trend is toward ecology, minimalism, quality and ethical products, less is more, valuing time and life experiences over materials, and a strong emphasis on rail transport. If society wants to increase people's well-being, it should promote equality, social safety nets, and the freedom to live a life of one's own choice, both at work and in leisure time, rather than material well-being.[13] Some of these changes are already evident. What we fail to consider is that these changes are not just small tweaks to existing society but are challenging many of the so-called truths of the economy and society. We are forced to ask, for example, whether more money is always better than less, what kind of work and working hours are optimal for human well-being, and what kind of economic equality is good for individuals and communities.

One compelling response to these challenges emerged in the early 2000s with the *degrowth* movement—an economic philosophy that fundamentally reframes how we think about progress, consumption, and prosperity. Rather than pursuing endless expansion, degrowth advocates for an economy that operates within environmental limits while actively promoting social justice and equity. This approach represents a profound shift in how we measure success. Instead of focusing solely on GDP growth or material accumulation, the degrowth framework embraces a more holistic understanding of well-being—one that recognizes the complex relationships between economic activity, human flourishing, and planetary health. It asks not just "How much can we produce?" but "What kind of life do we want to create together?"

Central to the degrowth philosophy is the principle of socially sustainable moderation. This means thoughtfully reducing overconsumption in wealthy societies while simultaneously addressing inequality and deprivation. The goal isn't universal austerity but rather a more equitable distribution of resources—scaling back excess where it exists while ensuring that everyone has access to what they need for a dignified life. This nuanced approach acknowledges that in a world moving toward ecological balance, living standards must still rise significantly in places where basic needs remain unmet, while moderating in contexts where consumption has far exceeded necessity.

We navigate each day with whatever resources we possess—financial, emotional, or otherwise—sometimes thriving, sometimes barely managing, occasionally reaching out for help, often pushing through alone. Yet no one emerges from life's challenges without wounds. In these inevitable struggles, cultivating humanity toward ourselves and others becomes not just helpful but essential for maintaining perspective and resilience.

Research consistently reveals compassion as one of our most powerful capacities for healing and growth—a skill that deserves nurturing both inward and outward. Yet self-compassion shouldn't become another impossible standard we set for ourselves, another way to fall short of our own expectations.

The truth is, extending compassion to ourselves often feels nearly impossible. Many of us have mastered the art of endurance, pushing forward without pausing to ask what we genuinely need or deserve. We stay busy enough to avoid these uncomfortable questions, filling our days so completely that reflection becomes impossible. Sometimes, when self-compassion feels out of reach, it's enough to receive it from others and simply notice how that feels—to let someone else's kindness become a bridge to understanding our own worthiness. There is little difference between the sexes in this respect; brain research shows that women are no more compassionate than men. However, women are usually brought up to be understanding, compassionate, and approachable, and they experience greater external pressure to show empathy.[14] Women often excel at offering compassion to everyone except themselves, having learned that self-care can feel selfish or indulgent.

For high achievers, self-compassion presents a unique challenge because it seems to contradict the drive that fuels their success. Accepting imperfection, acknowledging limitations, or treating failures with gentleness can feel like weakness, laziness, or surrender—emotions that directly threaten their identity as people who overcome obstacles through sheer determination. Yet this resistance reveals a fundamental misunderstanding: compassion isn't the opposite of achievement but its sustainable foundation. Without it, even our greatest successes can feel hollow, and our inevitable setbacks become sources of shame rather than opportunities for growth.

Self-compassion does not increase empathy toward others, but according to some studies it may reduce the psychological burden associated with empathy (emotional stress from a situation) and increase helping behavior toward others.[15] Although there is still little research on this, one possible reason is that we have more opportunities and resources to do good things when we are not so attached to empathetic responses and the negative emotional burden they cause. Self-compassion and compassion would therefore be a very good combination.

Life rarely looks exactly like we would like it to be. Yet here's what I think is true: life's purpose isn't to perfectly reflect who we think we should be but to express who we choose to become through our actions.

Regardless of our starting circumstances—whether we began with abundance or scarcity, privilege or hardship, clarity or confusion—we retain the power to choose how we show up in the world. This choice extends to every interaction with people, animals, and the living systems that sustain us all. It's the one realm where we maintain genuine control, the one certainty we can rely on—our next response to whatever life presents. This doesn't require heroic gestures or world-changing achievements. The most profound impact often happens through small acts that align with our unique capabilities and circumstances. Each of us possesses something valuable to offer: time that could comfort a lonely neighbor, money that could support a meaningful cause, or skills that could brighten someone's day.

Consider the gifts you might take for granted—a beautiful singing voice that could lift spirits, an intuitive ability to read emotions and offer exactly the right words, the practical skill to help others navigate confusing paperwork, or the culinary wisdom to transform simple ingredients into something memorable. Perhaps you possess the almost mystical knowledge of heating a traditional smoke sauna to that perfect temperature where relaxation becomes transcendent. Every skill, no matter how ordinary it seems to you, has the potential to create joy, solve problems, or ease burdens for others.

For those interested in maximizing their direct financial positive impact, here are some ideas that can help us channel our resources toward the greatest possible good:

Direct your financial resources strategically. Research organizations thoroughly to ensure that your donations create maximum impact per dollar spent. Look for transparency in how funds are used, evidence of measurable outcomes, and alignment with causes that address root problems rather than just symptoms.

Align your work with your values. Seek opportunities where your professional skills contribute to planetary or human well-being. This might mean transitioning to a mission-driven organization, advocating for sustainable practices within your current workplace, or using your expertise to support causes you care about through volunteer work or pro bono services.

Normalize conversations about collective action. Make discussing solutions and addressing injustices a natural part of workplace conversations, social gatherings, and online interactions. When we talk openly about positive change—whether that's supporting local businesses, addressing inequality, or protecting the environment—we help shift cultural norms and inspire others to act.

Integrate conscience into daily decisions. Choose products, services, and habits that minimize harm and support regenerative practices. This includes everything from transportation choices and food purchases to banking with institutions that align with your values and supporting businesses that treat workers fairly.

Embrace continuous learning and self-reflection. Approach each day with curiosity about how to live more intentionally. Question existing habits, stay open to new information that might challenge your assumptions, and remember that doing better tomorrow doesn't require being perfect today. Your life situation doesn't matter, because there is always something you can do, no matter how small. The most important thing is to see yourself as part of the good and strong forces in the world.

We need regular reminders that life contains possibilities beyond our current horizons—touchstones that gently expand our understanding of what's possible for ourselves and the world around us. It's essential to surround ourselves with things and ideas that stretch beyond the boundaries of our daily routines, larger and more inspiring than our immediate concerns. For some, this expansion comes through deep connection with nature—standing beneath ancient trees or watching ocean waves that have rolled for millennia. For others, it emerges through encounters with art, music, theater, or film that reveal new ways of seeing and feeling.

Sometimes the most profound growth happens through meaningful conversations with people whose life experiences differ vastly from our own, whose experience offers fresh perspectives we've never considered. You can recognize these moments by their distinctive quality: a simultaneous sense of being slightly dazed and deeply contemplative, accompanied by the startling realization that "things could be like that"—possibilities that seem both obvious and revolutionary once glimpsed.

Elevating your existence doesn't require expensive travel, exclusive social circles, prestigious career moves, or luxury experiences. What it demands is something both simpler and more challenging: mindful presence. Being fully present in our own lives, consciously engaging in personal growth, requires sustained attention—a commodity that feels increasingly scarce in our accelerated world. What emerges instantly rarely endures. True growth, like the rings of an ancient tree, accumulates slowly, building strength through seasons of abundance and scarcity alike.

FINAL WORDS

Each of us begins life from a different starting line. Some must struggle intensely to reach what others achieve effortlessly, fighting for opportunities that seem to fall naturally into other hands. Research on intergenerational patterns can feel overwhelming—showing how attitudes, beliefs, self-confidence, and our capacity for giving and receiving love all trace back to early childhood experiences. If these patterns were truly permanent, hope would indeed seem distant.

But the past is only one chapter of our story, not its final word. While it's important to acknowledge the obstacles and wounds we carry, they need not define our destination. Change becomes not only possible but probable when we seek support and encouragement from others who believe in our capacity to grow. Even the most entrenched patterns can shift when we stop trying to transform ourselves in isolation. Each of us moves through the world in our own distinctive way—using resources, forming relationships, and leaving our unique imprint on our immediate communities and the broader world. Everything we do carries meaning. There are no insignificant actions, because even the grandest changes emerge from small, persistent, conscious efforts to protect and nurture life.

Financial well-being offers us the opportunity to direct our energy toward what truly serves our values and vision for our lives. We often feel compelled to measure ourselves against external standards—calculating our carbon footprint, worrying about future generations, setting rigid criteria for what constitutes a worthy existence. Yet there are countless ways to contribute meaningfully, each drawing on different resources and strengths. What matters most is finding our authentic way to take responsibility for ourselves and our impact on the world.

Awareness alone can radically transform our actions. It requires no special self-discipline, willpower, detailed project plans, or constant effort.

Final Words

In its elegant simplicity lies its power. Awareness may give us what we need, though not always what we think we want.

Our self-help culture often promotes the belief that with enough effort, we can continuously refine ourselves into better versions—more evolved, productive, and useful. This idea particularly appeals when achievement brings satisfaction, security, and social approval. Who wouldn't want to bask in success and recognition? *Here I am! I can accomplish things others only dream of! Hard work has finally paid off!*

There's nothing inherently wrong with celebrating success, achievement, and financial well-being. We could celebrate even more—both small daily victories and major life milestones. However, it's dangerously easy to focus exclusively on individual achievements and heroic narratives when, in reality, most outcomes result from countless interconnected factors. How we engage with social media shapes our brain function and identity formation as well as our attention to environment and economy. Our beliefs about personal success and limitations affect our ability to respond to unexpected situations, our neurological health, our stress levels, and our capacity for empathy. Our power to influence the world around us strengthens through engaged relationships, mental flexibility, and resilience.

It is later than you think. We postpone life changes, waiting for the perfect moment that may never arrive. At life's end, people often regret not pursuing their dreams, prioritizing work over relationships, failing to develop deeper connections, or delaying joy indefinitely. Amid busy schedules and performance pressure, we forget small pleasures and meaningful moments.

Yet the freedom to pursue what truly matters to us isn't quite as simple as recognizing its importance. Behavior, emotions, and thoughts exist in intimate connection—change in one area ripples through the others. Solving one problem can untangle knots you never imagined loosening. The human mind operates as a neural network where changes create new pathways, shortcuts, faster routes, and varying levels of activation. Starting with the easiest change often enables others. Similarly, one idea can birth many others. One goal can sprout an entirely new life. Growing as a person ultimately means recognizing that we are free to make choices—and that this freedom, rather than being a burden, is our greatest gift both to ourselves and to the others.

Money Values

+ + +

I'd like to share a final meditation with you, one for which I'm deeply grateful to Dr. Suvi Laukkanen.

Begin by imagining a vast space in your mind. Simply a large, expansive space. If you're anything like me, your brain will immediately rebel, demanding specifications: "Large compared to what? Is it enclosed or boundless? Are there walls, windows, a ceiling? What exactly do you mean by 'space'?"

Let these questions arise and then gently set them aside. This space can be anything that feels genuinely expansive to you—a sun-drenched greenhouse with soaring glass walls, a hot-air balloon drifting through endless sky, a cathedral with vaulted ceilings, an aircraft hangar, a child's tree house with multiple rooms. Trust your imagination to show you what feels right.

Once you've settled on a space that resonates with you, close your eyes and **imagine that this space can actually exist within you.** Don't worry about the logistics—simply allow the possibility that you can contain something this large.

Now, **picture your entire identity—every aspect of who you are—finding a home within this inner space.** Your personality, beliefs, values, dreams, contradictions, fears, hopes, and ambitions. All the different facets of yourself, even those that seem to conflict with each other.

Let each part find its own place naturally. They don't need to fit together like puzzle pieces, perfectly interlocking. Nor do they compete for territory or diminish each other's presence. They simply coexist in this generous expanse you've created.

Take a moment to sense into this experience. How does it feel to contain this much complexity, this much possibility? Does the spaciousness feel overwhelming or liberating? Too vast or surprisingly intimate?

Notice whether this inner space allows for change, for growth, for parts of yourself you haven't yet discovered. Perhaps you'll become aware of some aspect of yourself that has been cramped, that's been asking for more room, more attention, more permission to exist fully.

Can you let it expand?

ACKNOWLEDGMENTS

I would like to express my warmest thanks to those people who have in many ways made it possible for this book to be written. Writing is always a very private process for me, so even my closest friends and family have not always been aware of everything that is going on with it. I always worry about time running out and whether it will ever be finished, but I don't want to burden others with my doubts. This was the case with this book as well; I took a lot of time to think, but in the end I believe that the slowness, doubt, and rewriting have been worth it.

I want to express my endless gratitude to all who agreed to be interviewed for this book. I have followed the wishes of changing the names, and sometimes combining the stories, if anonymity was requested.

Thank you all who have stood by my side during these years: The Riemenschneiders, especially Henna and Liina, who gave me inspiration—without their sheltering garden, apple tree, and confusingly unique pet rabbits this book would hardly have managed to find its first sentences. Emily Chan, who continues to be an ambassador of perseverance, calmness, and humor amid cultures. Rico Behlke, who has followed his own path, for his uncompromising and honest views over the years. Amy Whitehead, who in her own kindhearted way continues to uplift and motivate to seek new perspectives. Anniina Pesonen, whose visions illuminate the future and who has encouraged me to live fully with warmth and compassion. Sari Markkanen, who has always been a beacon of inspiration and fellow teacher of tough crowds. Bridget Harris, who has abundant financial wisdom and a generous heart. Annie Harper and Michael Rowe, who asked the right questions and opened a path less traveled. Lovely, determined, and bright Mila, who has the world ahead of her. Suvi Laukkanen, whose wisdom and always apt observations about life and society have helped me to look at things more deeply.

Always supportive Jake Bonar, who saw the potential in this book and believed it could happen.

Finally, thank you my dear partner Mika for love and unlimited kindness, in all the twists and turns of our lives, now and always. And my deepest gratitude to those who have patiently endured all the distraction, absence, and long days involved in writing this book: Sam, Elliot, and Amos, the best teachers of humanity and mindful being.

NOTES

CHAPTER 1: WE ALL HAVE OUR STORY ABOUT MONEY

1. Jung, 1933.
2. Guan et al., 2022.
3. Fligstein, Hastings, and A. Goldstein, 2017.
4. Krieger and Sheldon, 2015; City and Guilds, 2012.
5. Grable, 2013.
6. U.S. Census Bureau, 2024.
7. Hyytinen et al., 2019.
8. Heckmann, Stixrud, and Urzua, 2006.
9. Shim et al., 2009.
10. Norvilitis and MacLean, 2010.
11. Carmona and Vilarroya, 2025.
12. Abraham et al., 2014.
13. Cheng, Powdthavee, and Oswald, 2017.
14. Lagattuta, Sayfan, and Bamford, 2012.
15. Whitebread and Bingham, 2013.
16. Mohsen, 2022.
17. Harris et al., 2016.
18. Roberts et al., 2005.
19. Bleidorn et al., 2022.
20. Letkiewicz and Heckman, 2019.
21. Liu and Csikszentmihalyi, 2020.
22. YouGov, 2024.
23. Festinger, 1950.
24. Mental Health Foundation, 2019.
25. Sapolsky, 2018.
26. Gilbert, 2000.
27. Marmot and Brunner, 2005.
28. Anderson et al., 2012.
29. Wilkinson and Pickett, 2018.
30. Cingano, 2014.

CHAPTER 2: THE SOCIETY
1. Ferguson, 2008.
2. Niedzwiedz et al., 2016.
3. Sapolsky, 2023.
4. Henrich, 2020.
5. Mannerström, 2019.
6. Barna Group, 2020.
7. Auriol et al., 2020; Siegfried, 2019.
8. World Bank, 2012.
9. World Economic Forum, 2024.
10. Mitchell and Lusardi, 2008.
11. Laakso and Mehtonen, 2018.
12. Dweck, 1986.
13. Curran and Hill, 2019.
14. Stoeber & Stoeber, 2009.
15. Stoeber and Otto, 2006; Yarnell et al., 2015.
16. Zyphur et al., 2015.
17. Rosling, Rosling, and Rosling Rönnlund, 2018.
18. Baron-Cohen, 2011.
19. Chauvel and Leist, 2015.
20. Wilkinson and Pickett, 2009.
21. Ribeiro, Bauer, and Andrade, 2017.
22. Graham and Felton, 2009.
23. Carrell, 2014.
24. Saunders, 2010.
25. Layte, 2012.
26. Paskov and Dewilde, 2012.
27. Dickerson and Popli, 2016.
28. ATD Fourth World UK, 2019.
29. Bray et al., 2020.
30. Pew Research Center, 2023.
31. Kraus et al., 2012.
32. Alonso-Ferres et al., 2020; Taylor, 2011.

CHAPTER 3: THE NEUROSCIENCE
1. Hanson, 2009.
2. Opendak et al., 2016.
3. Hiraoka and Nomura, 2016.
4. Elliot, 2010; Joel et al., 2015.
5. Nielsen et al., 2013.
6. Elliot, 2010; Joel et al., 2015.
7. Rogowsky, Calhoun, and Tallal, 2015.
8. Sheridan et al., 2023.
9. LaBar and Cabeza, 2006.
10. Hartshorne, Tenenbaum, and Pinker, 2020.
11. Bak et al., 2016.

12. Merzenich, 2013.
13. Anandi, Sendhil, and Eldar, 2013.
14. Lenroot and Giedd, 2008.
15. Voss et al., 2017.
16. Eagleman, 2021.
17. Park et al., 2021.
18. Kahneman, 2013.
19. J. Kim and Garman, 2003.
20. Metzger et al., 1990.
21. O'Neill et al., 2005.
22. Kahn and Pearlin, 2006.
23. Hubler et al., 2016.
24. White et al., 2022.
25. Merzenich, 2013.

CHAPTER 4: THE EMOTIONS
1. Andrews, 2010.
2. Krys et al., 2016.
3. Feldman Barrett, 2017.
4. James and Lange, 1922.
5. Purves et al., 2001.
6. Russell, 1980.
7. Nummenmaa et al., 2014.
8. Nummenmaa, 2019.
9. Kanai et al., 2011.
10. Kagan, 2007.
11. Tan and Forgas, 2010.
12. Storr, 1992.
13. Danziger, Levav, and Avnam-Pesso, 2011.
14. Bechara and Damasio, 2005.
15. Warren, 2025.
16. American Psychological Association, 2023.
17. S. Kim, Thibodeau, and Jorgensen, 2011.
18. Elison, Lennon, and Pulos, 2014.
19. Nechita, Bud, and David, 2021.
20. Dearing, Stuewig, and Tangney, 2005.
21. Starrin, Åslund, and Nilsson, 2009.
22. B. Brown, 2007.

CHAPTER 5: GUIDING VALUES
1. Miller, 1955.
2. Schwartz, 2012.
3. Canevello and Crocker, 2010.
4. Cave and O'Hagan, 2022.

CHAPTER 6: MONEY-RELATED VALUES
1. Carroll, 1865.
2. Sarraute, 1959.
3. Felix and Garza, 2012.
4. Teng et al., 2017.
5. Dittmar, 2007.
6. Jiang et al., 2015; Zawadzka et al., 2022.
7. Dittmar et al., 2014.
8. Kasser, 2016.
9. Hart, Keller, and Perren, 2024.
10. Wilson, 2000.
11. Wilson and Musick, 2003.
12. Tabassum, Mohan, and Smith, 2016.
13. Grimm et al., 2005.
14. Newmyer et al., 2022.
15. Jenkinson et al., 2013; E. S. Kim et al., 2020.
16. Long and Fowers, 2020.
17. Safane, 2024.
18. U.S. Bureau of Labor Statistics, n.d.
19. U.S. Bureau of Labor Statistics, 2025.
20. Bian, Leslie, and Cimpian, 2018.
21. Good, Rattan, and Dweck, 2012.
22. Testa and Cavallini, 2021.
23. Fehr and Fischbacher, 2003.
24. Engel, 2011.
25. Freund and Blanchard-Fields, 2013.
26. Diener and Seligman, 2002.
27. Brooks, 2007.
28. Becchetti, Corrado, and Conzo, 2017.
29. Curry et al., 2018.
30. Harbaugh, 1998.

CHAPTER 7: THE MYTH OF HAPPINESS
1. D. Brown, 2017.
2. Tolstoy, 1886.
3. Lubomirsky, Sheldon, and Schkade, 2005; Baselmans and Bartels, 2018.
4. Røysamb, Ragnhild, and Vittersø, 2014.
5. Lucas, 2007.
6. Clark et al., 2006.
7. Armenta et al., 2014.
8. Lubomirsky and Layous, 2013.
9. Cummins, 2014.
10. Sheldon and Lubomirsky, 2009.
11. Hendriks, 2018.
12. Easterlin, 1974.
13. Easterlin et al., 2012.

14. Veenhoven, 2014.
15. Erasmus University Rotterdam, 2017.
16. Sen, 1999.
17. Dolan, 2015.
18. Seehuus, 2021.
19. Dehaan and Ryan, 2014.
20. Nickerson et al., 2007.
21. Pleeging, Burger, and van Exel, 2021.
22. Bauer, 2012.
23. Bruggen et al., 2017.
24. Arber, Fenn, and Meadows, 2014.
25. Vosloo, Fouche, and Barnard, 2014.
26. Maslow, 1943.
27. Prati, 2017.
28. Ferrer-i-Carbonell, 2005.
29. Finke, Howe, and Huston, 2016.
30. Summerville and Roese, 2017.

CHAPTER 8: ECONOMIC SYSTEMS AND SOCIAL EXPECTATIONS

1. Hawken, 1993.
2. Jun and Choi, 2015.
3. Jain et al., 2025.
4. Lee, Park, and Lee, 2016.
5. Alexander, 2010.
6. Atadokht et al., 2015.
7. Killingsworth, 2021.
8. Vassallo, 2023.
9. Grant, 2023.

CHAPTER 9: PREPARE YOURSELF

1. Gaardner, 2016.
2. Amstrong, 2012.
3. Klontz and Klontz, 2009.
4. Frankl, (1946) 2006.
5. K. Brown et al., 2009.
6. D. Stone, 2011.
7. Van Doesum et al., 2019.
8. Shaver et al., 2007.

CHAPTER 10: WORK AND LIVE WITH PURPOSE

1. Camus, (1942) 1955.
2. Hakanen et al., 2019.
3. Office of the U.S. Surgeon General, 2022.
4. Chandola and Zhang, 2018.

5. Ericsson, Krampe, and Tesch-Römer, 1993.
6. Steger 2019.
7. Hari, 2019.
8. Morris et al., 2022.
9. Arendt, 1958.
10. Holten, 2026.
11. Powdthavee and Stutzer, 2014.

CHAPTER 11: MONEY MANAGEMENT
1. Hill, 2023.
2. Chou, Bidhan, and Galinsky, 2016.
3. Wilkinson and Pickett, 2009.
4. Guan et al., 2022.
5. Berk, Dodd, and Henry, 2006.
6. Searle, Smith, and Cook, 2009.
7. French and McKillop, 2017.
8. Mischel et al., 2011.
9. Consumer Financial Protection Bureau, 2020.
10. DeSteno et al., 2014.
11. Dickens and DeSteno, 2016.
12. Cho, Geistfeld, and Loibl, 2014.
13. Shim et al., 2009.
14. Hershfield et al., 2011.
15. Massachusetts Institute of Technology et al., 2025.
16. Gratton and Scott, 2018.
17. Atwood, 1988.
18. Beauvoir, 1977.
19. CFA Institute, 2023.
20. She et al., 2021.
21. Pariser, 2011.
22. Noelle-Neumann, 1984.
23. Engeln, 2017.
24. Allcot et al., 2025.
25. Ramadhan et al., 2024.
26. Brynjolfsson and Eggers, 2019.

CHAPTER 12: BUILDING A VISION
1. Dillard, 1989.
2. Brunner, 2006.
3. Bukowski, 1983.
4. Chou, Bidhan, and Galinsky, 2016.
5. DeWall et al., 2010.
6. Ovidius, (8 CE) 1935.
7. Rosenthal and Jacobson, 1968.
8. Alderotti and Traverso, 2023.
9. A. Stone and Schneider, 2016.

10. Blumenberg and Siddiq, 2023.
11. Bloom, 2024.

CHAPTER 13: BEING THE CHANGE
1. Rumi, (13th century) 1995.
2. Arendt, 1958.
3. Diener and Seligman, 2002.
4. K. W. Brown and Kasser, 2005.
5. Wang and Huo, 2022.
6. Binder and Blankenberg, 2017.
7. Hyman, 2014.
8. Piff et al., 2012.
9. Putnam, 2015.
10. Myers, 2000.
11. Empower, 2023.
12. Harwood Group, 1995.
13. Barrington-Leigh and Galbraith, 2019.
14. Pang et al., 2023.
15. Rachel et al., 2018.

REFERENCES

Abraham, E., T. Hendler, I. Shapira-Lichter, Y. Kanat-Maymon, O. Zagoory-Sharon, and R. Feldman. 2014. "Father's brain is sensitive to childcare experiences." *Proceedings of the National Academy of Sciences of the United States of America* 111, no. 27: 9792–97.

Alderotti, G., C. Rapallini, and S. Traverso. 2023. "The Big Five Personality Traits and Earnings: A Meta-Analysis." *Journal of Economic Psychology* 94, Article 102570. https://doi.org/10.1016/j.joep.2022.102570.

Alexander, B. 2010. *The Globalization of Addiction: A Study in Poverty of the Spirit*. Oxford University Press.

Allcott, H., L. Braghieri, S. Eichmeyer, and M. Gentzkow. 2025. "The effect of deactivating Facebook and Instagram on users' emotional state." National Bureau of Economic Research Working Paper No. 33697. https://www.nber.org/papers/w33697.

Alonso-Ferres, M., G. Navarro-Carrillo, M. Garrido-Macías, E. Moreno-Bella, and I. Valor-Segura. 2020. "Connecting perceived economic threat and prosocial tendencies: The explanatory role of empathic concern." *PLOS ONE* 15, no. 5: e0232608.

American Psychological Association. 2023. "Stress in America 2023: A nation recovering from collective trauma." https://www.apa.org/news/press/releases/stress/2023/collective-trauma-recovery.

Anandi, M., M. Sendhil, and S. Eldar. 2013. "Poverty impedes cognitive function." *Science* 341: 976–80.

Anderson, C., M. W. Kraus, A. D. Galinsky, and D. Keltner. 2012. "The local-ladder effect: Social status and subjective well-being." *Psychological Science* 23, no. 7: 764–71.

Andrews, S. 2010. "Antonio Demasio probes the mind in his new book." *Medical Press*, November 12. https://medicalxpress.com/news/2010-11-antonio-damasio-probes-mind.html.

Arber, S., K. Fenn, and R. Meadows. 2014. "Subjective financial well-being, income and health inequalities in mid and later life in Britain." *Social Science & Medicine* 100: 12–20.

Arendt, H. 1958. *The Human Condition*. University of Chicago Press.

Armenta, C., K. Jacobs, S. Lubomirsky, and K. Sheldon. 2014. "Is lasting change possible? Lessons from the hedonic adaptation prevention model." In K. Sheldon and R. Lucas, eds., *Stability of Happiness: Theories and Evidence on Whether Happiness Can Change*. Elsevier Academic Press.

Armstrong, J. 2012. *How to Worry Less about Money*. MacMillan.

References

Atadokht, A., N. Hajloo, M. Karimi, and M. Narimani. 2015. "The role of family expressed emotion and perceived social support in predicting addiction relapse." *International Journal of High Risk Behaviors and Addiction* 4, no. 1: e21250.

ATD Fourth World UK. 2019. "Understanding poverty in all its forms: A participatory research study into poverty in the UK." https://www.atd-fourthworld.org/wp-content/uploads/sites/5/2019/10/ATD-POVERTY-REPORT_D.pdf.

Attwood, M. 1988. *Cat's Eye*. Toronto: McClelland and Stewart.

Bak, T., M. Long, M. Vega-Mendoza, and A. Sorace. 2016. "Novelty, challenge, and practice: The impact of intensive language learning on attentional functions." *PLOS ONE* 11, no. 4: e0153485.

Barna Group. 2020. The Connected Generation. https://theconnectedgeneration.com.

Baron-Cohen, S. 2011. *Zero Degrees of Empathy: A New Theory of Human Cruelty*. Penguin.

Barrington-Leigh, C., and E. Galbraith. 2019. "Feasible future global scenarios for human life evaluations." *Nature Communications* 10: 161.

Baselmans, B. M. L., and M. Bartels. 2018. "A genetic perspective on the relationship between eudaimonic and hedonic well-being." *Scientific Reports* 8, no. 1: 14610.

Bauer, M. 2012. "Cuing consumerism: Situational materialism undermines personal and social well-being." *Psychological Science* 23, no. 5: 517–23.

Beauvoir, S. de. 1977. *Old Age*. Penguin Books.

Becchetti, L., L. Corrado, and P. Conzo. 2017. "Sociability, altruism and well-being." *Cambridge Journal of Economics* 41, no. 2: 441–86.

Bechara, A., and A. Damasio. 2005. "The somatic marker hypothesis: A neural theory of economic decision." *Games and Economic Behavior* 52: 336–72.

Berk, M., S. Dodd, and M. Henry. 2006. "The effect of macroeconomic variables on suicide." *Psychological Medicine* 36, no. 2: 181–89.

Bian, L., S. J. Leslie, and A. Cimpian. 2018. "Evidence of bias against girls and women in contexts that emphasize intellectual ability." *American Psychologist* 73, no. 9: 1139–53.

Binder, M., and A. Blankenberg. 2017. "Green lifestyles and subjective well-being: More about self-image than actual behavior?" *Journal of Economic Behavior & Organization* 137: 304–23.

Bleidorn, W., T. Schwaba, A. Zheng, et al. 2022. "Personality stability and change: A meta-analysis of longitudinal studies." *Psychological Bulletin* 148, no. 7-8: 588–619.

Bloom, S. 2024. *The 5 Types of Wealth: A Transformative Guide to Design Your Dream Life*. Portfolio.

Blumenberg, E., and F. Siddiq. 2023. "Commute distance and jobs-housing fit." *Transportation* 50: 869–91.

Bray, R., M. de Laat, X. Godinot, A. Ugarte, and R. Walker. 2020. "Realising poverty in all its dimensions: A six-country participatory study." *World Development* 134: 1–10.

Brooks, A. 2007. "Does giving make us prosperous?" *Journal of Economics and Finance* 31: 403–11.

Brown, B. 2007. *I Thought It Was Just Me (but It Isn't): Making the Journey from "What Will People Think?" to "I Am Enough."* Gotham Books.

Brown, D. 2017. *Happy: Why More or Less Everything Is Fine*. Corgi Books.

Brown, K. W., and T. Kasser. 2005. "Are psychological and ecological well-being compatible?" *Social Indicators Research* 74, no. 2: 349–68.

References

Brown, K., T. Kasser, R. Ryan, P. Linley, and K. Orzech. 2009. "When what one has is enough: Mindfulness, financial desire discrepancy, and subjective well-being." *Journal of Research in Personality* 43, no. 5: 727–36.

Bruggen, E. C., J. Hogreve, M. Holmlund, S. Kabadayi, and M. Lofgren. 2017. "Financial well-being: A conceptualization and research agenda." *Journal of Business Research* 79: 228–37.

Brunner, L. 2006. "Review of the book *Deep Listening: A Composer's Sound Practice*." *Notes* 62, no. 3: 715–18.

Brynjolfsson, E., A. Collis, and F. Eggers. 2019. "Using Massive Online Choice Experiments to Measure Changes in Well-Being." *Proceedings of the National Academy of Sciences* 116(15), 7250–55. https://doi.org/10.1073/pnas.1815663116.

Bukowski, C. 1983. *Tales of Ordinary Madness*. City Lights Publishers.

Camus, A. 1955. *The Myth of Sisyphus and Other Essays*. J. O'Brien, trans. Vintage Books. Original work published 1942.

Canevello, A., and J. Crocker. 2010. "Creating good relationships: Responsiveness, relationship quality, and interpersonal goals." *Journal of Personality and Social Psychology* 99, no. 1: 78–106.

Carmona, S., and O. Vilarroya. 2025. "The transition to parenthood: Linking hormones, brain, and behavior." *Psychoneuroendocrinology* 172: 107247.

Carrell, A. 2014. "Scottish NHS boards pay hundreds of pounds an hour for locums amid psychiatry crisis." *The Guardian*, October 7. https://www.theguardian.com/society/2024/oct/07/scottish-nhs-boards-pay-up-to-837-an-hour-for-locums-amid-psychiatry-crisis.

Carroll, L. 1865. *Alice's Adventures in Wonderland*. Macmillan.

Cave, N., and S. O'Hagan. 2022. *Faith, Hope, and Carnage*. Canongate Books.

CFA Institute. 2023. "Gen Z and investing: Social media, crypto, FOMO and family." https://rpc.cfainstitute.org/sites/default/files/-/media/documents/article/industry-research/Gen_Z_and_Investing.pdf.

Chandola, T., and N. Zhang. 2018. "Re-employment, job quality, health and allostatic load biomarkers: Prospective evidence from the UK Household Longitudinal Study." *International Journal of Epidemiology* 47, no. 1: 47–57.

Chauvel, L., and A. Leist. 2015. "Socioeconomic hierarchy and health gradient in Europe: The role of income inequality and of social origins." *International Journal of Equity in Health* 14, no. 132.

Cheng, T. C., N. Powdthavee, and A. J. Oswald. 2017. "Longitudinal evidence for a midlife nadir in human well-being: Results from four data sets." *Economic Journal* 127, no. 599: 126–42.

Cho, S. H., L. Geistfeld, and C. Loibl. 2014. "Motivation for emergency and retirement saving: An examination of regulatory focus theory." *International Journal of Consumer Research* 38, no. 6.

Chou, E., L. Bidhan, and A. Galinsky. 2016. "Economic insecurity increases physical pain." *Psychological Science* 27, no. 4: 443–54.

Cingano, F. 2014. "Trends in income inequality and its impact on economic growth." *OECD Social, Employment and Migration Working Papers*, No. 163.

City and Guilds Career Happiness Index. 2012. Referenced in https://www.thehrdirector.com/features/health-and-wellbeing/remember-happy/.

References

Clark, A., E. Diener, Y. Georgellis, and R. Lucas. 2006. "Lags and leads in life satisfaction: Test of baseline hypotheses." IZA Discussion Paper No. 2526.

Consumer Financial Protection Bureau. 2020. "Perceived Financial Preparedness, Saving Habits, and Financial Security." CFPB Office of Research Reports Series No. 20-11. https://files.consumerfinance.gov/f/documents/cfpb_perceived-financial-preparedness-saving-habits-and-financial-security_2020-09.pdf

Cummins, R. 2014. "Can happiness change? Theories and evidence." In K. Sheldon and R. Lucas, eds., *Stability of Happiness: Theories and Evidence on Whether Happiness Can Change*. Elsevier Academic Press.

Curran, T., and A. Hill. 2019. "Perfectionism is increasing over time: A meta-analysis of birth cohort differences from 1989 to 2016." *Psychological Bulletin* 145, no. 4: 410–29.

Curry, O., L. Rowland, C. Van Lissa, S. Zlotowitz, J. McAlaney, and H. Whitehouse. 2018. "Happy to help? A systematic review and meta-analysis of the effects of performing acts of kindness on the well-being of the actor." *Journal of Experimental Social Psychology* 76: 320–29.

Danziger, S., J. Levav, and L. Avnam-Pesso. 2011. "Extraneous factors in judicial decisions." *Proceedings of the National Academy of Sciences* 108, no. 17: 6889–92.

Dearing, R. L., J. Stuewig, and J. P. Tangney. 2005. "On the importance of distinguishing shame from guilt: Relations to problematic alcohol and drug use." *Addictive Behaviors* 30, no. 7: 1392–1404.

DeHaan, C. R., and R. M. Ryan. 2014. "Symptoms of wellness: Happiness and eudaimonia from a self-determination perspective." In K. M. Sheldon and R. E. Lucas, eds., *Stability of Happiness: Theories and Evidence on Whether Happiness Can Change*, 37–55. Elsevier Academic Press.

DeSteno, D., Y. Li, L. Dickens, and J. Lerner. 2014. "Gratitude: A tool for reducing economic impatience." *Psychological Science* 25, no. 6: 1262–67.

DeWall, C., G. MacDonald, Gregory Webster, et al. 2010. "Acetaminophen reduces social pain: Behavioral and neural evidence." *Psychological Science* 21, no. 7: 931–37.

Dickens, L., and D. DeSteno. 2016. "The grateful are patient: Heightened daily gratitude is associated with attenuated temporal discounting." *Emotion* 16, no. 4: 421–25.

Dickerson, A., and G. K. Popli. 2016. "Persistent poverty and children's cognitive development: Evidence from the UK Millennium Cohort Study." *Journal of the Royal Statistical Society Series A: Statistics in Society* 179, no. 2: 535–58.

Diener, E., and M. E. P. Seligman. 2002. "Very happy people." *Psychological Science* 13, no. 1: 81–84.

Dillard, A. 1989. *The Writing Life*. Harper & Row.

Dittmar, H. 2007. *Consumer Culture, Identity and Well-Being: The Search for the "Good Life" and the "Body Perfect."* Psychology Press.

Dittmar, H., R. Bond, M. Hurst, and T. Kasser. 2014. "The relationship between materialism and personal well-being: A meta-analysis." *Journal of Personality and Social Psychology* 107, no. 5: 879–924.

Dolan, P. 2015. *Happiness by Design*. London: Penguin Books.

Dweck, C. 1986. "Motivational processes affecting learning." *American Psychologist* 41, no. 10: 1040–48.

Eagleman, D. 2021. *Livewired: The Inside Story of the Ever-Changing Brain*. Pantheon Books.

References

Easterlin, R. A. 1974. "Does economic growth improve the human lot? Some empirical evidence." In P. A. David and M. W. Reder, eds., *Nations and Households in Economic Growth: Essays in Honor of Moses Abramovitz*, 89–125. Academic Press.

Easterlin, R. A., R. Morgan, M. Switek, and F. Wang. 2012. "China's life satisfaction, 1990–2010." *Proceedings of the National Academy of Sciences* 109, no. 25: 9775–80.

Elison, J., R. Lennon, and S. Pulos. 2014. "Shame and aggression: Theoretical considerations." *Aggression and Violent Behavior* 19, no. 4: 447–53.

Elliot, L. 2010. *Pink Brain, Blue Brain: How Small Differences Grow into Troublesome Gaps—and What We Can Do About It.* Mariner Books.

Empower. 2023. "Financial Happiness." https://www.empower.com/the-currency/money/research-financial-happiness.

Engel, C. 2011. "Dictator games: A meta study." *Experimental Economics* 14: 583–610.

Engeln, R. 2017. *Beauty Sick: How the Cultural Obsession with Appearance Hurts Girls and Women.* Harper.

Erasmus University Rotterdam. 2017. World Database of Happiness. https://worlddatabaseofhappiness.eur.nl.

Ericsson, K. A., R. T. Krampe, and C. Tesch-Römer. 1993. "The role of deliberate practice in the acquisition of expert performance." *Psychological Review* 100, no. 3: 363–406.

Fehr, E., and U. Fischbacher. 2003. "The nature of human altruism." *Nature* 425: 785–91.

Feldman Barrett, L. 2017. *How Emotions Are Made: The Secret Life of the Brain.* Houghton Mifflin Harcourt.

Felix, R., and M. Garza. 2012. "Rethinking worldly possessions: The relationship between materialism and body appearance for female consumers in an emerging economy." *Psychology & Marketing* 29, no. 12: 980–94.

Ferguson, N. 2008. *The Ascent of Money: A Financial History of the World.* Allen Lane/Penguin Press.

Ferrer-i-Carbonell, A. 2005. "Income and well-being: An empirical analysis of the comparison income effect." *Journal of Public Economics* 89, no. 5–6: 997–1019.

Festinger, L. 1950. "Informal social communication." *Psychological Review* 57, no. 5: 271–82.

Finke, M., J. Howe, and S. Huston. 2016. "Old age and the decline in financial literacy." *Management Science* 63, no. 1: 213–30.

Fligstein, N., O. P. Hastings, and A. Goldstein. 2017. "Keeping up with the Joneses: How households fared in the era of high income inequality." *Socius: Sociological Research for a Dynamic World* 3: 1–15.

Frankl, V. 2006. *Man's Search for Meaning.* Beacon Press. Original work published in 1946.

French, D., and D. McKillop. 2017. "The impact of debt and financial stress on health in Northern Irish households." *Journal of European Social Policy* 27, no. 5: 458–73.

Freund, A., and F. Blanchard-Fields. 2013. "Age-related differences in altruism across adulthood: Making personal financial gain versus contributing to the public good." *Developmental Psychology* 50, no. 4: 1125–36.

Gaardner, J. 2016. *The World According to Anna.* Weidenfeld Nicolson.

Gilbert, P. 2000. "The relationship of shame, social anxiety and depression: The role of the evaluation of social rank." *Clinical Psychology & Psychotherapy* 7, no. 3: 174–89.

Good, C., A. Rattan, and C. Dweck. 2012. "Why do women opt out? Sense of belonging and women's representation in mathematics." *Journal of Personality and Social Psychology* 102, no. 4: 700–17.

References

Grable, J. E., S. Cupples, F. Fernatt, and N. Anderson. 2013. "Evaluating the Link Between Perceived Income Adequacy and Financial Satisfaction: A Resource Deficit Hypothesis Approach." *Social Indicators Research 114*(3), 1109 -24. https://doi.org/10.1007/s11205-012-0192-8.

Graham, C., and A. Felton. 2009. "Does inequality matter to individual welfare? An initial exploration based on happiness surveys from Latin America." In A. K. Dutt and B. Radcliff, eds., *Happiness, Economics and Politics: Towards a Multi-Disciplinary Approach*. Edward Elgar.

Grant, A. 2023. *Hidden Potential: The Science of Achieving Greater Things*. Ebury Publishing.

Gratton, L., and A. Scott. 2018. *The 100-Year Life: Living and Working in an Age of Longevity*. Bloomsbury Business.

Grimm, R., Jr., N. Dietz, K. Spring, K. Arey, and J. Foster-Bey. 2005. *Building Active Citizens: The Role of Social Institutions in Teen Volunteering*. Brief 1 in the *Youth Helping America* series. Corporation for National and Community Service.

Guan, N., A. Guariglia, P. Moore, F. Xu, and H. Al-Janabi. 2022. "Financial stress and depression in adults: A systematic review." *PLOS ONE* 17, no. 2: e0264041.

Hakanen, J., A. Ropponen, H. De Witte, and W. Schaufeli. 2019. "Testing demands and resources as determinants of vitality among different employment contract groups: A study in 30 European countries." *International Journal of Environmental Research and Public Health* 16, no. 24: 4951.

Hanson, R. 2009. *Buddha's Brain: The Practical Neuroscience of Happiness, Love, and Wisdom*. New Harbinger Publications.

Harbaugh, W. 1998. "What do donations buy? A model of philanthropy based on prestige and warm glow." *Journal of Public Economics* 67, no. 2: 269–84.

Hari, J. 2019. *Lost Connections: Why You're Depressed and How to Find Hope*. Bloomsbury Publishing.

Hart, L. M., R. Keller, and S. Perren. 2024. "Spielzeugfreier Kindergarten: Differentielle Effekte eines Präventionsprojektes zur Stärkung der Lebenskompetenzen von Kindergartenkindern" [Toy-free kindergarten: Differential effects of a prevention project to strengthen life skills in kindergarten children]. *Kindheit und Entwicklung* 33, no. 2: 103–10.

Harris, M. A., C. E. Brett, W. Johnson, and I. J. Deary. 2016. "Personality stability from age 14 to age 77 years." *Psychology and Aging* 31, no. 8: 862–74.

Hartshorne, J. K., J. B. Tenenbaum, and S. Pinker. 2020. "A critical period for second language acquisition: Evidence from 2/3 million English speakers." *Cognition* 177: 263–77.

Harwood Group. 1995. *Yearning for Balance: Views of Americans on Consumption, Materialism, and the Environment*. Merck Family Fund.

Hawken, P. 1993. *The Ecology of Commerce*. HarperBusiness.

Heckman, J., J. Stixrud, and S. Urzua. 2006. "The effects of cognitive and noncognitive abilities on labor market outcomes and social behavior." *Journal of Labor Economics* 24, no. 3: 411–82.

Hendriks, M. 2018. "Does migration increase happiness? It depends." Migration Policy Institute, June 21. https://www.migrationpolicy.org/article/does-migration-increase-happiness-it-depends.

Henrich, J. 2020. *The WEIRDest People in the World: How the West Became Psychologically Peculiar and Particularly Prosperous*. Farrar, Straus and Giroux.

References

Hershfield, H. E., D. G. Goldstein, W. F. Sharpe, et al. 2011. "Increasing saving behavior through age-progressed renderings of the future self." *Journal of Marketing Research* 48: S23–37.
Hill, N. 2023. *Wellness: A Novel.* Alfred A. Knopf.
Hiraoka, D., and M. Nomura. 2016. "The Influence of Cognitive Load on Empathy and Intention in Response to Infant Crying." *Scientific Reports* 6, 28247. https://doi.org/10.1038/srep28247.
Holten, E. 2026. (S. N. Hellberg, Trans.). *Deficit: How Feminist Economics Can Change Our World.* WH Allen.
Hubler, D. S., B. K. Burr, B. C. Gardner, R. E. Larzelere, and D. M. Busby. 2016. "The intergenerational transmission of financial stress and relationship outcomes." *Marriage & Family Review* 52, no. 4: 373–91.
Hyman, L. 2014. *Happiness: Understandings, Narratives and Discourses.* Palgrave Macmillan.
Hyytinen, A., P. Ilmakunnas, E. Johansson, and O. Toivio. 2019. "Heritability of lifetime earnings." *Journal of Economic Inequality* 17: 319–35.
Jain, L., L. Velez-Figueroa, S. Karlapati, M. Forand, R. Ahmed, and Z. Sarfraz. 2025. "Cryptocurrency trading and associated mental health factors: A scoping review." *Journal of Primary Care & Community Health* 16: 21501319251315308.
James, W., and C. G. Lange. 1922. "The emotions." In K. Dunlap, ed., *The Emotions.* Williams & Wilkins.
Jenkinson, C. E., A. P. Dickens, K. Jones, et al. 2013. "Is volunteering a public health intervention? A systematic review and meta-analysis of the health and survival of volunteers." *BMC Public Health* 13: 773.
Jiang, J., Y. Zhang, Y. Ke, S. T. Hawk, and H. Qiu. 2015. "Can't buy me friendship? Peer rejection and adolescent materialism: Implicit self-esteem as a mediator." *Journal of Experimental Social Psychology* 58: 48–55.
Joel, D., Z. Berman, I. Tavor, et al. 2015. "Sex beyond the genitalia: The human brain mosaic." *Proceedings of the National Academy of Sciences* 112, no. 50: 15468–73.
Jun, S., and E. Choi. 2015. "Academic stress and Internet addiction from general strain theory framework." *Computers in Human Behavior* 49: 282–87.
Jung, C. G. 1933. *Modern Man in Search of a Soul.* Harcourt, Brace and Company.
Kagan, J. 2007. *What Is Emotion? History, Measures, and Meanings.* Yale University Press.
Kahn, J., and L. Pearlin. 2006. "Financial strain over the life course and health among older adults." *Journal of Health and Social Behavior* 47: 17–31.
Kahneman, D. 2013. *Thinking, Fast and Slow.* Farrar, Straus and Giroux.
Kanai, R., T. Feilden, C. Firth, and G. Rees. 2011. "Political orientations are correlated with brain structure in young adults." *Current Biology* 21, no. 8: 677–80.
Kasser, T. 2016. "Materialistic values and goals." *Annual Review of Psychology* 67: 489–514.
Killingsworth, M. 2021. "Experienced well-being rises with income, even above $75,000 per year." *Proceedings of the National Academy of Sciences* 118, no. 4: e2016976118.
Kim, E. S., A. V. Whillans, M. T. Lee, Y. Chen, and T. J. VanderWeele. 2020. "Volunteering and subsequent health and well-being in older adults: An outcome-wide longitudinal approach." *American Journal of Preventive Medicine* 59, no. 2: 176–86.
Kim, J., and E. T. Garman. 2003. "Financial stress and absenteeism: An empirically derived model." *Financial Counseling and Planning* 14, no. 1: 31–42.
Kim, S., R. Thibodeau, and R. S. Jorgensen. 2011. "Shame, guilt, and depressive symptoms: A meta-analytic review." *Psychological Bulletin* 137, no. 1: 68–96.

References

Klontz, B., and T. Klontz. 2009. *Mind over Money: Overcoming the Money Disorders That Threaten Our Financial Health*. Crown Business.

Kraus, M. W., P. K. Piff, R. Mendoza-Denton, M. L. Rheinschmidt, and D. Keltner. 2012. "Social class, solipsism, and contextualism: How the rich are different from the poor." *Psychological Review 119*, no. 3: 546–72.

Krieger, Shirley, and Kennon Sheldon. 2015. "What Makes Lawyers Happy?: A Data-Driven Prescription to Redefine Professional Success." *George Washington Law Review* 83, 554–627.

Krys, K., M. Vauclair, C. A. Capaldi, et al. 2016. "Be careful where you smile: Culture shapes judgments of intelligence and honesty of smiling individuals." *Journal of Nonverbal Behavior* 40, no. 2: 101–16.

Laakso, L., and A. Mehtonen. 2018. "The relationship between child's gender and caregiver's actions in child's risk-taking situations." Pro gradu thesis, University of Tampere Faculty of Education.

LaBar, K., and R. Cabeza. 2006. "Cognitive neuroscience of emotional memory." *Nature Reviews Neuroscience* 7: 54–64.

Lagattuta, K., L. Sayfan, and C. Bamford. 2012. "Do you know how I feel? Parents underestimate worry and overestimate optimism compared to child self-report." *Journal of Experimental Child Psychology* 113, no. 2: 211–32.

Layte, R. 2012. "The association between income inequality and mental heath." *European Sociological Review* 28, no. 4: 498–511.

Lee, S., J. Park, and B. Lee. 2016. "The interplay of internet addiction and compulsive shopping behaviors." *Social Behavior and Personality: An International Journal* 44, no. 11: 1901–12.

Lenroot, R., and J. Giedd. 2008. "The changing impact of genes and environment on brain development during childhood and adolescence: Initial findings from a neuroimaging study of pediatric twins." *Developmental Psychopathology* 20, no. 4: 1161–75.

Letkiewicz, J., and S. Heckman. 2019. "Repeated payment delinquency among young adults in the United States." *International Journal of Consumer Studies* 43: 417–28.

Liu, T., and M. Csikszentmihalyi. 2020. "Flow among introverts and extraverts in solitary and social activities." *Personality and Individual Differences* 167: 110197.

Long, H., and A. Fowers. 2020. "Unemployment claims soar to 3.3 million." *Washington Post*, March 26. https://www.washingtonpost.com/business/2020/03/26/unemployment-claims-coronavirus-3-million.

Lubomirsky, S., and K. Layous. 2013. "How do simple positive activities increase well-being?" *Current Directions in Psychological Science* 22, no. 1: 57–62.

Lubomirsky, S., K. M. Sheldon, and D. Schkade. 2005. "Pursuing happiness: The architecture of sustainable change." *Review of General Psychology* 9, no. 2: 111–31.

Lucas, R. E. 2007. "Adaptation and the Set-Point Model of Subjective Well-Being: Does Happiness Change After Major Life Events?" *Current Directions in Psychological Science* 16(2), 75–80. https://doi.org/10.1111/j.1467-8721.2007.00479.x.

Mannerström, R. 2019. "Uncertain future plans—Personal identity among Finnish youth and its links with well-being, digital engagement and socio-economic circumstances." Doctoral thesis, University of Helsinki.

Marmot, M., and E. Brunner. 2005. "Social organization, stress and health." In M. Marmot and R. Wilkinson, eds., *Social Determinants of Health*, 2nd ed., 17–43. Oxford University Press.

References

Maslow, A. H. 1943. "A theory of human motivation." *Psychological Review* 50, no. 4: 370–96.
Massachusetts Institute of Technology, MIT Media Lab, Fluid Interfaces, KBTG, UCLA, and Harvard University. 2025. "Meet Future You." https://futureyou.media.mit.edu.
Mental Health Foundation. 2019. "Loneliness in young people research briefing." https://www.mentalhealth.org.uk/our-work/public-engagement/unlock-loneliness/loneliness-young-people-research-briefing.
Merzenich, M. 2013. *Soft-Wired: How the New Science of Brain Plasticity Can Change Your Life*. Parnassus Publishing.
Metzger, R. L., M. L. Miller, M. Cohen, M. Sofka, and T. D. Borkovec. 1990. "Worry changes decision making: The effect of negative thoughts on cognitive processing." *Journal of Clinical Psychology* 46, no. 1: 78–88.
Miller, W. 1955. "Death of a genius: His fourth dimension, time, overtakes Einstein." *LIFE*, May 2.
Mischel, W., O. Ayduk, M. G. Berman, et al. 2011. "'Willpower' over the life span: Decomposing self-regulation." *Social Cognitive and Affective Neuroscience* 6, no. 2: 252–56.
Mitchell, O., and A. Lusardi. 2008. "Planning and financial literacy: How do women fare?" *American Economic Review* 98, no. 2: 413–17.
Mohsen, J. 2022. "Personality trait level and change predict future financial well-being: A longitudinal study in Australia." *Personality and Individual Differences* 191: 111575.
Morris, L., M. Grehl, S. Rutter, M. Mehta, and M. Westwater. 2022. "On what motivates us: A detailed review of intrinsic v. extrinsic motivation." *Psychological Medicine* 52, no. 10: 1801–16.
Myers, D. 2000. *The American Paradox: Spiritual Hunger in an Age of Plenty*. Yale University Press.
Nechita, D. M., S. Bud, and D. David. 2021. "Shame and eating disorders symptoms: A meta-analysis." *International Journal of Eating Disorders* 54, no. 11: 1899–1945.
Newmyer, L., A. M. Verdery, H. Wang, and R. Margolis. 2022. "Population aging, demographic metabolism, and the rising tide of late middle age to older adult loneliness around the world." *Population and Development Review* 48, no. 3: 829–62.
Nickerson, C., N. Schwarz, E. Diener, and the Gallup Organization. 2007. "Financial aspirations, financial success, and overall life satisfaction: who? and how?" *Journal of Happiness Studies* 8: 467–515.
Niedzwiedz, C., E. Richardson, H. Tunstall, N. Shortt, R. Mitchell, and J. Pearce. 2016. "The relationship between wealth and loneliness among older people across Europe: Is social participation protective?" *Preventive Medicine* 91: 24–31.
Nielsen, J., B. Zielinski, M. Ferguson, J. Lainhart, and J. Anderson. 2013. "An evaluation of the left-brain vs. right-brain hypothesis with resting state functional connectivity magnetic resonance imaging." *PLOS ONE* 8, no. 8: e71275.
Noelle-Neumann, E. 1984. *The Spiral of Silence: Public Opinion—Our Social Skin*. University of Chicago Press.
Norvilitis, J. M., and M. G. MacLean. 2010. "The Role of Parents in College Students' Financial Behaviors and Attitudes." *Journal of Economic Psychology* 31(1), 55–63.
Nummenmaa, L. 2019. *Psychology of Emotions*. Sage Publications.

References

Nummenmaa, L., E. Glerean, R. Hari, and J. K. Hietanen. 2014. "Bodily maps of emotions." *Proceedings of the National Academy of Sciences* 111, no. 2: 646–51.

Office of the U.S. Surgeon General. 2022. "Workplace Mental Health & Well-Being." https://www.hhs.gov/surgeongeneral/reports-and-publications/workplace-well-being/index.html.

O'Neill, B., B. Sorhaindo, J. J. Xiao, and E. T. Garman. 2005. "Financially distressed consumers: Their financial practices, financial well-being, and health." *Financial Counseling and Planning* 16, no. 1: 73–87.

Opendak, M., L. Offit, P. Monari, et al. 2016. "Lasting adaptations in social behavior produced by social disruption and inhibition of adult neurogenesis." *Journal of Neuroscience* 36: 7027–38.

Ovidius. 1935. *Metamorphoses*. Harvard University Press. Original work published in 8 CE.

Pang, C., W. Li, Y. Zhou, T. Gao, and S. Han. 2023. "Are women more empathetic than men? Questionnaire and EEG estimations of sex/gender differences in empathic ability." *Social Cognitive and Affective Neuroscience* 18, no. 1: nsad008.

Pariser, E. 2011. *The Filter Bubble: What the Internet Is Hiding from You*. Penguin Press.

Park, A. J., A. Z. Harris, K. M. Martyniuk, et al. 2021. "Reset of hippocampal–prefrontal circuitry facilitates learning." *Nature* 591: 615–19.

Paskov, M., and C. Dewilde. 2012. "Income inequality and solidarity in Europe." *Research in Social Stratification and Mobility* 30, no. 4: 415–32.

Pew Research Center. 2023. "Nonresponse rates on open-ended survey questions vary by demographic group, other factors." https://www.pewresearch.org/decoded/2023/03/07/nonresponse-rates-on-open-ended-survey-questions-vary-by-demographic-group-other-factors.

Piff, P. K., D. M. Stancato, S. Côté, R. Mendoza-Denton, and D. Keltner. 2012. "Higher social class predicts increased unethical behavior." *Proceedings of the National Academy of Sciences* 109, no. 11: 4086–91.

Pleeging, E., M. Burger, and J. van Exel. 2021. "Hope mediates the relation between income and subjective well-being." *Journal of Happiness Studies* 22: 2075–102.

Powdthavee, N., and A. Stutzer. 2014. "Economic approaches to understanding change in happiness." In K. Sheldon and R. Lucas, eds., *Stability of Happiness: Theories and Evidence on Whether Happiness Can Change*. Academic Press.

Prati, A. 2017. "Hedonic recall bias: Why you should not ask people how much they earn." *Journal of Economic Behavior & Organization* 143: 78–79.

Purves, D., G. J. Augustine, D. Fitzpatrick, L. C. Katz, A. S. LaMantia, J. O. McNamara, and S. M. Williams, eds. 2001. "Physiological changes associated with emotion." In *Neuroscience*, 2nd ed. Sinauer Associates.

Putnam, R. 2015. *Our Kids: The American Dream in Crisis*. Simon & Schuster.

Rachel, M., K. Mehr, L. Sauers, and J. Silbert. 2018. "Examining the relationship between empathy for others and self-compassion in college students." *Educational Research and Reviews* 13: 617–21.

Ramadhan, R., D. Rampengan, D. Yumnanisha, et al. 2024. "Impacts of digital social media detox for mental health: A systematic review and meta-analysis." *Narra J* 4, no. 2: e786.

Ribeiro, W., A. Bauer, and M. Andrade. 2017. "Income inequality and mental illness-related morbidity and resilience: A systematic review and meta-analysis." *The Lancet Psychiatry* 4, no. 7: 554–62.

References

Roberts, B. W., D. Wood, and J. L. Smith. 2005. "Evaluating Five Factor Theory and Social Investment Perspectives on Personality Trait Development." *Journal of Research in Personality* 39(1), 166–84.

Rogowsky, B. A., B. M. Calhoun, and P. Tallal. 2015. "Matching learning style to instructional method: Effects on comprehension." *Journal of Educational Psychology* 107, no. 1: 64–78.

Rosenthal, R., and L. Jacobson. 1968. "Pygmalion in the classroom." *Urban Review* 3: 16–20.

Rosling, H., O. Rosling, and A. Rosling Rönnlund. 2018. *Factfulness: Ten Reasons We're Wrong About the World—and Why Things Are Better Than You Think*. Flatiron Books.

Røysamb, E., B. Ragnhild, and J. Vittersø. 2014. "Well-being: Heritable and changeable." In K. Sheldon and R. Lucas, eds., *Stability of Happiness: Theories and Evidence on Whether Happiness Can Change*. Elsevier Academic Press.

RTTNews. 2020. "U.S. weekly jobless claims spike to 3.3 million." Nasdaq, March 26. https://www.nasdaq.com/articles/u.s.-weekly-jobless-claims-spike-to-3.3-million-2020-03-26.

Rumi, J. 1995. *The Essential Rumi*. C. Barks, trans. Harper. Original work published in 13th century.

Russell, J. A. 1980. "A circumplex model of affect." *Journal of Personality and Social Psychology* 39, no. 6: 1161–78.

Sapolsky, R. 2018. *Behave: The Biology of Humans at Our Best and Worst*. Random House.

———. 2023. *Determined: A Science of Life without Free Will*. Penguin Press.

Sarraute, N. 1959. *The Planetarium*. George Braziller.

Saunders, P. 2010. *Beware False Prophets: Equality, the Good Society and the Spirit Level*. Policy Exchange.

Schwartz, S. 2012. "An overview of the Schwartz theory of basic values." *Online Readings in Psychology and Culture* 2, no. 1, article 11.

Searle, B. A., S. J. Smith, and N. Cook. 2009. "From housing wealth to well-being?" *Sociology of Health & Illness* 31, no. 1: 112–27.

Seehuus, S. 2021. "Gender differences and similarities in work preferences: Results from a factorial survey experiment." *Acta Sociologica* 66, no. 1: 5-25.

Sen, A. 1999. *Development as Freedom*. Oxford University Press.

Shaver, P., P. Lavy, C. Saron, and M. Mikulincer. 2007. "Social foundations of the capacity for mindfulness: An attachment perspective." *Psychological Inquiry* 18, no. 4: 264–71.

She, L., R. Rasiah, H. Waheed, and S. Pahlevan Sharif. 2021. "Excessive use of social networking sites and financial well-being among young adults: The mediating role of online compulsive buying." *Young Consumers Insight and Ideas for Responsible Marketers* 22: 272–89.

Sheldon, K., and S. Lubomirsky. 2009. "Change your actions, not your circumstances: An experimental test of the Sustainable Happiness Model." In A. K. Dutt and B. Radcliff, eds., *Happiness, Economics and Politics: Towards a Multi-Disciplinary Approach*. Edward Elgar.

Sheridan, M., et al. 2023. "Measuring the impact of structural inequality on the structure of the brain." *Proceedings of the National Academy of Sciences* 120, no. 255: e2306076120.

References

Shim, S., J. J. Xiao, B. L. Barber, and A. C. Lyons. 2009. "Pathways to life success: A conceptual model of financial well-being for young adults." *Journal of Applied Developmental Psychology* 30, no. 6: 708–23.

Starrin, B., C. Åslund, and K. W. Nilsson. 2009. "Financial stress, shaming experiences and psychosocial ill-health: Studies into the finances-shame model." *Social Indicators Research* 91, no. 2: 283–98.

Steger, Michael F. 2019. "Laboratory for the Study of Meaning and Quality of Life," http://www.michaelfsteger.com/.

Stoeber, J., and K. Otto. 2006. "Positive Conceptions of Perfectionism: Approaches, Evidence, Challenges." *Personality and Social Psychology Review* 10(4), 295–319.

Stoeber, J., and F. S. Stoeber. 2009. *Domains of perfectionism: Prevalence and relationships with perfectionism, gender, age, and satisfaction with life. Personality and Individual Differences*, 46(5), 530–35.

Stone, A., and S. Schneider. 2016. "Commuting episodes in the United States: Their correlates with experiential wellbeing from the American Time Use Survey." *Transportation Research Part F: Traffic Psychology and Behaviour* 42, part 1: 117–24.

Stone, D. 2011. "Cultivating financial mindfulness: A dual-process theory." In D. J. Lamdin, ed., *Consumer Knowledge and Financial Decisions: Lifespan Perspectives*. Springer.

Storr, A. 1992. *Human Aggression*. Penguin.

Sufane, Jake. 2023. "Over Half of Americans Are Planning for Major Job Changes in 2024." Nasdaq, December 21. https://www.nasdaq.com/articles/over-half-of-americans-are-planning-for-major-job-changes-in-2024.

Summerville, A., and N. Roese. 2017. "Dare to compare: Fact-based versus simulation-based comparison in daily life." *Journal of Experimental Social Psychology* 44, no. 3: 664–71.

Tabassum, F., J. Mohan, and P. Smith. 2016. "Association of volunteering with mental well-being: A lifecourse analysis of a national population-based longitudinal study in the UK." *BMJ Open* 6: e011327.

Tan, H., and J. Forgas. 2010. "When happiness makes us selfish but sadness makes us fair: Affective influences on interpersonal strategies in the dictator game." *Journal of Experimental Social Psychology* 46, no. 3: 571–76.

Taylor, S. E. 2011. "Social support: A review." In H. S. Friedman, ed., *The Oxford Handbook of Health Psychology*, 189–214. Oxford University Press.

Teng, F., Y. You, K. Poon, Y. Yang, J. You, and Y. Jiang. 2017. "Materialism predicts young Chinese women's self-objectification and body surveillance." *Sex Roles: A Journal of Research* 76, no. 7-8: 448–59.

Testa, A., and E. Cavallini. 2021. "The effect of European employment policies on job precariousness and well-being in 30 countries." *International Journal of Environmental Research and Public Health* 18, no. 24: 13222.

Tolstoy, L. 1886. *The Death of Ivan Ilyich*. Various editions.

U.S. Bureau of Labor Statistics. 2025. "Employed persons by detailed industry, sex, race, and Hispanic or Latino ethnicity." Labor Force Statistics from the Current Population Survey, 2024. Last modified January 29, 2025. https://www.bls.gov/cps/cpsaat18.htm.

———. n.d. "Frequently Asked Questions." https://www.bls.gov/nls/questions-and-answers.htm.

References

U.S. Census Bureau. 2024. "Poverty in the United States: 2023." https://www.census.gov/library/publications/2024/demo/p60-283.html.

Van Doesum, N., et al. 2019. "Social mindfulness: Prosocial the active way." *Journal of Positive Psychology* 14, no. 6: 1–11.

Vassallo, S. 2020. *Neoliberal Selfhood*. Cambridge University Press.

Veenhoven, R. 2014. "Long-term change of happiness in nations: Two times more rise than decline since the 1970s." In K. Sheldon and R. Lucas, eds., *Stability of Happiness: Theories and Evidence on Whether Happiness Can Change*. Elsevier Academic Press.

Vosloo, W., J. Fouche, and J. Barnard. 2014. "The relationship between financial efficacy, satisfaction with remuneration and personal financial well-being." *International Business and Economics Research Journal* 13, no. 6: 1455–70.

Voss, P., M. Thomas, J. Cisneros-Franco, and É de Villers-Sidani. 2017. "Dynamic brains and the changing rules of neuroplasticity: Implications for learning and recovery." *Frontiers in Psychology* 8.

Wang, J., and Y. Huo. 2022. "Effect of materialism on pro-environmental behavior among youth in China: The role of nature connectedness." *Frontiers in Psychology* 13.

Warren, J. "Guided Meditations and Talks." https://jeffwarren.org/explore/meditations.

White, N., K. Packard, J. Kalkowski, et al. 2022. "Improving health through action on economic stability: Results of the finances first randomized controlled trial of financial education and coaching in single mothers of low-income." *American Journal of Lifestyle Medicine* 17, no. 3: 424–36.

Whitebread, D., and S. Bingham. 2013. *Habit Formation and Learning in Young Children*. Money Advice Service.

Wilkinson, R., and K. Pickett. 2009. *The Spirit Level: Why Equality Is Better for Everyone*. Penguin Books.

———. 2018. *The Inner Level: How More Equal Societies Reduce Stress, Restore Sanity and Improve Everyone's Well-Being*. Penguin Books.

Wilson, J. 2000. "Volunteering." *Annual Review of Sociology* 26, no. 1: 215–40.

Wilson, J., and M. Musick. 2003. "Doing well by doing good: Volunteering and occupational achievement among American women." *Sociological Quarterly* 44, no. 3: 433–50.

World Bank. 2012. "World Development Report 2012: Gender Equality and Development." http://hdl.handle.net/10986/4391.

Yarnell, L. M., R. E. Stafford, K. D. Neff, E. D. Reilly, M. C. Knox, and M. Mullarkey. 2015. "Meta-Analysis of Gender Differences in Self-Compassion." *Self and Identity*, 14(5), 499–520.

YouGov. 2024. "Who are high income earners in the US and what do they think?" https://business.yougov.com/content/49463-who-are-high-earning-americans-and-what-do-they-think.

Zawadzka, A. M., J. Borchet, M. Iwanowska, and A. Lewandowska-Walter. 2022. "Can Self-Esteem Help Teens Resist Unhealthy Influence of Materialistic Goals Promoted by Role Models?" *Frontiers in Psychology* 12, 687388.

Zyphur, M., et al. 2015. "Income, personality, and subjective financial well-being: The role of gender in their genetic and environmental relationships." *Frontiers in Psychology* 6: 1493.

www.ingramcontent.com/pod-product-compliance
Lightning Source LLC
LaVergne TN
LVHW041956060526
838200LV00002B/43